THE RAPTURE DIALOGUES
DARK DIMENSION

By Terry James

VMI Publishers
Sisters, OR

Published by

a division of VMI Publishers
Sisters, Oregon
www.vmipublishers.com

ISBN: 1-933204-18-4

Library of Congress Control Number: 2005938977

Author Contact:
wtjames1@swbell.net
Terry James
P.O. Box 1108
Benton, AR 72018

DR. TIM LAHAYE
co-author of the *Left Behind* series, writes:

"With a solid background in Bible prophecy, my good friend and colleague, author Terry James, has penned a highly suspenseful and thought-provoking novel entitled The Rapture Dialogues. *An incredible tale involving mysterious UFO sightings, secret government cover-ups, international warfare, and frightening encounters with extra-dimensional beings, this fascinating work is intriguing, unique, and entertaining."*

Acknowledgments

My most profound thanks, and my love to Angie Peters for all the superb editorial work on this novel. Also, for her encouragement in the process.

All my love to Margaret, my wife, who once again put up with my many hours in my study, concentrating on the writing of this book.

My very special thanks and love to Terry James, Jr., my son, who contributed so much to the project. Also, my love to my son, Nathan James, who does much to assist with my work.

And, to Jeanie Hedges, my love and thanks for her research help and moral support.

Great appreciation and love to my father-in-law, Stephen P. Sullivan, CMsgt. ret. U.S. Air Force, for his thoughts on the military aspects involved in the writing.

And, my thanks and love to Dana Neel for all of her help in getting this book to you, the reader.

My very special thanks to my good friend Dave Wilson for his expert advice and counsel on the aviation matters involved in the story's creation.

To all others who have contributed to bring this book to publication, my deep gratitude. —TJ

Prologue

February, 1947- Qumran, near the Dead Sea

Mustafa Kihbolah sensed someone or something watching him, an eerie chill running down his spine. He glanced around, and satisfied himself that he was alone. The Arab 12-year-old squinted through the mid-morning brightness, thinking the dark split that gaped in the rocky surface above was a mirage playing a trick on his vision. He bent to pick up a stone from the ground. Shading his eyes with his left hand, he threw the rock upward toward the gap in the jagged boulder, but it slammed against the surface just above the opening.

The Bedouin boy grabbed another stone from the hard-packed, sandy ground and flung it with all his might. This time his aim was good and the cave's black mouth swallowed the rock. He threw another, his aim again good. His effort was rewarded with sounds he hadn't anticipated, like something breaking. Like the times he and the other boys threw big stones into the pit just outside their town where all the old and broken bowls and other vessels made of clay were thrown away.

Mustafa cocked his head, and again shaded his eyes with his sun-browned fingers together in a salute, trying to see into the dark void of the cave. Looking at the opening from that distance provided no answers.

He struggled up the sand and rock-strewn embankment. He dropped to his knees just in front of the hole, feeling the sand eat into the callused skin covering his kneecaps. The boy dug his fingertips into the earth, scooping as much as he could manage away from the cave's mouth. A few minutes of hard digging exposed enough of the opening that he could crawl forward into its now somewhat sunlit interior.

Discolored jars made of clay lined the wall at the back of the small cave. He counted seven of them. One was broken. The one his stone had struck. His eyes widened and a smile replaced the frown of puzzlement that had been there a moment before.

He had never seen vessels like these. They were very old. Probably left by someone who had long ago moved by caravan through the area of Khirbet Qumran.

Mustafa brushed aside the shards to see what lay within the broken jar. An old, brittle piece of parchment, rolled up, with faint writing of some sort. Part of the material crumbled when he tried to stretch it, and he thought better of further examination, not wanting to do any more damage.

He tried to pull the tops from the other jars, but succeeded only in cracking two of the vessels. These might bring something of value in trade in the marketplace. Better not to touch the jars again, he thought. This was a job for one of the heads of the tribe.

He scrambled on hands and knees from the cave, jumped to his sandaled feet and half-hopped, half-tumbled down the steep incline, landing on his back at the bottom of the embankment. Before he moved again, he caught a glimpse of something bright in the azure winter sky. He lingered for a moment, resting on his elbows with his legs sprawled, searching the sky above the jutting cliff and the small cave from which he had just come.

Far above, an object glinted while it hovered.

The boy blinked several times to clear his eyes so he could better take in the strange sight. His pupils dilated, and grew almost as large as the dark brown circle surrounding them. He stared, unblinking, transfixed. He muttered words in a language he didn't speak—in a deep, guttural voice that was not his own.

The thin, shimmering disk remained hanging in place for a moment, and then was gone.

* * *

Taos, New Mexico—the same hour

His mom would be mad. The thought caused the seven-year old boy to pump harder on the pedals of his bicycle.

A bag with the wing of a balsa model glider plane sticking out of it dangled by its straps on the handlebars while the bike swayed left, then right with each furious pump on the pedals.

He never had been out this late after dark, and he knew he was in for it.

"Hey, Mark!" the other boy, pumping his pedals just as hard, shouted from fifty feet behind. "Wait up!"

The two boys slowed a bit once they had joined again, both puffing hard from having just worked their way up the grade of blacktopped road toward their homes a half-mile away.

The boy in the lead stopped and slid his right leg down the bicycle until he stood on his right foot, holding the handlebars. He looked to the black sky.

"What's the matter?" Billy Masterson asked, stopping beside his friend, then looking up to see what Mark Lansing was seeing.

"What's that?" Billy asked, his eyes widening when he saw the shining object that hovered far above in the night sky. "That's no star!" he said. "Let's get outta here!"

Billy worked his pedals as never before, leaving the other boy frozen in position, holding his bike's handlebars while standing on his right foot with his left knee crooked over the bicycle. His eyes were wide, his pupils dilated, covering almost entirely the bright blue irises. His face brightened when a light stream emerged from the glowing object.

The boy's mouth moved while he stared without blinking. His voice was not that of a 7-year old child. The strange voice growled from somewhere deep within him, words from another place, another time.

***

Boothbay, Maine—the same hour

Chopping and delivering firewood was not the teenager's favorite thing. Outdoor activity of any sort did nothing to stimulate his spirit of adventure, like his father wished for his son. He liked books, and writing, and talking about things of loftier pursuit.

It was about to snow. Everyone could sense it in the small community of loggers and fishermen. Something in the cold air singed the nostrils in that special way. You just knew it was going to snow.

Christopher Banyon grabbed the thick severed tree section and set it on the end that didn't slant, so it would stand upright. He stroked hard with the axe, and the length of wood split into two parts.

Yes. There they were, just like everyone had been saying. The first large flakes of snow. It promised to be a big one, the seasoned loggers and fishermen of Boothbay predicted.

The kerosene lamp lit the wood well enough. But he wished he had finished the firewood splitting chore while it was still daylight, like his father had ordered that morning before heading out for the sawmill. Now, here he stood, at 9:30 at night, swinging an axe and stacking wood, wishing he were somewhere warm.

He would move somewhere warm when he grew old enough, he promised himself for the thousandth time. Even the heavy mackinaw failed to keep the chill from invading his young bones. He would move to Texas, when he got the chance. He heard good things about Texas…Texas was flat, and you could see forever. There were not so many trees to chop, and split, and carry. Texas was, if nothing else, warmer than Boothbay, Maine in February.

A sound seemed to whisk by his ear, carried by the wind that began whipping. Had his dad called from their log home 50 yards in the distant blackness?

Another noise – a series of sounds, very much like someone talking to him. Not yelling, but talking. Soft, gentle, whispered words.

He leaned on the axe handle and searched the surrounding darkness just beyond the lantern light's glow. He heard it again. The voice spoke louder –with more clarity.

"Christopher," the voice said.

"Who is it?" the teenager asked, trying to determine from which direction the voice came.

"Feed my sheep," the voice said above the wind's whine. "You must feed my sheep," the voice said again.

Chapter 1

July 3, 1947
(11:28 MST, somewhere over New Mexico)

James Morgan pulled the stick slightly toward him. The yellow Piper J-3 responded with its usual momentary hesitation. It wasn't at all like the P-51BS he had flown over Europe. He could almost feel it now, a phantom sensation four years after the fact.

The P-51BS's British Rolls-Royce Merlin engine would have thrust his body backward into the cramped seat, the g-force pushing his butt hard into the uncomfortable fanny-pack parachute he wore. The Piper was gentle, and strained to follow its command when its elevators flipped upward. He missed his P-51.

He missed the blood gushing hard through the carotids in his neck. He missed the powerful dynamics acting against his whole body while he made the turns and twists, the inverted dives in the effort to position the shuddering fighter behind the Messerschmitts he engaged in air combat.

"What's that?!"

Clark Lansing's words from the seat behind his own snapped the pilot from his remembrances.

"That a balloon?" Lansing questioned again, straining to see the shimmering object at 2 o'clock.

Morgan leveled the Piper's nose with the horizon and tilted the right wing downward so they both could get a better look.

"That's no balloon," James Morgan said, like his passenger

sitting behind him, trying to get a better view of the gleaming object. "It's going as fast as we are. We're not all that fast, but we're a lot faster than any balloon I've ever heard of."

Neither man spoke, but each watched the thin, cylindrical object that seemed to be cruising at the same speed and in the same direction a mile or so from them.

The object grew, filling the right window's vista. It had tilted and swooped to within a hundred yards of the Piper.

The disk-shaped object glistened so brightly it hurt the eyes, despite their military issue sunglasses. The metallic-looking craft swept above the small plane, and Morgan twisted the stick to the right and pushed forward, trying to avoid collision.

* * *

11:30 MST,
White Sands Proving Grounds, New Mexico

"Look at this, Ernie!"

The radar operator called for the man copying statistics onto a clipboard.

"What do we have here?" the operator said, seeing the reflection of an airborne object at the top right of his radar screen. He swore beneath his breath, then said louder, "It's one of those unidentifieds again, Ern. It just turned at a right angle that's impossible for any aircraft."

The thin, older man leaned over the radar operator's right shoulder to see for himself.

"Yep!" Ernest Dowling said, watching the blip reflecting something inexplicable. "It's just like the one I saw back in '42. But, then the image wasn't so good."

Neither man said anything for a few seconds, watching the blip with fascination while it continued to move at impossible speeds and angles.

"That's the third in a week," the standing man said. "I better call it in."

Dowling started to engage the microphone switch when Alan Budwing called to him again, his stare fixed upon the screen. Dowling moved to behind Budwing's right shoulder again.

"Another one. Would you look at that!"

James Morgan and Clark Lansing had a much closer view of the objects, which moved away from them so that the disks became pinpoints of light, then, in the next instant, loomed larger than ever just outside the plane's window.

One of the disks tilted and rocked in cradle fashion, while the other moved above the Piper. It slid over the top of the plane, then eased into place just outside the left window and hung there. It rocked like the other disk had done, grew to become a hundred times brighter, then shot up and out of sight.

"What are these things...?" Morgan said, still dazzled by their brightness, turning his body and head as far as he could to glance at Lansing.

His passenger was gone! Both Clark Lansing and the disks were gone!

* * *

"No. We don't know what to make of it, sir," Dowling said into the microphone to the colonel on the other end of the transmission.

"Look here, Ernie! Looks like they might've collided!" Alan's frantic words drew Dowling's eyes to the screen.

"Sir. Those things, whatever they are, seem to have come together, then dropped off radar," Dowling said in a calm, professional voice.

* * *

The little yellow piper's engine strained to reach the dirt runway near Socorro. The rear seat empty. The harness still fastened. The disks. Clark Lansing ...vanished.

When he landed, James Morgan was desperate to tell someone about what had happened. He had tried to radio, but got nothing but static, as if the Piper's radio was broken.

He called the local marshal's office. The deputy taking his call chuckled when he told the officer about the disks, about his friend Clark Lansing vanishing from the passenger seat.

The deputy seemed to become a bit more serious when James told him that he and his passenger were former pilots and had flown combat missions out of the same squadron early on over Europe, before Clark, a physicist, had been recalled to the States to work on a secret project at White Sands.

The officer began talking in quiet, soothing tones, as if he suspected he had a mental case on the line. Maybe this guy had some kind of shellshock. Maybe he went nuts, and pushed his passenger out of the plane or something.

"You come in to the office, Mr. Morgan. We'll go over this. Have a nice cup of coffee and a donut, and just get all the facts, okay?" the officer said.

The deputy marshal was cordial enough while James sat explaining the disks, their experience, his friend's sudden disappearance. But the instinctive law enforcement adversarial posturing was there, just beneath the surface of civility. James Morgan was the lawman's suspect, not his guest.

"You and ... what's the young man's name—Mr. Lansing— have any problems? You know, you guys get along okay?"

James responded before he realized the implications of the deputy marshal's question. "No, we didn't have any problems. Like I said, we've been close since the war."

Realizing the officer's intent, James' face reddened. "What? Are you trying to say I unbuckled my harness, climbed over the seat, unbuckled his harness, managed to fight him, then throw him out? All of that, and then buckle his harness again, climb back into the seat, and land the airplane?" he said, his voice rising in anger.

The big deputy said nothing, but sipped from the cup of black coffee.

"We were in the same squadron. We've been close friends in these years since…" James pushed away from the table and stood. "I've told you everything. I'll be at my house," he said, turning to walk toward the door. "You've got the address."

"Oh, we'll find you when we want you, son. Don't worry about that," the man said without changing expression.

The door burst open just as James reached for the knob. Another deputy hurried in, glanced at the young man about to leave the room, then at the bulky officer still sitting at the small desk.

"Jock. Man, you just won't believe what happened!" the thin, balding deputy exclaimed.

"What's wrong now, Timmy?" James' interrogator said, looking over the top of the coffee mug while he sipped.

"Something's crashed out by the old McKay place."

"What kind of plane?"

"It was no plane, according to the guys who've seen it. It's some kinda flying disk, shaped like a saucer!"

James Morgan listened, then slipped out of the room.

* * *

May 15, 1948—an airfield in Israel

The acrid smoke of exploding ordnance burned in his throat and lungs. He coughed, fumbling with his harness, then cranked the P-51's canopy forward and locked it into place. That did little to help him breathe better while he pushed the button that started the propeller spinning, its powerful engine creating with each piston stroke puffs of white smoke that added to the stifling air in the cockpit, despite its now closed and locked position.

Breathing came easier when he strapped the mask on his face.

A fireball exploded a hundred feet in front and to the right, and he used the left brake at the top of the rudder pedal to cause the tail wheel to swing to the right. Debris from the bomb showered the cockpit. He revved the engine and steered toward the runway. No time to worry about where the next enemy ordnance would land. He must get airborne –now!

He was behind the throttle of his beloved P-51BS again, and it felt good. Even with the probability that he would die before he made it off the narrow, bomb-pocked runway, it felt good.

At only 26, with a combat resumé that listed 14 single-handed Messerschmitt kills, James Morgan had little trouble convincing the Israelis he would be a productive asset in the battles that would come with Ben Gurion's declaration of Israel's nationhood. He preferred the just-formed U.S. Air Force to do his flying, but this was the only war of significance around. The United States had lent his services upon his agreeing to take up his commission again. He had been given one grade up from where he left right after the war.

He could rejoin America's military air arm anytime. The brass had agreed to his volunteering for the small group of American pilots who were sent, without announcement, to bolster Israel's chances of survival once independence was declared. He had jumped at the chance to join the fight. And there were those who were more than eager to send him to the Middle East. Perhaps it was a death wish on his part—to forget the secret he harbored in his troubled thoughts. Because of the same secret—he was convinced—they sent him with the unspoken hope he wouldn't be coming back. For now, he had to avoid the last crater in the runway by lifting the fighter just before reaching it. For now, he would kill as many Arab planes as they could put in his path. Or die trying.

A dozen thoughts raged within his smoke-saturated brain…

…The battle-hardened Israeli colonel with the scarred face and eye patch who had slammed his fist into James' stomach, just to "see how the American gut is constructed these days."

The caustic-mannered officer grinning before welcoming him into the Israeli service.

...His mother's farewell hug, her cheeks streaming with tears. Her instructions about staying away from danger.

...His teenage sister asking him if she could use his phonograph and record collection until he got back.

...Laura, beautiful, fresh-faced Laura with the tear-filled green eyes. His wife of two years, holding their one-year old daughter, begging him not to volunteer for the fight he, God help him, couldn't resist joining.

The P-51's throttle was all the way forward, the fighter's engine screaming while it strained to gain altitude. The ground below exploded at various places as the Arab forces pressed their attack.

James leveled the aircraft and began searching the skies for an enemy target of opportunity. He didn't have to look too hard or too long. They seemed everywhere. Diving, firing, dropping their belly loads of high explosives.

His Israeli friends, who had only nine, for the most part, outdated fighters, were doing their parts, sending one enemy airplane after another earthward. They fought with skill and ferocity he had not seen, even in the most intense times of air battle over Europe.

James downed a Fairchild F-24R Argus after several seconds of tailing it, and watched it plunge, trailing a black stream of smoke.

For the moment, there was a lull, and he moved alongside an Israeli ally, looking into the cockpit for any signal the pilot might give that would indicate where their next engagement could be found.

A blood-saturated, gaping hole where part of the leather helmet should have been, the pilot's head slumped forward, the canopy on the left side, shattered.

The German-made AviaS-199 Sakin flew in formation with him, although the pilot was as dead as any corpse James had ever seen. Yet, the aircraft seemed as in control as his own.

Suddenly the Israeli plane banked sharply right and downward. James prepared to watch the fatal plunge, when the diving plane leveled off. What happened next would be something he would rarely tell anyone, ever, no matter how long he lived. Who would believe it?

The Sakin locked on to an enemy aircraft and began firing, knocking it from the sky. James watched while the same Israeli fighter downed two more enemy planes, not wasting a single burst of machine gun fire.

Within seconds, the enemy aircraft broke off the engagement and fled back toward their desert nests. James looked for the fighter with the dead pilot, but couldn't find it. Another Israeli pilot pulled his P-51 Mustang beside Morgan's left wing and signaled they should go home.

When he began his descent toward home base, Morgan caught a glimpse of a bright object in the distance. It was disk-shaped. It accelerated toward the east at incomprehensible speed, then vanished.

Chapter 2

Austin, Texas, May, 1967

Lori Morgan bristled in silent rage while Dr. Charles T. Morrison paced back and forth in front of the lectern 15 rows below her seating level. The spotlight from high above the professor of biology exaggerated the balding of his head. His words echoed throughout the amphitheater in caustic tone and cadence.

"While we study life, the baby killers sweep the villages of Vietnam with 50-caliber machine gun fire. American hotshot flyboys drop bombs on and strafe helpless women and children, while desecrating what were once pristine forests that kept the earth cleansed..."

Lori had heard enough. She stood from her theater seat and made her way past the knees of her fellow graduate students, her face reddened against the flaxen colored hair pulled back and knotted in a bun.

While Lori's long, slacks-covered legs carried her toward the double doors at the top of the amphitheater, a shorter, dark-haired female student tried to catch up to her.

"You know he noticed you leave," Ginger Knox said, finally able to pull along beside her friend.

"What about you? He noticed you chasing me," Lori retorted, pushing through the doors and onto the concourse that led to an atrium and beyond to the University of Texas grounds.

"He doesn't know me from anybody. But he knows that you are Dr. Waldren's favorite grad student," Ginger said, trying to catch her breath.

"Yeah, well, I'm not sitting still to listen to some panty-waist anti-war professor call my father a flyboy who murders women and children."

"But your dad just trains them, doesn't he?"

"He's done his share in Korea, and Vietnam... even World War Two," Lori said, slowing and bending to pick up a crumpled cigarette package that had been discarded just off the broad sidewalk. She stood again and deposited the package in her purse.

She saw Ginger's eyes welling with tears, and reached to touch her.

"I'm sorry, Gin," Lori said, embracing her friend. "This is where Joey was hit, isn't it?"

Ginger didn't answer, but nodded.

"It's hard to believe it's been less than a year since that monster did what he did," Lori said, picking a tissue paper from her purse and offering it to her friend.

"He was a good brother, Lori. Why him?"

Lori said nothing, but put her arm around the shorter girl while they began walking toward the looming 307-foot tower, from which on August 1, less than a year earlier, Charles Whitman had murdered 14 people and injured dozens more with a high-powered rifle.

Ginger said, "You see that guy up there? He's looking at us."

Lori looked upward toward the tower that was now within 50 feet. A man, wearing a dark suit, stood in a sixth-floor window, large binoculars trained on them.

When the man saw that they were looking upward at him, he slowly removed the instrument from his eyes, put on a pair of dark sunglasses, and left the window. He walked into a small office just off the hallway that circled the interior of the tower, picked up a phone receiver from a desk and dialed. He spoke into the mouthpiece moments later.

"The Morgan girl is here. Shall we implement DD101?"

The man listened, hearing the words, "Not now. There's plenty of time."

* * *

Aboard Air Force One, over Memphis, Tennessee, May 1967

"Why have I not been let in on this 'til now? Why did I have to learn about it over cocktails at some dinner party? You boys told me the Roswell thing was all to do about nothing. Looks to me like Eisenhower thought otherwise."

Lyndon Johnson scanned the document just handed him by Jarrod McConnell, one of a half-dozen National Security Agency advisors.

"Listen to what he had to say in this memorandum. No, I guess it's a letter. It's dated November 4, 1953."

Johnson pulled the reading glasses low on the bridge of his nose, and strained to look downward at the document while he began to read:

> *I cannot overemphasize the need for the utmost discretion and understanding in exercising the authority set forth in these documents. Accordingly, I would like you to find some way to brief the various Authorizing Commanders on the subject to ensure that all are of one mind as to the letter and spirit of these instructions. Preferably, I would like to see this done in a closed meeting to be arranged through the Director of the National Security Agency, yourself, and representatives of the MJ-12/Special Studies Project. I specifically want Project JEHOVAH director Professor Albert Einstein and Doctor Robert Oppenheimer to inject any useful comments to the briefing as they are most informed on the physics related to the subject. Perhaps the annual Quantico conference could provide an opportunity to do this without the publicity that would call attention to a special meeting.*

> *Sincerely,*

> *Dwight D. Eisenhower*

The President glanced again at the document taken from the "Deep Files" of NSA. He looked first at McConnell, then at the director of the NSA.

"I want to know what the hell's going on with this Majestic-12, and Project Jehovah matter," Lyndon Johnson said. "Is there something to this flying saucer stuff, or not?"

The director cast a sheepish look at his underling, glanced at Johnson, and looked again to McConnell.

"Get all the files we have on MJ-12, Project Jehovah, White Pebble Majcomsec Intelligence Eyes Only, and get it to Bergstrom as quickly as possible," the director ordered.

When McConnell had left Johnson's mid-fuselage office, the President kneaded his nose where the reading glasses had sat. He massaged his eyes, his temples, then after licking the palms of his huge hands, slicked back his silvered hair.

He leaned back in the big desk chair bolted to the cabin's floor and crossed his legs at the ankles, plopping his cowboy booted heels up on the desktop.

"Maybe those lights I saw as a boy growing up in Texas weren't my imagination after all," he said.

* * *

Same hour, Randolph Air Force Base, Texas

There would be no more sorties until the President had come and gone. The two white T-38 Talons taxied from the south end of the runway, turned right and began the long roll up the vast concrete ramp toward Talon 3, where the sleek birds belonged.

Randolph Air Force Base, headquarters for Air Training Command, was, in the mind of the instructor pilot sitting in the back seat of the lead plane, the most beautiful air base in the U.S. James Morgan peered between the hangars on their left and enjoyed glimpses of the red-tile roofed, cream-colored Spanish motif buildings while his student pilot in the front seat taxied them toward Talon 3.

"Looks like we're the last today," Morgan said into the microphone imbedded in the plastic and rubber oxygen mask covering his nose and mouth. He unsnapped the mask and let it swing to one side.

"Yes, sir," the second lieutenant said, guiding the T-38 using rudder pedals while depressing the nose wheel steering button on the bottom of the leading edge of the grip stick.

When these two parked and were put in the hangar, preparation would begin in earnest for receiving Air Force One, tail number 26000. The inevitable aircraft entourage would accompany Lyndon Baines Johnson to Texas for a weekend at the LBJ Ranch not many miles to the northwest.

Morgan guided the mask to his mouth. "You did pretty good today, Shelton. You going to celebrate tonight?" the lieutenant colonel in the back asked roughly.

"I don't know, sir. Thank you," the 23-year-old pilot said with military stiffness.

"Come on, kid. Lighten up. We'll be off duty here in a few," Morgan said, seeing the exhaust temperature rise a bit above the normal range on one of the cockpit gauges.

"Yes, sir," Lt. Clayton Shelton said, looking for the excessive temperature his instructor pilot had been fretting about for the last 15 minutes of flight. "My EGT still looks good, sir," Shelton said.

"Guess we're going to have to write her up," Morgan said, thumbing through the checklist attached to his right knee by Velcro straps.

"Yes, sir. It seems to be just your number two gauge," Shelton said.

"Yeah. Probably just a gauge. Hate to make these boys work on an engine tonight. Friday night is no time to have to pull a J-85. I'm just going to tell the crew chief that we think it's the gauge," he said, knowing that the flight chief for Talon 3 would mark the plane's forms with a red X until the bird's J-85 number two engine was checked out.

With cockpit pressure vented, James Morgan pulled the cockpit lever on the aircraft's interior wall upward, and his canopy popped loose and flipped up. The younger man did the same.

The lieutenant swung the bird to the left by pushing the left rudder pedal, then slowed the aircraft by touching the top of the rudder pedals several times. He pushed fully on the right pedal, still depressing the button on the bottom of the control stick's handle with his little finger. The young pilot watched the crew chief wearing the sound-suppressing ear muffs while he stood in front of the long yellow parking spot. The man in the green fatigues, with three blue-trimmed, white chevrons and a star in their midst, held his arms and hands in the air. He then pointed downward and to the left with his left hand, while continuing to hold his right arm in the air. He waved his right hand toward himself, while pointing with his left hand.

The nose wheel turned sharply right, then straightened, and the crew chief again put both arms and hands in the air, continuing to signal for the pilot to come forward. At just the right moment, the crew chief crossed his arms at the wrist, and the lieutenant stopped the T-38 by pushing forward with the balls of his feet on the top of the rudder pedals.

Another enlisted member of Talon 3 hurried to place the two sets of wooden, yellow-painted chocks, each set having two of the blocks attached by short lengths of rope. He put one block on each side of the bird's left main wheel tire, then hurried beneath the flat belly of the T-38 to repeat the procedure on the other wheel.

The crew chief held one hand fully aloft, palm forward, until the other enlisted man had finished the job. He then dropped his hand and moved to the yellow cockpit ladders.

"Hold up a minute, Shelton. I want to check this engine a little before we shut her down," Morgan said, concentrating on the Exhaust Gas Temperature gauge for the number two engine while he applied braking pressure to the top of the rudder pedals and manipulated the right throttle with his left hand, revving the engine several times.

The right EGT gauge fluctuated erratically.

"I really think it's the gauge, Shelton," the instructor said. "What you think?"

"Yes, sir."

Morgan grinned, hearing uncertainty in the young man's voice. Although the pilot training gave some attention to mechanical troubleshooting, the youngsters weren't supposed to be experts on everything –just experts on flying high-performance jet fighters to the point they were the best in the world.

At 46, he was confident that he had reached that goal. But, it didn't come without a lot of testing in aerial combat. It couldn't be achieved sitting in a pretty little white trainer whose honeycombed wings could barely fend off bird strikes, much less 20 mm cannon fire.

Still, he was glad to be at Randolph for now. He and Laura had it better than ever before. She deserved to have him come home every night. She had been an understanding wife like few others.

They had married in 1945 following his discharge after World War II. Then came the strange year with the Israeli air force.

He had retaken his commission in 1948, flew F-84s, then F-86s, over the Korean Peninsula. He had been shot out of the air once, luckily parachuting into friendly territory. A couple of his fellow flyers hadn't been so fortunate. They died prisoners of the North Koreans.

He was forced to take a desk job for a time right after the Korean Conflict, as they called it. He couldn't figure why they didn't call it a war. It certainly was that, and only the State Department's diplomatic "striped-pants set," as President Truman called them, could see it as merely "conflict."

He knew in the back of his mind that somebody lurked behind the decision to put a thumb on his career progress, rank-wise. To keep him in his place, so that he knew they would not forget they were ever vigilant concerning the secret he carried. He had been allowed to rejoin as an active fighter pilot in late 1958. The reassignment came just in time; he had become bored stiff with the nerve-jangling corporate-like structure and all of the attendant politics involved.

Although he welcomed the chance to get back to doing what he loved, the result of his forced time as a desk jockey was that uninterrupted flyers of his age were now full bird colonels or higher, while he was only a lieutenant colonel as of about six months ago.

He had the experience and all those medals. None was more qualified to lead in combat duty, they told him. He was, however, age-wise, "on the edge of physiological effectiveness" in the eyes of those who called the shots. Since he had downed several Mig 17s and other enemy aircraft over the jungles of Vietnam, he should now be content to lend his invaluable experience to training the young men whose turn had come to carry on in the best tradition of the Air Force's top guns.

Randolph Air Force Base was a gravy assignment. But, he thought, giving the engine another rev and pulling it back to idle, he would like to have one more go in combat. He would like to engage the Migs over Vietnam in an F-4 or F-105 just one more time. The Phantom and the Thunderchief were his birds of choice.

"Okay, young man. Let's shut her down and start our weekend," Morgan said, pulling both throttles fully back with his gloved left hand.

The engines whirred to a halt and the instructor pilot opened the map box to his right. He pulled from it the clear plastic covered loose leaf form for the airplane everyone called "Triple Nickel," alluding to the last 3 numbers, 555, painted black on the bird's bright white vertical stabilizer.

After removing the ejection seat safety pins from the map box and inserting them in the seat's T handle, he documented the malfunction, which he viewed as an "EGT gauge problem, number two engine."

When he had pulled the g-suit hose from its connector on his g-suit, he reached to the clasp at his waist to pop open his lap belt. He handed his helmet to the airman, exited the cockpit, and stepped onto the ladder the crew chief had hooked over the edge of the cockpit's canopy rest.

Morgan explained the problem, as he saw it, handed the form to the crew chief, and then looked down at the yellow parking spot, where the nosewheel tire sat directly at its center.

"You got it dead on, Shelton," the older man said clinically. "Guess you owe me a beer at the club tonight. Wasn't that our bet?"

"I don't think so, sir," the lieutenant said in military tone.

"Oh? That's how I remember it," the ranking officer said, beginning to walk toward the awaiting dark blue Air Force van.

"No, sir. That's not how I remember it," the young pilot said watching Morgan wrestle with his parachute, trying to loosen it, then jump it higher on his aching back.

"Well, son. I got a silver leaf here that remembers better than you and your gold bar remember," James Morgan said with an amused twinkle in his eye.

"Yes, sir," the lieutenant replied, with a smile in his voice. He and the other pilots in training knew well this man's good-natured, bantering ways. Although it was an unspoken rule that instructors and their students didn't fraternize, Col. Morgan often bought rounds for all of his young charges. He was their favorite instructor. He would, as he always did, pay off his bet when he lost the wager on whether he or a student stopped precisely on the rounded end of the yellow parking spot painted on the concrete. Rarely did he collect on a bet he won.

"I'll be glad to get out of this g-suit," the older pilot said once they sat down on the long board running the length of the big van's interior.

They greeted the other two pilots when they entered the van a minute or so later.

"Looks like the boss will be on schedule," Maj. Chuck Bender said, taking his seat beside his own second lieutenant student pilot.

"Looks like," Morgan replied, as the van began its quarter-mile roll southward down the street in front of the flight shacks and hangars to the right.

They moved past Base Ops, and saw, as they headed toward their point of departure, the Air Force personnel rolling the big plush units and even bigger air conditioning units and auxiliary power units into place in preparation for the arrival of Air Force One.

* * *

Laura Morgan looked into the mirror above the upright piano while she dusted and polished the instrument's mahogany surface. She guessed she didn't look all that bad at 44; at least everyone told her she was pretty. After all, she did have a daughter who was almost 23.

The officers' wives, usually not too kind to each other, nonetheless always had questions about how she stayed so slim and kept her skin so young looking. She mentally chastised herself for the momentary daydream. She found such self-centeredness repugnant, and, she thought to herself now, such indulgence was a sure sign one was getting old.

She moved to the stereo, and after rubbing its surfaces with her dust rag, she knelt to pull a record from its place. She selected her favorite Barbra Streisand album and started it playing before returning to the cleaning.

She glanced at the clock. 3:35. She mentally translated to Military Time, 15:35. James would be driving in before long. His day of training the "eaglets," as he called them, was shortened today. The President was coming in for one of his once or sometimes twice-a-month visits to the LBJ ranch.

Her husband worried her lately. That is, worried her more than usual. Somehow, his physicals always turned out to be good reports. Col. James Morgan, according to the flight surgeons at

Lackland's Wilford Hall, was in great shape for a man approaching his 47th birthday.

But, they didn't see him during those early morning hours. Times when she would look for him and find him standing on the balcony of their 10th floor apartment staring into the heavens. They didn't see the shaking, almost convulsing, while his unblinking eyes gazed into the star-filled nights, his mouth sometimes muttering things she couldn't understand.

"Guess I'm just sleepwalking," he told her. "Nothing to worry about," he assured, promising to mention the episodes to the flight surgeons.

They had told him at his most recent physical that everything looked perfect. "Some people just do unusual things in their sleep, like sleepwalk. Just be sure to lock your balcony doors so that you'll have to be awake to open them. Wouldn't want to have one of our best pilots thinking he can take off from up there without his T-38," they had joked.

The Morgans had had a special, complicated locking system installed on the heavy-framed French doors. Maybe that would at least keep him off the balcony during his sleepwalks.

"Super L!"

Laura smiled, hearing her husband's pet name for her. She remembered, with another smile, the night he gave it to her.

All he could talk about was the new fighter he was training to fly. She had told him, while they lay in bed that night in the early 1950s, that he loved the F-100 Super Saber so much that maybe he should go make love to it rather than to her. His response had been that the plane was only a Super Saber, but that she was "Super L." The name had stuck, she remembered with fond reflection while she walked into their foyer.

They embraced when he had put the attaché case in the foyer closet and shut the door.

"How'd it go today, Smilin' Jack?" Laura said, kissing him.

"Not bad, not bad," James answered, and returned her kiss.

"Got a drink for a thirsty stranger, my dear?" he questioned in a seductive tone.

"Tea, Coke, or coffee?" Laura responded.

"How 'bout bourbon and branch water, in honor of the commander-in-chief coming to town?"

His drinking had never been a point of contention between them. But lately he was heavier into the hard stuff than usual. She didn't like him drinking at all. Never had. But, she thought, probably it bothered her more now because of her recent conversion to Christianity and her membership in the Presbyterian Church. She must remember to not preach to him.

He went to the little bar near the French doors leading to the balcony and started putting together his drink. He knew she wanted him to quit, and he planned to. Just not today.

"Speaking of strangers, Babe, someone called about 20 minutes ago. He said he's the son of somebody you know. Didn't give his name," Laura said.

"Oh?"

"Said he's TDY to Randolph for the weekend."

"Did he say he would call back?"

"No, but I told him to call anytime before seven this evening."

"Well, he'll catch up with me if he really wants to. Probably will hang out at the Officer's Club some while he's here. Somebody will point me out to him."

* * *

Marine Capt. Mark Lansing watched the Boeing 727 touch down on the east runway, its tires sending blue-white puffs of smoke behind before settling for its rollout. It was the chartered plane that carried the press, and went everywhere the President went. Its arrival was a sure tip that Air Force One wasn't too far behind.

The much smaller Lockheed Jet Star had already arrived and was parked not more than a hundred feet from where he stood gripping the chain-link fence, put there only a few hours before to keep the public from stepping onto the flight line when the President was at Randolph.

The Jet Star was a beauty, although a little on the pudgy side, he surmised, admiring it from behind his aviator sunglasses. It looked a bit stumpy, he knew, because it provided headroom other smaller jets didn't. Even the six foot three President could walk without having to lean forward in this aircraft.

It was painted and decorated in the blue, white and gleaming silver colors of the 707, the same one that had delivered President Kennedy to Dallas, then back to D.C. that fateful day four years earlier. The Jet Star was used to take the President to the landing strip at the LBJ ranch. It required fewer feet of runway.

He wondered what kind of feel it had when the pilot controls called upon it to perform. What kind of acceleration it produced when pushed to full throttle, when the four engines, two on either side of the fuselage just below the vertical stabilizer, roared to full power. Like all passenger jets, it had no afterburners. After the F-4s ABs, nothing would feel like much of a kick, he mused.

The chartered 727, a bright orange and multi-color schemed Braniff airliner, began its roll northward toward where he stood. He thought it would be a bore to fly such a plane for a living.

His choice was the F-4C. It was a fighter-bomber without peer. Maybe a few could go faster by a few knots, but none with the devastating combination of thrust, speed, firepower and ordnance capability existed. That, figuring in its athletic maneuverability and tank-like strength, made the F-4C Phantom the most awesome plane to command on the planet.

He felt sorry for the 727's pilot and crew, shuffling the herd of, for the most part, anti-military, anti-war Washington press corps around. He even felt for the colonel who flew LBJ's big, beautiful bird. The plane that was now at full flaps, nose slightly up, its white and chrome-like belly shimmering in the afternoon Texas sunlight.

Air Force One glided almost noiselessly above Universal City, its silver-edged wings seeming not to vary a single degree up or down. Momentarily the back most of its many tires sat softly on the runway. Unlike with the press plane, there were no puffs of smoke.

The engines roared mightily when the thrust-reversers began to slow the aircraft.

Lansing's own hulking aircraft sat drooping in its green, brown, and tan camouflage just a hundred feet or so north of where the press plane finally came to a stop. The ramps of stairs were rolled to the doors, both front and back, and men and women spilled from the Braniff, watched carefully by Air Police from the hangar roofs, and by uniformed and plain-clothed Air Police on the tarmac.

The reporters and overflow White House personnel made straight for Base Ops, the cream colored, red-roofed building of several stories across the street directly behind him. They conversed, laughed, and made shuffling, rustling crowd noises like everyone else, he thought, wondering how they could at the same time seem so ordinary, and spew such anti-American garbage with their typewriters, cameras, and microphones.

It was good that Lt. Col. James Morgan was here, not on TDY, leave, or something other. Mark Lansing's thoughts turned to the reason he requested temporary duty at Randolph Air Force Base. He needed the cross-country hours and on-going flight education, of course, but the real assignment was personal. He had to talk to Morgan. His sanity might well be at stake, depending upon the results of their meeting.

The Presidential 707 came to a stop 200 feet in the distance. The crews hurried to make all of the necessary attachments involving the air-conditioning units and the auxiliary power before the engines were shut down.

A huge, dark blue Air Force tractor-trailer rig moved between Air Force One and Mark, around whom people started to gather.

"I wonder if he'll shake hands today?" a young mother holding a toddler said, shading her eyes with her other hand to watch for activity around the van and the big plane. Mark started to answer, but saw her question was to a woman standing on her right.

People had spread along the long security fence, and now were piling up several rows deep. He knew when he saw a number of dark-suited men with walkie-talkies scanning the crowd and moving to strategic positions on the other side of the fence that President Lyndon B. Johnson and entourage would soon be moving and smiling among the people.

* * *

19:10 MST

"Excuse me, ma'am, are you Col. Morgan's wife?"

Laura looked from her companion at the table into the intense, blue eyes of the young man in civilian clothes.

"Yes, I'm Laura Morgan."

"I'm sorry to interrupt, ma'am," Mark Lansing said, leaning slightly forward to be heard above the noises of conversation and waiters serving Randolph Officer's Club patrons. "Ma'am." He nodded his unspoken apology in the direction of the woman sitting directly across from Laura.

The woman stood, smiling, and said, "That's quite alright. I have to meet my husband." With that, she left.

"Yes?" Laura asked.

"I called your home for Col. Morgan earlier today," Lansing said, pausing to collect his thoughts.

"Yes," Laura smiled, reaching her right hand to take his. "I remember that call."

"Do you know if the colonel might talk with me for a minute or two? It's about my father. Your husband and my dad were in the Army Air Corps together."

"Why, I think so," Laura said brightly. "I don't think you gave me your name on the phone."

"Oh, I'm sorry, ma'am. I'm Mark Lansing. Capt. Mark Lansing."

He could see the woman's expression change to the search

mode, trying to remember. Her eyes widened, and her mouth opened in a smile when she recognized the name.

"You're Clark and Jennifer's son?" She asked the question with excitement, while she pushed her chair back and stood.

"Yes, ma'am."

Laura embraced him and he grinned, returning her hug.

"We haven't seen you since…it must have been 1950!" She again tried to remember. "Yes! It was 1950. You were, let me see, you were 10 years old!"

"Yes, ma'am," he said, his voice dropping in volume, embarrassed from the fuss.

"Sit down here, Mark," Laura said, seating herself and patting the table in front of the chair, which he moved to take his seat.

"Jenny—" Laura's tone became soft. "How's your mother, Mark?"

"She's married. Met a guy in '57. He's a few years older than Mom. He's a retired brigadier…Army. "

"And, is she happy?" Laura asked the question softly, genuinely. She remembered the years after Jenny lost her husband, while memory of the tragedy reframed the circumstances of that distant past.

Jennifer had nearly gone insane. As had her own husband, James.

Clark Lansing had disappeared, and there was never an explanation. Jenny was told only that Clark never showed up that day for the flight in the Piper. The two men were going to look at some land the military wanted to purchase. Neither of them was any longer in the Army Air Corps, which, by July of 1947, had become the United States Air Force. But, officer friends hired them as consultants. They were to recommend whether to buy the land once they had looked it over.

James had told the story to the marshal and the military authorities. He told them Clark had in fact shown up that morning. That they had flown toward the prospective piece of land. Told them the disks had appeared, flew around and over them, then disappeared. When he looked to the passenger seat, Clark was gone, his safety harness still locked in place.

James had fought to preserve his own sanity, as well as that of Jennifer Lansing. He did everything he could to comfort her and her seven-year-old son.

He begged them to let him tell Jenny the story the way it really happened. Threatened to tell it all, just the way it had unfolded. The frightening time flooded Laura's mind in a flash of vivid remembrance. If James ever told that Clark Lansing disappeared, with flying saucers involved—an Air Force colonel had told both of them—James Morgan would go to prison for murder. He could make the choice. Go to prison for murder, or rejoin the Air Force at a rank one step higher than when he left, with his promise that he would never again talk about what happened during the same time that the infamous UFO incident occurred near Roswell.

His "military imprisonment," as James called it, guaranteed he wouldn't talk, being subject to orders and to consequences of the Uniform Code of Military Justice. The colonel had said in a grim voice, "You will be safe and protected from prying ears and eyes with us."

Laura didn't like what it did to her husband, but there were no alternatives to the government's way of dealing with James' inadvertent role in the strange phenomenon. They promised him a safe, enviable assignment and combat if he wanted it, when opportunity presented itself.

They had gone along with the lie. They had no choice. But the lie had taken its toll. The sleepwalking and the drinking were getting worse.

"Mom seems to be doing well," Mark said. "I don't get to see her enough these days."

"And, you're a captain in the Air Force now," Laura said patting his hand.

"No, ma'am. The Marine Corps."

"Well, we'll try not to hold that against you, Capt. Lansing," Laura teased, seeing a handsome man of over six feet tall with thick, blonde hair, and shoulders like a fullback, but remembering the 10-year-old she saw last in 1950.

"What do you do?"

"Fly F-4Cs," he answered, glancing upward at the waiter. "I'll just have some club soda, please."

"F-4s! The colonel will be very envious of you. He wants more than anything to go over there and fly F-4s again," Laura said.

"I understand he's training guys. There's nothing more important than that right now," Mark said.

"Well, Mark, don't let him hear you say that. He says he hears that every day from Air Training Command."

"Yes, ma'am. It must be hard when you want to be in combat."

"Sure is," James Morgan said in a gruff, loud voice.

Mark stood when the lieutenant colonel approached the table.

"You the guy looking for me?" the older man said, eyeing the younger.

"Yes, sir. I'm Mark Lansing."

James Morgan searched Lansing's features for any spark of familiarity.

"You're Clark's son?" he said softly, finding the resemblance to his remembered friend.

"Yes, sir," Mark said in an equally subdued tone, feeling, somehow, his father's presence. This man had been his dad's best friend. He tried to sense what the two had in common that had made them close friends.

"Sir, I'm sorry to be abrupt, but there's some things, weird things, going on. Things I've found out about Dad. I know that you two made the flight in that Piper that day he…"

Mark Lansing let his thought go.

"Guess we need to go somewhere where we can talk," James Morgan said after a troubled pause of several seconds while looking into the eyes of his long-lost best friend's son.

Chapter 3

He chose a noisy lounge on the north side of San Antonio. There were no listening devices, and no prying ears here. He had watched very closely to see if they were followed.

"Now, Mark," he began, while they waited for the lounge hostess so they could order drinks. "What, exactly, do you want from me?" Morgan's tone was blunt.

"Sir, I don't know, exactly, what I want," the younger man said. "I can tell you about things happening to me, about things I know."

"Okay. Let's have it," Morgan said, leaning forward on his elbows to hear above the cacophony of noises.

Mark glanced up at the approaching barmaid. Both men ordered drinks, then waited until she left before returning to their eye-to-eye, elbows-on-the-table posture.

"As I said, I know Dad made that flight with you that day, the day he…disappeared."

"How do you know?" Morgan said.

"I talked to a guy who was a deputy in the marshal's office the day you reported about the…whatever it was. A guy named Tim Sooter."

"And what did he tell you?"

"That you told them Dad was riding with you in that J-3. Said you told them flying saucers buzzed the plane. That Dad vanished, his lap belt still locked."

"You believe them?" Morgan said in a slightly incredulous tone.

"Not then. But I do now, Colonel. You better know I believe them now," Mark Lansing said, leaning forward to make his thoughts known in a way that would leave no doubt that he meant what he was saying.

"I've seen them, Col. Morgan. I've talked with them," he said, eyes narrowing, fists tightening with the intensity of his tone.

"You've talked to who?" Morgan asked, clasping his fingers together and leaning further forward to hear Mark's words better. "The deputy marshals? The military, the FBI? Who?" Morgan's question was heavily tinged with skepticism that bordered on irritation.

The younger man's eyes searched his surroundings for the right answer.

"I don't know. I'm not sure. They aren't ..." he stammered, still searching his thoughts for the way to explain. "They aren't—*normal* conversations. They're more like...dreams."

James Morgan unclasped his fingers and leaned back in the chair. He reached to take the glass filled with ice and bourbon. He sipped the drink, then measured the man across the table before speaking. "You mean you've been talking to someone in your dreams, your sleep?"

"No, sir. It's not like that. These aren't dreams. They're like, I don't know how else to say it. They are like trances. But, trances when I'm fully awake. Fully aware."

Morgan sipped the drink again, then placed the glass on the table and rotated it back and forth between his right thumb and fingertips. He spoke, not with disbelief in his voice, but with curiosity.

"These—conversations—tell me about them."

The man hadn't immediately got up and left, thinking he was talking with a head case. The thought gave Mark boldness.

"It happens more often now," he said, sipping on his drink, then, like Morgan, fidgeting with the glass by rotating it on the table's top. "It began one night when I was home—well, visiting Mother at Taos. Something in my mind told me to go outside. I was in bed, about 2 in the morning, or so. I got up and went onto the patio. It's like I couldn't do anything else but go out on that patio that morning."

Morgan studied Mark's expression from across the table. He drank hard from his bourbon and rocks.

"That first time, I couldn't understand what they were saying. But before long I understood them, even though they were speaking some totally crazy language I knew nothing about."

"Who? Who was talking to you?" Morgan said, moving forward to hear Mark's word over the lounge noises.

"I don't know, Colonel. I always see just outlines, shadowy outlines. Human outlines, with no features. They seem outlined by a thin edge of light."

"What did they say?"

"I don't know."

"You don't know?" Morgan said with irritation. "I thought you said you understood them."

Mark sipped the drink, going over in his mind the same question posed by James Morgan. The question he had asked himself many times.

"I knew I understood at the time. But I can't remember anything. That is, I remember only that they were there, that we talked, that what we talked about was…something I knew I understood at the time. But I can't remember anything now."

"And you say it's always the same. You have the same experience over and over?" James said after several seconds.

"Pretty much the same. Only one time do I remember from the…conversations. I know Dad is with them. They have him with them," Mark said, his voice becoming shaky with emotion. "The one thing I always remember is that they tell me they took him from the plane that day, and he is with them."

James Morgan's right hand started trembling while he held the drink. He felt the blood drain from his face, his body becoming weak to the point he felt faint.

"Sir, are you okay? You don't look very well," Mark said,

rising from his chair to grasp the older man's forearm.

The colonel took a deep breath and downed the remainder of the bourbon.

"No. I don't feel well at all."

Laura met them at the door. She took her husband's right arm when she saw Mark steadying him.

"What's wrong?" she asked, helping the younger man.

"I don't know," Mark said, helping James sit in a living room chair. "He just got weak and dizzy."

"I'm feeling better now," James said, trying to shake off the weakness that had come on suddenly at the lounge twenty minutes earlier.

"Maybe we should call Col. Schmidt," Laura said, touching James' brow with the back of her right hand.

"No. I'll be okay, Super L," he said, gently brushing aside her mothering gesture.

"Think I better lie down for a bit," James said after a minute of trying to clear his head. When he tried to rise from the deep, soft chair, he was too weak, and slumped back into the seat.

He tried again, this time succeeding with the help of both Laura and Mark Lansing.

"Really. I'll be fine. Just want to rest for a while," he said, shuffling, with their help, to a bedroom.

"We've got to finish this, Captain, before the weekend is gone," he said, lying on his back, while Laura adjusted two pillows to make him comfortable.

"Yes, sir. I'll give Mrs. Morgan the number where you can reach me."

Laura closed the bedroom door when they left the room.

"He doesn't seem short of breath," she said. "He didn't complain of chest pains or anything, did he?"

"No, ma'am," Mark said.

"I'm worried about him. He's always been so healthy," she said.

"Has he been feeling like this much lately?" Mark said,

walking toward the apartment's foyer.

"Please. Sit for a while. I think we should talk." Laura took Mark's arm and led him into the small den. She sat across from him when he was seated.

"James has always been so healthy, Mark. Never even a sneeze," she said, her face taking on an expression of worry.

"But for about six months, since he was promoted to lieutenant colonel, really, he's—he's been having these…" She tried to find the words. "He's been walking in his sleep, and…"

She was obviously considering whether to tell him about the problem. He moved to put her at ease.

"Look, Mrs. Morgan, you don't have to tell me, but if you do, it won't go further, I promise."

She remained silent, considering the words of the young man who despite their past relationship, was still a virtual stranger. James was very private, and she knew he wouldn't want the matter discussed.

"Let me just say that this, this dizziness, or whatever, came on him suddenly when I told him about something that's pretty private in my own life."

He could see that he had softened her resistance to discussing the problem.

"I was telling the colonel about my own bouts at night. My, sleepwalking, if that's what it is. When I told him, that's when he seemed to become dizzy and feel faint."

She sat forward, and became tense when she talked. "Yes. That's got to be it! This thing has him on edge. It has us both on edge," she said, nearly coming to tears.

"He's so afraid he's going to lose flight status. But, I know it goes deeper. Much deeper," she said, her throat tight with emotion.

"It's the thing about Dad, isn't it?" he asked.

She said nothing, but straightened as if she had been punched in the ribs.

"I know my dad was on that Piper with the colonel that day.

I told him about it. That's what caused his…his weak feelings, I think."

"Who told you? Nobody knows but he and I…and…" She thought better of saying more.

He provided the words for her. "The military who were in charge of the Roswell thing?"

"Oh, Mark," she said, the tears finally spilling over her cheeks.

"We wanted to tell your mother, and you. They told us that if we did—if we told anyone—James would be charged with murder. They would see to it that he paid for Clark's disappearance."

Mark moved to Laura's side on the sofa and put his arm around her shoulders, patting her hand with his free hand. "It's okay. I know neither of you would do anything to hurt us. You did the only thing you could."

He moved to a table at the end of the sofa, took a tissue, and handed it to her.

"Thank you, Mark. That will mean a lot to James, as well as to me."

"I've had these sleepwalking episodes, or whatever they are, for months. About six months, like the colonel, I think," he said, then paused for a moment when a thought came.

"Before I go on, let me ask. Exactly what happens when the colonel has one of these…?"

"I've found him out on the balcony, just looking off into space. He's usually talking, muttering, in words I can't understand. Sounds almost like a foreign language."

She stopped to dry her tears, then continued. "I always lead him back to bed without his waking."

"Does he remember these sleepwalks?" Mark's question came with increased urgency in his voice.

She nodded "no." "He never remembers," she said.

"Has he told the flight surgeons?"

"Yes."

"What do they say?"

"They say all the tests are just fine. It's normal for some people to sleepwalk, they tell him."

"But, he's never done it before? Never walked in his sleep—until six months ago?"

"No, never. Not that I know of, anyway."

Mark stood, rubbing his eyes and temples. It had been a long day, and the two drinks he had were making his head spin. He wasn't used to drinking the hard stuff.

"I talk in my episodes, too. Only sometimes I remember a few things. Sometimes I know what the conversations are about, even though they are in some kind of language I can't understand," he said, looking at her and cocking his head in an expression that said he was as confused about it as he knew she was from hearing it.

"These episodes, I talk with these people I can't really see. I don't even know if they're people. They're just dark, shadowy human-like figures, outlined by strange, thin lines of light. They told me, made me know somehow, that Dad was taken from the J-3 that day in 1947. They say he's with them."

She was dumbfounded. What did it mean? She watched him take his seat in the chair across from her, not knowing what to say to break the silence.

"What on earth is going on?" she managed, finally.

He snapped out of his deep thoughts with her words. "What on earth? Or somewhere else?" he said with amused irony in his tone.

"You probably think I'm completely nuts, but I've reached the point I don't care what anyone thinks. I need answers."

The doorbell chimed before he could say more.

"Hope that's Lori," she said, rising from the sofa and walking through the foyer to the door.

"Sorry, Mom," the young woman said when her mother opened the door.

"Forgot your keys. Found them on the floor by your nightstand," Laura said, hugging her daughter.

Mark Lansing stood, seeing the tall female who walked into

the den with Laura.

"Mark, this is our daughter, Lori. She's home from UT for the next couple of weeks."

* * *

"Thanks, Lori," Mark said, bending low to look beneath the rag top to see the face of the young woman who had driven him from the apartment building to Randolph Air Force Base.

"No problem," she said holding the TR-5's steering wheel and smiling at him.

He wanted to say more to her. The drive was too short, and there hadn't been time to break the ice.

Laura had whispered to him, after she asked Lori to drive him to Randolph's officer guest quarters that her daughter knew nothing about what they had talked about. Mark had nodded understanding. The conversation on the drive to the base had been mostly about what Lori was studying at the University of Texas.

She showed no interest in him. She did mention a boyfriend she had a date with Saturday night.

He watched the little red British sports car drive away, considering that he wished he, too, had a date tomorrow night. Instead, he would spend time pouring over training manuals preparing for the advanced simulator training he faced starting Monday.

Something gnawed at the back of his thoughts. He wondered if it would work. He went to the bed and sat on its edge, once he entered his temporary apartment. He reached for the phone and dialed.

"Hello?" Laura answered.

"Sorry, Mrs. Morgan, to be calling so late. Oh, Lori should be home shortly. She just let me off. Thank you again for the ride."

"I've been thinking about what we talked about, Mark," Laura said. "We need to talk again. I just can't believe these things are…"

"Yes, I know. I've got to find out what's going on. And, that's what I wanted to ask you about," Mark said.

"Oh?"

"Would it be possible – that is, could you, would you try something that might help us find out things?"

"If I can," she said with apprehension in her voice.

"Will you try to tape-record the colonel's words, if and when there is another sleepwalking episode?"

Chapter 4

H e was glad he chose the small snack bar just behind Base Ops rather than accept the invitation to go with the two pilots who were also TDY for continuing flight training on the simulators. Few people were having breakfast at this early hour on Saturday morning, just as he had figured.

He enjoyed the semi-solitude, eating at a leisurely pace, sipping black coffee, and perusing the *San Antonio Light* for the latest news from Vietnam. President Johnson was taking some heavy hits from the swelling numbers of protesters opposed to the war.

There hadn't been any when LBJ landed, though, he thought. Although, he considered further, the press corps—especially the D.C. press corps—was itself a growing, surreptitious, anti-war protest movement.

He read on the second page that Johnson would be returning to the White House Monday. He glanced at page 3, scanning it from top to bottom. He started to bring the pages together to turn to page 4 when a small headline in the lower left side of page 3, which made a fleeting, residual impression on his brain, caused him to again pull the pages apart.

"UFO sighted near SA"

His eyes devoured the brief piece:

"Two light-like objects were reported hovering over an area northwest of San Antonio," Bexar County Sheriff's Deputy Michael

Cox said early Saturday morning.

'We were called about 2:20 in the morning to check out some weird lights flying around and hovering,' Cox said. 'We saw them. They didn't look like they were in any hurry to leave,' he said.

The San Antonio Light checked with San Antonio International Airport, and with military bases in the area. None reported recording the objects on radar."

The brevity of the article irritated him. Before, he would have smiled, shaken his head at such a ludicrous report, then moved on. But that was before...

Probably, they inserted the short piece at the last minute, just before they had to get out the early edition.

"There you are!"

At first, Mark couldn't distinguish who had shouted. The bright morning light streaming through the doors of the snack bar where the young woman stood blinded him for the moment.

She walked past several empty tables, pulled a chair from his table, and sat down.

"Lori. What are you doing here?" he said, not knowing what else to say.

"That's a great greeting from somebody I've spent my Saturday morning sleep-time tracking down," she said with mock irritation.

"Okay, I'll do it right. Lori! Great to see you!"

"Better, much better," she said with a deadpan expression.

"Dad sent me to find you. He didn't say why. What have you two got going?"

"Nothing. Just some aircraft stuff."

"Yeah, well. Your very, very sleepy chauffeur has arrived—if you can come," Lori said.

The morning sunlight playing upon her golden-hued hair seemed almost electric while he watched her graceful, feminine form moving a few steps in front of him toward the little TR-5.

She gesticulated while she walked and talked. He heard her words, but was too busy admiring her to know what she was saying. She was a welcome sight for eyes not yet ready to fully accept the day.

She swung her long, slacks-wrapped legs—athletic, yet feminine—into the sports car, and set the four cylinders rumbling with the twist of a key.

"Dad will meet us at the Taj," Lori said when she turned right from the parking lot onto the street between the snack bar on their right and the swimming pool on the left.

"The Taj?"

"The Taj Mahal," she said, surprised he didn't know.

"It's the centerpiece of Randolph. You've seen it. It's the building that looks like the real Taj Mahal. It's the big building you'll run into when you go straight from the front gate. You probably saw it last night when I brought you on base."

"I imagine I was too busy looking at you," Mark said, looking at her now.

She said nothing, but looked at him and laughed brightly.

Both were silent, the thought-provoking meaning of his words hanging in the air between them.

Less than four minutes later they pulled in beside the tan Chrysler belonging to Lori's father. Lt. Col. James Morgan, in dress blues, walked toward them down the long sidewalk leading from a side door to the Taj Mahal.

"There's Dad now," she said, seeming to become shy as she searched for the right words.

"Mark—What are you doing tonight?" she asked.

"I haven't given it much thought," he lied, knowing that he needed to study the manuals.

"Want to go out, or something?" Lori said, cocking her head in a beautiful, little girl way, her eyes looking into his for the answer she wanted.

"Sure. That would be great," he said, numbed by the surprise invitation, but exhilarated at the same time.

He started to ask what had happened to the date she already had for Saturday night, then thought himself crazy for even considering the question.

"About 1800 hours?" she said with a pleased smile.

She was a military brat, no doubt about it, he thought. Learned military time before civilian time, probably.

"Great!"

Her father bent to speak to his daughter. "Thanks for getting him, Sunshine," he said. "Be careful going home."

The colonel noticed the looks between the two just before Lori put the TR-5 in reverse and left the men standing beside Morgan's big Chrysler.

"Looks like you're feeling better this morning, sir," Mark said, shaking the colonel's hand.

"I would feel better dead than I did last night," Morgan said.

"Let's go somewhere. Gotta lot to talk about," the colonel said, opening the door to the sedan.

Ten minutes later they sat parked near the practice tees of Randolph's golf course. They watched the early morning golfers honing their driver and iron skills, hitting balls northward toward the base's southernmost taxiway.

"Laura said she told you most everything going on with this sleep-walking business," James said.

"Yes, sir. We talked about your, your episodes," Mark said, not wanting to make an abrupt jump into the subject, but anxious to know everything.

"She tell you about me saying Clark's name over and over, during some of the earlier episodes?" James put the question, knowing the younger man had not been told the particulars.

Mark sat mute for a moment. "She didn't tell me that," he said.

"I don't remember any of it. God help me, I can't remember a single thing that has happened during these things," James said. "It happened again last night. Rather, early this morning," he said.

"Did your wife know about this last incident?"

"Yeah. She recorded what I said, just like you asked her to," James said. Mark wasn't sure whether his tone reflected approval.

"It was probably a good idea," James said.

He reached beneath his seat and pulled out a recorder.

"Won't do any good to hear it, unless you understand gibberish," Morgan said.

"But, it's interesting, and a little scary, that it doesn't sound like me. I mean, it doesn't sound like my voice."

"Laura found me staring out the French door window panes. Guess the new locks work, because otherwise, I'd probably be standing out there on the balcony, staring up as usual."

"And you were saying something?"

"I was mumbling gibberish. That's all I hear. I was muttering things in a voice that didn't sound like mine," James said, putting the recorder on the seat between them.

He pushed the "Play" button, and a deep, guttural voice spoke.

"It runs for about a minute, total, then I must have stopped. Laura led me to bed, and I woke up once I was back in the sack."

Mark listened intently. He turned the recorder so he could get at the controls. He rewound the reel-to-reel tape and punched "Play."

The voice wasn't that of the colonel. It was much deeper, and it wasn't speaking gibberish.

"It's in some sort of language. I'm almost sure of it. Do you speak any foreign languages?"

"No, well, except for a little war-time French and Italian, if you know what I mean?" James said with a light chuckle.

"Yes, sir," Mark said with a smile. "But, you've never learned a language?"

"No."

"It sounds familiar, but I can't make it out," Mark said, rewinding and replaying the tape again.

"Are any colleges nearby, nearer than Austin?"

"Yeah. We have a couple in SA, and one in San Marcos," Morgan said.

"Then they would most likely have language departments, right?"

"Yeah, kid. That's a good idea."

Mark was glad to hear cheeriness in the colonel's voice for a change.

"Why don't you and Lori take it down to Trinity or one of those others in San Antonio?"

Morgan's tone became less businesslike, more accommodating. "You know, Lori kind of likes you, Mark. I can see that you two get along. She knows her way around SA. Think you might be able to break away from the simulators for an hour or two next week?"

She must have mentioned him, for her father to make such speculation. The thought pleased him.

"Yes, sir. Most sessions will end by noon, I think."

"Well, she'll be out of school this week. Why don't you try to find out what I've said on this stupid tape?" The colonel's serious demeanor returned. "Of course, I still think it's just nonsense."

"You might be getting into something you'll regret, son," Morgan said, a bit more softly.

"Something has already involved me, colonel. I'm going to find out what it's all about. Are you sure we want Lori in on this?"

"Just don't let her know what the tape is about. Tell her it's for some project or the other you're working on for the Corps."

"Yes, that should work," said Mark.

Treading gently, the younger officer said, "Colonel, I know you're to keep quiet on the things that happened in 1947, and things that've happened since. Are you under some sort of official clearance, or are these things that you and they, whoever they are, have an unofficial understanding about?"

"Let's just say they wouldn't be pleased if they knew we were discussing these things now," Morgan said.

"Are these UFOs part of some weapons development program, you think?" Mark asked.

"If so, what's this dream stuff about, these mumblings, and all that?" Morgan said gruffly.

"Could be a psychological or mind control project of some kind," Mark said.

"Could be, I guess. They'd have to lace my food, or drinks. I've thought about that. I've been very careful anytime I'm eating or drinking away from home."

"Could it be some of the sound-wave experiments, or some sort of other new technology they're working with?"

"Don't know. Whatever it is, it must be happening to both of us. Maybe they've manipulated us into coming together like this," Morgan said.

"What if it really is something, you know, something other than has a rational explanation?"

"You mean something from out there somewhere?" James motioned toward the sky.

"Yes, sir. What if these things are from out there?"

"They aren't," said the older man. "Somebody's playing with our thoughts, but the answers can be found down here."

"Maybe we'll know the source once we understand what you've said on this tape," Mark said.

"I doubt it. Sounds like nonsensical jabbering."

"I don't think so, sir. I know I've heard that language before," Mark disagreed.

"Maybe in your own trances," Morgan said with a laugh of irony-laced supposition.

* * *

Mark heard a knock on the guest quarters' door. He glanced at his black aviator's watch. Exactly 1800 hours, he thought, looking into the bathroom mirror and straightening the collar on his blue oxford-cloth shirt.

"How's that for punctuality?" Lori said when he opened the door.

"Can't fault you for punctuality," he said, glancing at his watch.

"You and Dad get your...aircraft business...taken care of this morning?"

Her hesitating tone made him wonder if she was letting him know that she understood that she was not being let in on the true nature of the matter.

"Yeah. We took care of things," he said.

Mark, urged to do so by its owner, drove the little TR-5 at a brisk clip along Loop 410, and headed west on the outer northern edge of the sprawling city San Antonio had become. Lori kept him changing lanes at the proper times to prepare for exchanges and off ramps as they came to them.

"I know something's up, you know?" she said.

"What's up?"

"Mom and Daddy have been acting really strange about Dad's problems sleeping. Does that have anything to do with you two meeting today?"

Mark said nothing, refusing to lie to her.

"It does, doesn't it?"

"Really, Lori. I'm not free to discuss our conversations..."

She interrupted. "There! Turn there, we're going to turn on San Pedro."

He glanced in the rearview mirror, the side mirrors on both sides, and then whipped the sports car into the next lane on the right.

"You've got to tell me. I'm their daughter. I've got to know!" Now there was anger in her voice.

"And, so, that's why I was asked out on a date," he said.

"Well, yes. I guess so."

She brooded in silence for several seconds, then said with renewed gentleness, "I'm sorry, Mark. That's not fair to you. It is the reason I asked you out. But, that's not the only reason. You're not too bad looking, you know?" She leaned closer to him, tugged at the right sleeve of his shirt, and smoothed the spot she had pinched.

"Oh, so now it's the 'good cop,' instead of the 'bad cop' approach."

Rather than offending her, the remark amused her. She really did like Mark Lansing, she decided, looking at the handsome profile, whose features the passing and approaching vehicle lights highlighted.

They pulled into the parking lot in front of the Zeider Zee restaurant.

"There's one!" she said, pointing to the only open parking spot anywhere in view.

A few minutes later they were seated, had given their orders, and waited for service.

Mark looked into the blue eyes that sparked with quick wit and a deeper intelligence beyond that. Her face, already the prettiest he had seen, was emblazoned in its beauty by the shadow casting of the flame that flickered at the center of the table between them.

He was not easy to fluster, Lori thought, looking into the eyes that were obviously studying her. She imagined him in uniform, the full-dress Marine uniform. He would be the prototype for a United States Marine officer recruitment poster.

"So you fly F-4s," she said, not really wanting to talk about aircraft, or even military things.

"The F-4C," he said.

"There's a difference? Isn't an F-4 an F-4?" she said.

"No. You see, the F-4 C is the ultimate…" he cut himself off, realizing he was being had by the teasing of someone who had grown up hearing one of the best fighter pilots in the world talk about aircraft.

She spoke after a few seconds of silence. "Look, Mark. I've got to know what's going on with my father. Mother wants to tell me, but won't. Do you or do you not know anything I should know? They're my parents. I have a right to know."

He sipped from the wine that had been put at his fingertips moments earlier. He wiped his lips with the cloth napkin, looked down in thought.

"It's because they don't want even the slightest possibility of your getting hurt, Lori," he said, knowing he had started down a trail he would not be able to get off of.

"Your dad isn't going to like this," Mark said, knowing that she was right. Lori had every right to know it all.

Over the next few minutes, he told her everything.

"You have the tape?" Lori asked, when she had heard it all.

"Yes. It's at my quarters at Randolph."

"We don't have to wait until next week to find out what Dad is saying on that tape. I know this language professor at Trinity. He's giving a lecture tonight."

* * *

"It is Hebrew."

The gray-bearded, balding professor rewound the tape and pressed "play" again, then listened intently. This time, he spoke above the tape's voice.

"*Time is fleeting...time is now...the taking...the taking away...*"

Dr. Hertzog Kretchner pushed the "stop" button, rewound a short amount of tape, then put his ear closer to hear better while he tried to translate.

"Here it changes to Greek," he said, turning his face upward so the words could flow into his right ear.

"*The removal of all ...of all in opposition...to...the eternal... the eternal design.*"

"It doesn't sound like him at all," Lori said. "It sounds like a ghoul."

"It changes from Hebrew to Greek," Kretchner said, seating himself in a chair beside the recorder.

"What's this all about?" he asked.

"It's just that we recorded someone while he slept—you know, as a joke. He's always talking in his sleep," Mark lied.

"Oh? Is he Jewish?" the professor of linguistics asked, pulling his wire-rimmed glasses from his nose, then removing the handkerchief from the pocket of his tweed jacket and rubbing the thick lenses.

"I don't think so," Mark said.

"Well, I tell you," the professor said in an Israeli accent, "this man speaks both languages fluently."

Kretchner put the glasses back on his nose. "He speaks Hebrew like a scholar, and Greek like a philosopher."

The professor paused a few seconds, then spoke again.

"Interesting, interesting," Kretchner said, his brows narrowing.

"Why is that?" Lori said.

"It's just that it's kind of strange. The inflection, the nuance and cadence of the way it's spoken is archaic. It's of another age. I'm certain that the way this man is speaking went out of common usage a couple thousand years ago."

He stood from his chair and looked at his watch.

"Well, I must be off," Kretchner said. "They actually want me to hear this…this gorilla, or orangutan, or something. They want me to try to determine what this beast is trying to tell them."

He rolled his eyes, shaking his head.

"Bring back the tape of this one, anytime." He tapped the tape recorder with the tip of his right index finger. "I will enjoy doing something civilized for a change."

Fighting traffic again on Loop 410, Mark spoke while glancing at all of the mirrors at his command. "Did you tell your dad I told you all about this?"

"Not yet. I told Mom. She'll break it to him in that special way she has with him. That will be better, believe me."

"Yeah, well, he'll probably come gunning for me."

Mark eased the TR-5 into the left lane and accelerated to pass a semi rig to the right.

"Not when Mother is through working her magic."

"Let's hope not," he said, trying to find a new opening in an adjacent lane.

"Mom really likes you," Lori said.

"And what about *you*? Do you like me?"

The question caught her off guard, and she looked away. She didn't answer, and he started to press the matter. He thought better of it, and said instead, "I wonder what his ramblings mean. 'The taking away. Time is now. The removal of all in opposition to the eternal design.'"

Again she was silent.

"I wonder if I talk during these episodes," he said finally, trying to fill the conversational vacuum he felt he had created.

"I wonder why you can remember you had these—whatever they are—and Daddy can't remember his. Maybe there's no relationship at all," she said, as if talking to herself.

"How often do you have them?"

"Last one was about a week ago or so," he said, finally able to scramble the small car into the moving vacancy in the lane to their right. "Probably about due for another one. I would really like to know."

"We need to find out, don't we?" Lori said.

"Yes. I guess we do."

"I'm out of school for another ten days," she said.

"I won't have to get back to my home base until a week from today," he said, glancing at Lori, who looked straight ahead.

Silence ruled inside the little car for a minute. Lori spoke, finally.

"Yes."

He looked at her, puzzled by her suddenly speaking.

"What?" he said.

"The answer is yes. I definitely do like you."

* * *

She would take him up I-35 to New Braunfels and introduce him to some "real German food," Lori promised just before they parted 30 minutes earlier. He would eat *escargot* still wiggling, he thought, if it meant he could do so sitting across from her, looking at her all afternoon.

He picked up the training manuals from the chair and plopped them on the small tabletop near the bed. The manuals—when would there be time to study them?

He would rise early and get in a couple of hours on the simulator studies in order to be prepared for Monday's sessions. He had managed to convince his CO that he needed the training, and that Randolph was the place to get it. Now, he would have to produce some results to show the old man.

He splashed his face with water, while the reason for his being allowed the Randolph TDY ran through his thoughts.

The growing need to integrate Tactical Air Command's advanced weapons with the latest instrument flying technology made Capt. Mark Lansing's TDY choice easy for the commanding officer to approve. TAC was on a fast track timeline to get as many pilots as possible into theater. Mark was chosen by the Marine Corps to be an exchange pilot between the Corps and the Air Force. He was, in effect, the prototype in anticipation of integrating more pilots of the various armed services. He could not disappoint TAC—or the Corps.

He brushed his teeth and stretched out on the bed, still in the pants he had worn most of the day. Almost before his head touched the pillow he had fluffed, he sat up. He would at least have a quick look at one of the manuals, he decided.

He retrieved the 2-inch thick paperback book and lay back down. He read the same paragraph for the third time, and knew it would be a fruitless effort. His eyelids grew heavier by the second, and he laid the manual aside.

He removed his socks and pants, and flung them at the chair several feet away. After turning out the lamp on the small nightstand, he stretched back and pulled the covers to his chest.

He had just begun the descent into sleep when his senses burst to full alertness. His surroundings filled with a dim greenish glow that illuminated the whole room. Attempting to sit upright, he found he was unable to move even his now wide-open eyelids.

Another trance! Only this time he was fully conscious, aware of every nuance of what was happening to him.

The paralysis relaxed its grip, and he was able to move his head to a position that allowed him to peer into the fog-like glow. A voice spoke, at first in volume that was barely audible. It grew louder, and was in a language he didn't understand. It sounded like Hebrew, the same as the tape he and Lori had taken to be interpreted.

Why was he now so completely in control of his thoughts? Rarely did the trance-like states allow for more than a few seconds of lucid thought. He understood everything happening now, while he heard the voice and saw the mass form somewhere in the pale greenish light.

Though the voice continued speaking a language foreign to him, his mind translated the words. It had never happened like this before, he thought, while the form of a dark, human-like figure coalesced in the eerie mist.

"Mark. It is me. It is your father, Mark," the deep, throaty words were spoken in a mechanized drone.

Dad?! Could it be?

He strained to see something he could recognize within the black, rolling mass that was the face, highlighted by a sliver-thin line of light. No detectable features. Just a cloud-like, rolling boil of smooth, black nothingness.

He tried to call out to his father, tried to shout, "Dad!" He could manage only a whimper within his own mind. Again, the paralysis seized him. He could only stare into the human-shaped storm within the glow.

"We, you, I, and a few others have been chosen," the voice said in what must be Hebrew, Mark thought. At the same time his mind translated, the words gripped his emotions as he remembered

the father he hadn't seen since he was seven years old.

"You will be contacted, son. You must do what they ask," the voice continued, as translated somehow by his cognitive processor.

"This is reality, Mark. It is not a dream. You will know. It will be validated when the time is right."

Mark's brain began shutting down. His eyes started to involuntarily close while he felt the blackness engulfing him just before his mind slammed shut to the world around him.

Chapter 5

Laura joined the singing of "It is Well With My Soul" at the chorus. It was a soothing anthem, its words seeming to soften her edginess while she sang.

"It is well...with my soul. It is well, it is well...with my soul."

When the congregation began the next stanza, the door to the right of the choir opened and the young Presbyterian minister, in full-robed splendor, walked to the front of the choir and stood, joining them and the congregation on the next chorus.

Laura had been a Christian for only a few months and a member of the church for even less time, but she felt like these people were her life-long family members. James and Lori were happy for her, but refused to join her. She didn't push. She prayed, instead, that they would one day decide to join her.

James always said that he believed in God, but he wasn't ready to sit and listen about "hell fire" just yet. He would, he said, come see what all the Bible talk was about when it came closer to time for needing an asbestos suit. He would take out the preacher's fire insurance policy then.

Her daughter...Laura felt guilty. She hadn't taken Lori to Sunday school when she was a little girl. Or even read her stories from the Bible. Laura had attended church on special occasions throughout the years. Lori had accompanied her a few of those times—on Easter and Christmas—but said that church wasn't for her. That God would judge her fairly. She wasn't too bad, Lori had joked. She said she would take her chances.

The cavernous echoing of the pipe organ sounds lifted her spirits every time she heard them, and they roared with magnificence now, punctuating the final words of the hymn in sync with each word from the congregation: "It is well with my soul!"

When the singing was done and announcements were made, Rev. Christopher Banyon ascended the few steps to the carved oak pulpit. He gripped the lectern on either side and began in the familiar strong voice.

"My dear, wonderful people of St. Paul Presbyterian Church. Your pastor comes today to confess a sin of omission. I humbly ask your forgiveness."

There was a rustle in the pews, the women fidgeting nervously, glancing at each other and straightening to hear the young pastor's next words. The men, for the most part, were stoic, their concentration totally on the preacher's face.

Laura was afraid this was the announcement she didn't want to hear—that he was being transferred to another pastorate. She, too, fidgeted a bit before she settled to listen.

"I confess to you, as I already have to our Father in Heaven..." He paused, as if to gather strength for the words he must say.

"I have been slack in delivering to you the whole word of the Living God."

Banyon scanned his audience, lowered his eyes in thought, and again looked across the congregation.

"The Lord has told me...that is, He has spoken to my spirit, in my quiet time of prayer and study of His Word, the Bible."

The young pastor straightened, and spoke with increased confidence, as if suddenly infused with new determination.

"We have, that is, the world has, entered the time of the end. God's prophetic truth must, without dilution, without hesitation, be proclaimed here, now, beginning with this congregation of St. Paul Presbyterian Church!"

An uneasy shuffling, mumbling sound rippled softly through the pews. What was this? Prophecy?

"I know, I know..." the pastor said in calming tones. "We've never even read from the Book of the Revelation or from some of the Old Testament books of the prophets. It's a totally unheard-of concept."

He paused before he spoke, his voice taking on the intonation of a much older, more seasoned preacher.

"The Lord has told me, convicted me in my very core being, that all is *not* well with my soul, as we sang a few moments ago."

He scanned each face again. "All will not be well with our souls—yours and mine—until we determine to get into the whole Word of God, including the Lord's words on prophecy yet future. Beginning here. Beginning now. We shall begin learning what our denomination and most others have shunned. We will look into eschatology...and that's just a fancy word for end-time things. Because, my brothers and sisters of St. Paul, it is my belief that we are indeed very near the time when God will intervene into the affairs of man like He did in past ages."

Rev. Banyon opened the big Bible in front of him on the podium.

"Turn to the Book of St. Luke, chapter 17."

When the paper rustling quieted, Banyon spoke again.

"The words of the Lord Jesus. St. Luke, chapter 17, verse 26: 'And as it was in the days of Noe, so shall it be also in the days of the Son of man.'"

* * *

James Morgan drank from the glass containing three jiggers of Jack Daniel that had been poured over two ice cubes. He had been at it again the night before. The sleepwalking, the mumbled words were coming with more frequency.

Hebrew, Greek. What was that all about? The words that said in Hebrew, then in Greek—ancient Hebrew, and ancient Greek at that—that there was coming a "taking away."

Part of his agitation was due to his lack of sound sleep. Part, maybe most, stemmed from Mark Lansing bringing his daughter into this…whatever it was.

He downed the whiskey, set the glass on the table, and vowed that was to be his only drink of the day. It did, in fact, seem to calm him a bit, and he thought that now some dry toast might soothe his indigestion.

He wished for Laura. He needed her stroking, her loving gentleness. But she was doing the thing she truly loved more and more these days. She loved that church, loved hearing the young preacher spouting whatever he spouted. It was good for her. He would never discourage her from going to the church. And he was grateful that she wasn't the type to nag him, to preach to him about joining her on Sunday mornings.

What about Mark Lansing?

Obviously he was an outstanding fighter pilot and an officer with great promise. But he didn't hesitate to get his little girl involved in something she didn't have any business getting involved in. It was reckless of him.

He felt the first tingle of the drink. He welcomed it, because it brought relief to his sleep-deprived nerves.

What was the connection? Could it be his own sleepwalking and weird mumblings to Mark Lansing's trances, if that's what they were?

Had to have something to do with the incident with Clark and the disks in 1947…but what?

What about the boy's dream, or whatever it was last night? Sounded stranger than even his own episode.

Mark told him all about it before Mark and Lori had left for New Braunfels. How it wasn't like a dream. It was, the boy said, as real as standing there telling Lori and him about it.

Said it was Clark—his father—talking to him. But in a strange voice. Like the voice on the recorder the professor had translated.

Hebrew, then Greek. What did it mean?

Mark said he understood all of this…dream…vision, or whatever it was. Said it was in a language he didn't know—probably the ancient Hebrew the professor talked about—but that he understood it perfectly.

Said the thing, the human-like form who said he was Mark's father, told him he would know beyond a doubt that it was real, that he would be contacted.

What did it all mean?

His ruminations snapped to a close when the doorbell rang.

"Col. Morgan," the taller of the two men said, producing a leather card wallet, which he opened and showed James.

"We're with the Presidential Mobile Ops."

"Secret Service?"

"Yes, sir," replied the perfectly groomed man in the dark blue suit. "May we come in?"

"Sure. What's this about?"

The shorter man said, while he followed Morgan and his partner into the living room, "It's about your relationship with Capt. Mark Lansing, sir."

"What about it?"

"We've been sent by a..." the taller agent said, looking without expression into James' eyes, "...a group within a certain clandestine services entity. They are concerned that you've become too involved in giving Capt. Lansing information he has no need to know."

"You see, Colonel," the other man interjected, "there are things involved that must not go beyond a select circle of people within certain agencies."

"You're talking about these dreams and visions we're both having?"

The agents said nothing, but stared at Morgan, who said, "How can I tell him anything that's going on. I have no idea myself!"

"All the more reason to keep quiet," said the taller agent. "These are matters of top security concerns, Colonel, I assure you."

"It's the disks."

James Morgan's words cut the air between him and the agents, who let them hang there for several seconds.

The shorter agent said, "No one has said anything about ... disks."

"Then what the..." Morgan calmed himself. "What is it all about?"

"We can't say more for now. Will you come with us, sir? There's someone who needs to speak with you," the taller man said.

"Do I have a choice?"

"We aren't here to force you to do anything you don't want to do, sir," the other man said.

"Where are we going?"

"Just a few miles. To Randolph, sir," the tall, dark-haired agent said in a solemn tone.

* * *

Neither of them was thinking of food. They sat at the little German restaurant picking at the cuisine for which the small town was noted.

"You're sure it wasn't a nightmare? You said it wasn't like the other...whatever they are..."

Lori watched Mark while he picked at the *wiener schnitzel*. He shook his head with a negative nod.

"I don't know, Lori. It was different, in that I understood fully every word. I mean, I knew it was the Hebrew language...sounded like the same Hebrew form that your dad spoke on the tape. But I understood in English. In the other trances, I rarely understand anything at the time. I sometimes remember bits and pieces afterward."

"And, you're sure it was your father?"

"Not at all." He sat forward, his elbows on the table.

"It was in that strange, growly voice, like your father's voice on the tape. But for some reason, I did sense it was my dad."

"Do you think this is some kind of mind alteration, or something like that?" Lori said, moving the food around on her plate, but not eating.

"If it was just a nightmare, it was the most realistic I've ever had. But, I don't know why anyone would choose me to manipulate my mind."

"You said the figure that claimed to be your father said you would be given proof? That he is alive, that you must work together in some way?"

"Crazy, huh? Maybe that's a reason somebody might want to use mind control—to get me involved in something or the other," Mark said, feeling his stomach growl with queasiness not unlike he felt when taking an F-4 into a sudden dive.

"The figure, whomever, whatever, he—it—was, said I would be contacted."

Both were silent for several moments.

"Then I guess there's nothing we can do for now. We'll just have to wait and see if you're contacted," Lori said, her upbeat tone suggesting she was going to take the conversation in a more desirable direction.

* * *

Rev. Christopher Banyon thundered with passion completely foreign to his soft-spoken way.

"The times of Noah just before God judged mankind in the Great Flood were filled with evil and perversion. Our day is rapidly reaching the same state of vileness!"

The congregation sat in a fearful state of concentration upon the young man who punctuated the air with his right fist. The huge, gaping sleeve of the gray and burgundy robe swung wildly while he made his points.

"The angels of darkness came down to earth. They saw human women. They had sexual relations with them at every opportunity. The result was a hybrid offspring that literally corrupted the bloodline, the genetic make-up of humanity."

His voice quieted and he paused, tightly gripping the lectern's top on either side.

"The Lord had to destroy all but the eight people who had not been touched by the contamination."

Laura Morgan, like the others, never had heard the young pastor speak with such power. As if he was being used somehow by the Lord above to channel His words.

"My denomination doesn't accept this view. Most seminaries of most denominations do not accept this view. But God has shown me, through His Word, through my prayer and meditation…"

Banyon paused, looking around at the faces that looked to him to be frozen in time and place.

"…that this is the true account of the Genesis, chapter 6 story. It was not a purely human evil that caused God to have to intervene directly by sending the global flood in order to cleanse the earth. It was the direct contact with humans by Lucifer's fallen angels that caused the need for the elimination of all flesh, all people who lived on the planet, except Noah and his family."

He paused again, his forehead beading sweat, his throat constricting and dry because of the intensity of the sermon he had spent the past 45 minutes preaching with all his might.

"It is happening again," he said, then let his eyes dart from face to face to see their expressions. The many faces were still locked in awestruck silence.

"We have entered the time that Jesus foretold would break upon the world when His coming again draws near. I've been shown by our omniscient Lord that we are now in a time like it was in the days of Noah, the days just before he and the seven others entered the Ark."

* * *

"What's this all about?"

James Morgan's question broke the several minutes of silence in which the three men had been riding. They drove southward on the road adjacent to the flight line on the western side of Randolph

Air Force Base.

"Sorry, Colonel. We really don't know, exactly," the taller, slimmer agent said from the passenger-side seat while the other agent drove the dark blue government sedan toward the dark-glassed portable structure setting on the west-side flight line, 50 yards from the hangars.

"That's the President's mobile command center. Are we going there?" Morgan said, moving his head to see the structure that loomed ahead.

"Yes, sir," the agent riding shotgun said.

The squat, one-room edifice, completely encased by thick, nearly black glass-plastic composite windows, was set in place any time LBJ came to the San Antonio area. Although no one really knew all of its functions and purposes, it had communications that could reach from where it sat to anywhere in the world, any time, 24 hours a day, 7 days a week.

It sat there now in the brilliant Texas sun, ominous in its presence, a few blue Air Force vehicles parked nearby.

James felt his anxiety rising, the Jack Daniels' effects not strong enough to help him maintain the composure he wished for now. What, he wondered, could be so important as to bring him to the President's mobile command center on a Sunday afternoon? Maybe he would meet some extraterrestrials...

His silent musing brought an inward smile, while the agent brought the car to a stop near the portable building's main entrance.

An agent, probably Secret Service, Morgan surmised, opened the door when the men walked up the few steps. He said nothing, but stepped to one side to allow the three men to walk into the big room. No one else was in the building.

Tables and desks were arranged throughout the room, with five television monitors atop pedestals. A number of phones were scattered about the desks' tops. James noticed there was only one red phone. He glanced more closely. "White House/LBJ Ranch" was printed on its broad base, which housed several batteries of buttons.

"He will be here in eight minutes," the agent who had opened the door said. The others nodded.

"How's the wife and kid?" the 30-something agent said to the stockier of the two men who brought James to the command center.

"Fine. She'll be 13 this week," the agent responded.

"Thirteen!" the agent who had asked said. "Now you're in for it..."

"Yeah. That's what I hear," the man said, scanning through the dark glass to determine if the objective of their wait was in sight.

"You have a daughter, Colonel," the taller agent who had brought him said. The revelation that the man knew the fact told James they had looked into his personal life. The thought wasn't comforting.

"Got any advice for Agent Ballard?"

"Patience," Morgan said. "They do outgrow some of it."

He started to ask the agent how he knew about his daughter. It wasn't necessary. James knew how, and why. They all knew. Since the incident when his friend Clark Lansing had disappeared, they knew everything about him, about his family...

"They are here," the man who had let them in the command center said. The other two men almost snapped to attention. James remained seated.

"Good afternoon, sir," the greeter said when a short man with graying, thinning hair walked through the door, followed by several other men. The man nodded to the agent who held the door open, but said nothing. His eyes darted quickly until he found James Morgan.

"Col. Morgan," he said with a smile that seemed almost a grimace. He offered his hand.

James, after rising from the chair, felt the short, powerful grip, the hand having a tinge of roughness. This was a hand used for things other than pushing pencils. Probably handled the roughened bars of weights in regular workouts.

"I'm Bob Cooper," the 50-something year old man said, pumping James' hand cordially. "I work at the Defense Department."

"Yes, sir. I know who you are," Morgan said, wishing he hadn't.

"Oh? Well. I don't know whether that's good or not," Cooper said with a slight laugh. "I'm in covert operations. We're supposed to have low profile."

Bet that's hard to do, when you're always in the news, summoned to testify before Congress, James wanted to say, but only thought it.

"Good to meet you, sir," James did manage to say. He studied the blue-gray eyes that studied him back.

"Well, I hope you can still say it's nice to know me after we've had our talk," the deputy director of Covert Operations for the U.S. Department of Defense said. The words were matter-of-fact. Neither threatening, nor joking.

"Gentlemen," Cooper said, looking at the men who had accompanied him, then glancing at the other two agents. "Col. Morgan and I will be fine here. We need some privacy, if you don't mind."

"Sir. You have the meeting at 3:30," one of his assistants said.

"Yes. Please give me at least 30 minutes with the colonel."

With that, the assistant left the command center with the others.

The stocky man wore a perfectly tailored gray suit. Probably a thousand dollars or more, James thought, not knowing why he would be so observant about such a minor thing when his stomach was churning like a taffy-twisting machine.

"I think you know, at least in a general sense, what this is about, Colonel," Cooper said, turning from his pacing to face Morgan.

"Has something to do with my talking with Capt. Lansing, I was told," he said firmly, his growing agitation overpowering his nervousness.

"Sit," the deputy director said with a motion of his right hand, not demanding, but bidding.

Both men took seats at a long table, directly across from each other.

"Colonel, I think you realize that you've breached the... understanding...this government has always had with you since... the incident."

James Morgan said nothing for several seconds, but felt anger beginning to rise. He said, "What are you people doing to me? What are these nightmares, or visions, or whatever they are, Mr. Cooper?" His question was tinged with the emotional fire he felt.

"What nightmares?" The deputy director seemed genuinely in the dark.

"You don't know about my sleep-walking, the staring into the sky, the mumblings?"

James saw in the man's eyes a vacant look, the eyes shifting as if watching marbles roll back and forth along the table-top. He seemed to try to recall any intelligence he had stored on the matter. Deputy Director Robert G. Cooper was a good, very practiced liar.

"You've had these nightmares of what?" Cooper asked.

"I can't remember them, but my wife has had to bring me in from the balcony outside our apartment a number of times."

"How do you know they are associated with the things we're talking about? Your agreement to keep these matters to yourself?"

James felt the temperature of anger increase a degree. "I didn't agree to go insane," he said.

"These things haven't been brought to our attention, Colonel. Your physicals don't indicate any mental abnormalities, according to the reports I've seen."

Both men sat without speaking for several seconds before Cooper broke the silence. "What does this have to do with Capt. Lansing? Why are you telling him these things about the incident?"

"How do you know what I told the captain?" James said with

defiance in his tone. "Never mind. I know you have your ways. I don't begrudge security."

"Col. Morgan...we must keep this matter within the proper confines. We went over all that with you a long time ago. Hasn't the government lived up to our side of the agreement? Haven't you had the assignments you requested?"

James said nothing, analyzing the deputy director's words for peripheral meanings.

He wanted to lambaste Cooper about the matter of the slowness of his attaining rank, but thought better of it. His question could be easily deflected with something like an assertion that that area wasn't within Cooper's jurisdiction. It would make himself seem petty and self-serving.

"Capt. Lansing came to me, Mr. Director. He's got problems himself. Along the same lines that I have," James said with a calmer demeanor.

"How? You mean he has these nightmares, or whatever?"

"Come, now, Mr. Director. How can you know that I told him about Clark Lansing, his father, and not know about my and his problems when we sleep?"

The deputy director's face took on a steely expression. He leaned forward on his elbows, his fingers clinched against his chin while he spoke.

"Okay, Colonel. We'll quit playing cute games. We know all about your mental...shall we call them for now...glitches? We know about Capt. Lansing's visitations."

The blunt admissions made James' mind snap to increased alertness. The word, in particular, struck like an ice pick in the eye. "Visitations!"

"You haven't any idea what is involved here, Colonel, believe me. You don't want to know," Cooper said, his icy tone stabbing through the tension between them.

"Colonel, you are hereby ordered by your government to keep these things confined to the circle, which you have seen fit to expand."

The deputy director sat back in the chair and eyed Morgan, who sat, elbows on the table, his fingers intertwined over his mouth, his thumbs supporting his chin.

"And, that circle, I have to tell you, now includes your daughter."

* * *

James poured the Jack Daniels over the ice cubes, gave the liquid a few sloshes by circling the glass in the air, and then downed the liquor. He thought that he had just broken his vow to have no more drinks today.

He poured more, thinking how he might as well break the vow right.

"Okay, Smilin' Jack, you wanna tell me about it?"

Laura's tone was light, but James knew her question was serious. She wanted answers. He didn't feel like keeping secrets any more, the drinks already beginning to loosen his tongue.

"They've involved our girl in this thing…"

The words sounded as disturbing to himself as to his wife.

She didn't say anything for several seconds, trying to understand his meaning.

"The Roswell thing?" she said, then, realizing it was the only thing that could disturb him to this extent.

James took another swallow of the Jack Daniels.

"Said it's my fault for widening the circle of people who know about the…the incident," he said, his words almost without emotion.

"No less than the deputy of Covert Operations for the DOD— Robert Cooper. He ordered me to shut my yap, or else."

"Or else what?" Laura asked, her mind racing. What did it mean? Her daughter would be under the prying eyes and ears of the government?

"Who knows?" James said, starting to pour another drink.

Laura snatched the glass from his hand, poured the ice into the sink, put the Jack Daniels bottle in the cabinet and shut the door.

"We need you rational, Jimmy. Not flying higher than one of those jets you love so much," she snapped.

The name sobered him. She never used the name "Jimmy" unless she was getting angry with him.

"I know, SuperL. I've got to think this thing through."

"We both have to think it through," Laura said, her anger beginning to rise above her concern for their daughter. "They're not going to get away with interfering in Lori's life!"

* * *

Lori sat in the chair beside the table in the small apartment's living room, the phone to her ear.

"Mom. We're back. Had a great time at New Braunfels, ate some German stuff, then drove up to see some friends at San Marcos. You remember Jodie and Melissa?"

Mark was skeptical as he reclined with his legs stretched out the length of the sofa. But Lori seemed to know her parents would go along with the plan.

"Listen, Mom. I don't know how else to say it. I'm spending the night at Mark's officer quarters."

Mark watched Lori's blue eyes sparkle, her nose crinkling with a stifled laugh while she heard her mother go berserk at the other end of the line.

"Oh, Mom. Have a little faith," Lori said, and then listened again for several seconds.

"Mom, Mom! Now listen to me for just a second, and I'll explain."

Lori paused, looking over to Mark and winking.

"Okay. It's strictly a scientific venture. Seriously, Mother, we want to see if Mark has another of the sleep things like Dad goes into. I'm going to sit up and try to record it to see if he says anything."

Mark watched Lori thinking, her expression having lost its

humorous glow.

"Is Daddy okay?" she asked in a concerned voice.

Mark twisted from his reclining position and swung his legs into a sitting position.

"If you think I should be with you, I'll ..."

She listened to Laura, her expression displaying mild surprise.

"Okay. See you in about half an hour when I pick up some things. Goodbye."

"Something wrong?" Mark said.

"Mother said Dad's gone to bed. He's upset."

"About what?"

"Me. She said somebody from the Department of Defense chewed him out today. Said they practically threatened him. He told her they've included me in their...how do you say it?...their surveillance operation."

She sat beside him on the sofa.

"What do you think it means?"

"Your father knows what it means. It makes him sick, and I don't blame him," Mark said, more to himself than to Lori.

"It's the whole thing about Roswell, the disappearance of my dad. You now know everything, and they want to make sure that knowledge about those things stays confined to as few as possible."

Both were quiet, thinking their separate thoughts. Finally, Lori spoke.

"Nobody believes that stuff. Why are they even concerned? Only kooks and nuts think anything of the UFO reports."

"That's why Col. Morgan is more concerned than ever, the reason it concerns me."

"I don't understand," Lori said, gripping his right arm and laying her face against his shoulder.

"It means there's got to be something to all of this alien sightings stuff."

Lori stood at the small kitchen sink an hour and forty minutes later, drying the few dishes Mark had left strewn along the countertop over the days since taking up residence.

"Why are you worrying with those?" he asked, watching her from the kitchen table where he stood brushing his teeth.

"If you knew me, you would know I'm a cleannik," she said, continuing to dry a saucer with a hand towel. "Besides, it would just pile up if somebody didn't..."

Mark now stood beside her. He rinsed his mouth out and spit in the sink, then rinsed again.

He wiped his mouth with a nearby towel and threw his arms around her, pulling her close.

She pushed away at first, but relaxed when he kissed her, deeply, but tenderly.

When their lips parted, she looked into his eyes, her face reddened by her surge of emotion. She blew her breath through pursed lips, as if letting steam escape.

"You shouldn't do that if you don't mean it," Lori whispered.

"Did it feel like I meant it?" Mark asked softly.

She said nothing, but nodded yes, her eyes glancing downward, then back to meet his.

"I love you, Lori Morgan," he said, just before their lips came together again in a lingering kiss.

He surprised himself with the words he had long been sworn never to say to any girl until his flying time for the military was finished. He had watched as his friends fell one by one to their loves, and to the SAMs of Vietnam. He must never follow their mistakes...

All reservations went out the window in one moment of epiphany, when he saw this beautiful young woman standing there at his kitchen sink—looking every bit the domestic wife. Two days with her and he knew, knew without the slightest doubt whatever, there was none other for him.

"Wow," she said softly, thinking how foolish the word sounded in her own ears, but not caring whether it sounded foolish to him.

"You take the bed," Mark said. "I'll take the sofa."

They continued to hold each other close. Lori looked upward into his eyes.

"You don't have to take the sofa...you know? It's a double bed," she said.

Mark didn't respond for a moment, but took her by her hand. He stopped with her at the door to the small bedroom. He kissed her again, and they embraced for a long minute of silence.

"I'm not a guy with great character or anything," he said, looking deeply into the trusting eyes that wanted only to show him she loved him in return.

"Some guys would say I've completely lost my mind, and, maybe I have," he said. "But, I do love you, Lori. I want to prove it by doing something I probably would never do with any other girl. I...I want to wait. It's important for both of us that we wait."

He saw tears trickle in thin streams from the corner of one of her eyes, then from the corner of the other. He reached to brush them away with an index finger.

"Do you understand?"

She said nothing, but nodded yes, her eyelids lowering before looking again at him.

She loved him too, with all her heart, all her being. His insistence that they wait sealed her love for him with a burning, searing certainty that the heat and throes of passion could never have.

The tears came again, and he kissed them away.

"Lori, I do love you," he said.

Chapter 6

hristopher Banyon tossed fitfully. Lightning illuminated the bedroom, each flash followed by crashing thunder that rattled the window near his bed.

He sat up in the bed and swung his legs and feet over the side. He lifted the blind after moving the curtain to one side. Rain blew hard against the window, and when the skies flickered, he strained to see the street just down the slope that was the side portion of his yard. Swift water, a foot above the curb gushed down the street.

Banyon turned the little knob of the lamp sitting atop the nightstand. Nothing…

He went from the bed to the wall switch and flipped it up. The result was the same.

The young pastor started to go through the bedroom doorway, catching the little toe of his right foot on the thin leg of the chair sitting against the wall. He cursed, stopped to bow his head, more from the pain and to catch the breath the pain took from him than to seek forgiveness.

"Forgive me, Lord," he nonetheless said beneath his breath before limping farther into the darkness.

He thought to phone Susie, but realized that he should first check the time. He looked at the electric clock on the living room wall, able to read it when the lightning lit the room.

"2:15," he said.

He felt his way along the sofa to one of the end tables and fumbled to find his wallet and wristwatch. He held the watch's face close to his eyes, and turned it so he could see the hands when next the lightning flashed.

"3:10," he told himself. The electricity had been out for—he figured in his head—almost an hour. That was close enough.

Susie, like him, was living alone for the time being. She would be frightened—should have called him by now. Why hadn't she, he wondered, feeling his way toward the phone that sat in the little hallway's alcove.

He took the receiver from its cradle. The line was dead. He hit the buttons a number of times with his index finger, trying to get a dial tone.

"Well, that's why she hasn't called," he thought out loud, replacing the phone's receiver.

He wished they were already married. If they were married now, like he had wanted in the first place, she wouldn't be alone in her apartment, across town. She wouldn't have to lie frightened in her bed, her lights most likely out, unable to call him. He wouldn't have to be alone, worrying about her in this storm...

Instead, theirs would be a June wedding so both their parents and other relatives and their friends could arrange to attend.

The house, no matter how well furnished, was empty without Susie. The house the ladies at St. Paul's Church had fixed up for them. The parsonage they would share in just a few days...

The whole house suddenly flashed with light. The very air surrounding him seemed to explode at the same time with a tremendous clap of thunder.

Something nearby had been struck, and he hurried over to the big picture window. When he pulled the cord of the heavy draperies, all was dark, except for brief episodes of lightning that lit the storm-driven rain and trees just outside the front window.

A sudden chill began somewhere at the top of his spine and descended rapidly throughout his body. He started to pull the other cord to close the draperies.

He had to blink to make sure he wasn't imagining what he thought he saw. There. Near the largest of the trees. A black, human-like form, outlined in a thin, glowing light, looked to be facing the window—and him!

A terrible human-like figure—large, dark and looming—began to walk toward him. Its head—yes, there was definitely a head on the form! Red, flaming eyes glaring! The fiery eyes raged at him while it walked through the rain. The body, the arms, the legs seemed to emit faint sparks of electricity while it stalked him, getting larger. Getting ever larger!

He wanted to scream, but couldn't. He could only watch, and think frantic thoughts.

"My God! Help me, oh, Lord!"

The gigantic form of a nightmare trudging toward the picture window—was it a nightmare? From his childhood? After watching a horror show in some afternoon matinee?

No! The beast was real, and it was coming for him!

From out of nothingness within the lightning-illuminated blackness just outside the picture window, another figure, blazing with light, appeared and locked in what looked to be hand-to-hand fighting with the dark, menacing form. The lightning grew more horrific, the thunder deafening and earth shaking while the two combatants locked in immortal combat.

Christopher averted his eyes from the brilliance of the conflict that generated light more dazzling than the lightning. When he next looked, the battling forms were gone. He saw only the trees, the rain, the shimmering occasional lightning.

He jumped when the telephone in the hall rang. He pulled the draperies shut and made his way toward the phone while the storm continued to rage.

Any diversion from the terrifying thing he had seen—or had imagined he had seen—was welcome at this moment. Yes. He had just imagined it.

At least the phone was back in service, he thought, reaching to pick up the receiver.

"Hello?"

The line seemed as dead as before.

"Hello…"

Dead. Probably trying to reconnect it, get it working.

Banyon started to hang the receiver on its cradle, but hesitated when he thought he heard a voice.

He pressed the receiver hard against his ear, hearing only a tin-echoing static. Then, the static dissipated.

"Christopher—"

The voice was a whisper, sounded as if it were a human whisper blowing through the line.

"Christopher…" the wind-like voice repeated. Banyon started to respond, but the words wouldn't come.

"As in the days of Noah, so it shall be. Watchman watch. Therefore, watch for the bene elohim…"

The voice grew louder, like a rushing wind, and trailed off.

"Watch for the bene elohim…" the voice repeated just before the line went dead.

* * *

The second lieutenant saluted when Capt. Mark Lansing approached.

Mark returned the salute, wondering if the door out of which the lieutenant had exited the huge, stucco-façaded building was the one he needed.

He stopped and turned to call after the young officer who wore a flightsuit.

"Lieutenant!"

"Yes, sir?" the pilot in training said, walking quickly back the few paces.

"Is this the Advanced Simulator Facility?" Mark questioned, gesturing toward the building.

"Yes, sir. Through the door, to the right, then to the left down the long hallway. You can't miss it."

"Thanks."

Half a minute later, Mark saw the sign jutting from above the double doors along the right wall of the hallway.

"Flight Simulation Operations" the sign read in white letters etched in a black background.

He walked to a gray metal desk where a WAF, gold bars on the collar of her blue uniform dress, was sitting.

"Lieutenant..." Mark looked at the nametag above her right breast pocket, "...Simmons," he said, once she had gotten off the phone.

"Yes, sir?"

"I'm to do some ILS, Weather Weapons Systems upgrade training this week."

She looked at his nametag, but he said, "Lansing, Mark."

He started to give his service number, but she read it to him, instead.

"Yes. That's me," he said with a smile.

"Sir. You have been re-routed," the young, black lieutenant said.

"Re-routed? What, exactly, does that mean?"

"You're wanted on the flight line, sir," she said, standing and fingering through a number of stacked papers.

"Yes. Here are your orders," she said, handing him several pieces of the white pages, and keeping several for her files.

"What's this about?" he asked, flipping the pages, seeing that, indeed, his orders for TDY status had been changed.

"Sorry, Captain, sir. I really can't help you."

"Yeah," he said, still thumbing through the pages. "Well, thanks."

"You are to report to Lt. Col. Gerald Lazenby. His office is right through there," she said, pointing to a door against a nearby wall.

Momentarily he stood outside an office marked "Lt. Colonel Gerald B. Lazenby" on the frosted windowpane that was the top half of the door.

The lieutenant colonel met him at the door as he turned the knob and opened it.

"Just who are you, Captain?" the lanky officer asked with a curious tilt to his question.

Mark said nothing, watching the officer pick his blue cap with the silver leaf stuck to its side from the desktop.

"You must be somebody," Lazenby said, walking in front of Mark and starting down the hallway.

"Come on, Captain," the man said, putting on the cap as they reached the side door.

Mark thought they were going to go to the Air Force sedan sitting in the spot marked with the lieutenant colonel's name.

"I can't wait to see what this is all about," Lazenby said, striding quickly past the sedan, walking on the sidewalk that led down the side of the massive hangar building that had long ago been converted to a flight training facility.

"You got your orders, Captain?" Lazenby asked.

"Yes, sir."

"You'll need 'em," he said, stepping up his pace.

Mark had to strain to keep up with the older, longer-legged man. They were making a beeline for the Base Ops a hundred yards or so north of the training facility.

"What's this about, Colonel?" Mark said, pulling alongside the long-striding officer.

"You got me, Captain. All I know is they told me to deliver you personally to the Secret Service at Base Ops."

"Secret Service?"

"Yep. Said have you there no later than 8:10. We'll make it with time to spare," the lieutenant colonel said, his voice indicating a lighter mood than before.

"You're an F-4 pilot. I haven't had time to look over your record. You spent any time over 'nam?"

"A little..."

"Wonder what the blazes they want with a Marine F-4 pilot. You got a relative in Congress?"

"No, sir. No relatives that I know of."

"And you haven't any idea what this is about?"

"No, sir. Not a clue," Mark said.

"Well, the training they've pulled you from is considered the top priority, once assigned. At least this is the first case I've seen that's taken a combat pilot off the training docket once it's set."

The late May morning was unusually warm and muggy after the heavy rain the night before, and Mark found himself breaking a sweat by the time they reached the red-carpeted front portico of Base Ops. He followed the lieutenant colonel through the front double doors, like Lazenby, pulling his tan USMC cap from his head as he entered. The cold air of the air-conditioning felt good, but quickly turned uncomfortable because of the sweat-soaked T-shirt between the uniform shirt and his body.

Mark glanced at the big, round, white-faced military clock on the cream-colored wall of the lobby.

"08:02," he thought.

He stood by while Lazenby spoke to the first lieutenant behind the long, mahogany countertop that partitioned the lobby area from his recessed office.

The lobby was filling with people. Mark recognized them as members of the Washington press corps. Something was up— involving the President.

Gerald Lazenby, having finished his business with the first lieutenant behind the counter, came to Mark. He glanced around the large room, which had become more populous since he began his conversation with the Base Ops officer.

"According to the lieutenant, the Presidential party will be leaving earlier than they thought. Wasn't supposed to leave until fifteen hundred hours."

"Wonder what's up," Mark said, seeing a large party of the press corps come through the double doors.

"Nothing surprises me anymore when the man is in the vicinity," Lazenby said, watching three men in dark suits approaching, having just emerged from somewhere within the Base Ops interior.

"Capt. Mark Lansing?" one of the young men said, pulling his identification from inside his suitcoat.

"Yes, sir, I'm Capt. Lansing," Mark said, glancing at the I.D. the Secret Service agent presented.

"Thank you, Colonel, for bringing the Captain," the agent said. "We can handle it from here."

The man introduced the other agents by name. Then, addressing Lazenby, he said, "We've been instructed to escort Capt. Lansing to the President's plane."

The lieutenant colonel reluctantly left, when he realized this would be the extent of what he would be told about the strange change of orders for Capt. Lansing.

A flush of puzzlement overcame Mark's thoughts: the President's plane?

All he could think of was that it had something to do with the strange whatever it was night before last. Had something to do with his father, or whomever, or whatever had talked to him.

The things the dark vision being told him that night quickly ran through his mind.

"*We, you and I, and a few others have been chosen,*" he recalled the voice saying in what must have been Hebrew.

"*You will be contacted, son. You must do what they ask,*" the voice had instructed in the unknown language, but he had understood perfectly in English.

"*This is reality, Mark,*" the thing that said it was his father had told him. "*It is not a dream. You will know. It will be validated when the time is right.*"

The words echoed again in his head. The words the dream-creature, or vision-being or whatever it was, had said: "*You will be contacted, son. You must do what they ask.*"

"We need to get to the flight line, Captain," the agent who seemed the one chosen to talk, said. "Let's go this way," he said, motioning with toward the doorway at the side of the first lieutenant's open office, the doorway through which the agents had entered the Base Ops lobby.

Moments later they exited a side door into the bright morning light. They walked quickly, Mark flanked by the young Treasury men. Other Secret Service agents, holding walkie-talkies, watched the four men from their various vantage points, some of them talking into the devices.

Mark scanned the hangar rooftops. The Air Police were there, scoped rifles at the ready.

"What's this about, guys?" Mark said trying to sound nonplused.

"It won't be long, Capt. Lansing. You will know all about it," the agent who had done all the talking said while they traversed the white concrete of the flight line toward the President's gleaming 707.

Mark watched the aircraft grow larger while they walked. The same plane—26000—had flown President John F. Kennedy from Fort Worth to Dallas November 22, 1963, then flew his dead body back to Washington that same evening. The very airplane—he remembered now, approaching to within 70 feet of its rearmost portion—in which then-Vice President Lyndon Johnson had taken the presidential oath of office before leaving Dallas' Love Field.

The walkie-talkie held by one of the men at Mark's side squawked, and the agent spoke into it in what was obvious code-language. The agent listened, and responded.

"The man is about to land," he said to the other agents.

"We'll wait here, Captain," the man who seemed to be in charge said.

All eyes watched the horizon at the north end of the runway. Their wait was not long. The Presidential Jetstar flared before settling just as smoothly as had 26000 on Friday, when Mark had watched it land.

They watched while the Jetstar's thrust-reversers slowed the plane for its landing roll-out, then its right turn onto the taxiway immediately adjacent to the runway. All four men caught a glimpse of an Air Force sedan pull to within 20 feet of them on their right.

An Air Force tech sergeant in dress blues got out of the driver's side, while an officer got out of the other side of the front seat. Each of the men opened the back doors of the vehicle.

Two men emerged from the rear seat. Mark recognized them as Lt. Gen. Sam Maddox, Commander of Air Training Command, and Brig. Gen. Frank Matson, Commanding Officer of Randolph Air Force Base.

He anxiously wondered what he was doing here, standing between Secret Service agents, in the same company as commanding generals, and soon, the President of the United States.

The small Presidential jet taxied quickly, its pilot wasting no time in delivering the commander-in-chief to within 50 feet of Air Force 26000, whose engines began whirring as the noisy plush units fed them forced air. The plane would be ready to move out instantly, when the President gave the order.

"Let's move to the aircraft," the agent in charge said, nudging Mark's arm to start him moving toward the rear stairway leading upward to the back door of the 707.

The agents, when they had gotten their man where they wanted him to be, stood stiffly, looking around the area. They occasionally looked in the direction of the Presidential party, which had disembarked.

The President was easy to spot. Dressed in a golden-tan sports jacket and light tan trousers, his silver-haired head towered above others in the party.

Mark watched as several other people joined the generals in a line near the aircraft that had brought the President from Bergstrom Air Force Base.

Surrounded by a contingent of Secret Service agents, and followed by several people who had accompanied him to Randolph, the President moved slowly along the line of greeters, stopping to chat briefly with each person. He patted Gen. Maddox on his right shoulder, after returning the general's salute, walked a few feet past him, then returned to whisper a few words in his ear. Both men laughed heartily.

Probably a dirty joke, Mark thought, standing at semi parade-rest near the bottom of the stairway-ramp to Air Force One.

Mark thought it odd that there weren't more people around the big aircraft. Just himself and the agents, who spread out a bit, leaving Mark standing alone, feeling miniscule amidst the Presidential atmospherics.

Lyndon Johnson ambled in a determined course toward the stairway. A number of dark-suited young men, some carrying walkie-talkies, some carrying bags of different kinds, hurried to keep up with his long strides.

Mark's knees felt a bit rubbery, like after a hard sortie of aerial combat practice. What was this all about? Him, a captain, standing almost by himself, with the President approaching, forevermore looking like John Wayne on a mission from which he wouldn't be deterred.

"You will be contacted, son. You must do what they ask."

The voice! He heard it as plainly as if the words were spoken right in front of his face. But, the voice wasn't the guttural growl, like in the trance. It was the remembered voice of his dad!

"You must do what they ask," he heard his father say again.

"You doing okay today, son?"

Lyndon Johnson's shouted Texas drawl jerked Mark's thoughts back. He snapped to attention and saluted the President, who half-waved, half-saluted back, and then stuck out his right hand.

"Yes, sir," Mark said, burying his hand in the President's huge, fleshy hand. The warm, enormous hand was unlike any he had shaken.

"You been waitin' long, partner?" Johnson asked above the loud whine of the plush unit. He then shouted again before Mark could answer.

"You're gonna be asked to do some special things for your country, son. I want you to show 'em you've got what it takes."

"Yes, sir," Mark said, not knowing what else to say, not having even a spark of an idea what this giant presence of a man was talking about.

"Atta boy! Good!" the President said, smiling broadly and

gripping Mark on both shoulders, and slapping him gently, as if trying to compress one shoulder together with the other.

Johnson turned to go to the stair ramp.

"Don't let me down, now, Captain. Your President is countin' on you. Your country is counting on you," Lyndon Johnson said loudly, then bounded up the ramp and into Air Force One.

"Captain," a voice behind Mark said after the President had moved through the aircraft's rear hatch.

He turned to see a man of stocky build in a dark blue suit approach, a tight smile on his face.

"I'm Bob Cooper," the short, graying middle-aged man said, offering his right hand.

* * *

Laura Morgan sat at the little table recessed in the apartment's wall. She turned the page of the Bible, and read in silence.

"Genesis 6:13: 'And God said unto Noah, The end of all flesh is come before me; for the earth is filled with violence through them; and, behold, I will destroy them with the earth.'"

She looked up from the page with an expression of deep contemplation.

"What's so interesting?" Lori, wearing her father's big, well-worn blue terrycloth robe, took her seat in the booth bench across from her mother.

"Oh... good morning, baby," Laura said, reaching across to squeeze her daughter's hand, which held a mug of steaming black coffee.

"Just reading my Bible," Laura said.

"Must be something pretty good this morning. You had a look of total concentration."

"Our pastor has started giving sermons on something I've never heard, or even thought of."

"Oh, yeah? Well that would probably cover just about everything in there for me," Lori said lightly. She could see her flippant words did not please her mother.

"Sorry, Mom. I mean that I know I should read that book once in awhile," Lori said.

"Yes, you should," Laura agreed. She smiled and reached again to pat the hand that held the mug on the tabletop.

"What's he saying that has you so fascinated?"

"Out of the blue he started talking about prophecy. About how the Bible says things will again be like they were during Noah's time," Laura said.

Both were silent for a few seconds before Lori spoke.

"That's just a story about the flood covering the whole earth, all the animals in the Ark."

"No. I don't think so," Laura disagreed.

"Oh, Mom. I know it's a story meant to teach a lesson. Make everybody do the right things, live right. But, surely you can't believe that the whole earth was covered by water."

Her mother said nothing, her expression saying she considered her daughter's words, and rejected them.

"All those animals, Mother. How could Noah have even rounded them up? Much less gotten them in that boat. And, can you imagine the smell? The job of cleaning up after them?"

"Rev. Banyon says we should take the Word of God literally, except where the Bible expressly says it's a parable, or allegory, or symbol," Laura said.

Lori could see it would do no good to debate further, so she decided not to.

"He says in Noah's time, just before the Flood, fallen angels came to… seduce… the daughters of men. He says that he believes this sort of thing will happen again, the nearer it comes to the second coming of Christ."

"Angels are men? I thought angels are usually pictured as women," Lori said before sipping the hot coffee.

"No. They are always depicted in the Bible as male," her mother said.

"Then I've got one," Lori said happily. "His name is Mark

Lansing."

Laura studied her daughter's face, the wrinkle-free face of youth. Glowing and perfect, without a dab of make-up.

"You really like him?" Laura said as she sipped from her own mug of coffee.

"Mom." Her voice became almost a whisper as she leaned forward and looked into her mother's eyes. "Mark told me he loves me."

"Loves you?!" Laura's words came out louder than she intended. "You two have only known each other for a couple of days. How can he say he loves you?" Lori expected that reaction. Her mother's surprised disbelief amused her.

"What happened? I mean, men will say a lot of things to…" She let the thought transfer to her daughter's mind.

Lori calmly drank from the mug, watching her mother's expression that said she awaited an answer.

"Mom. You just won't believe it. He must be one of your angels. Not from the fallen angels, but from the others."

She told her mother that she actually did sit up most of the night, waiting for the trance-like visitation that never came.

When Lori had told her mother all but the fact that her daughter had been willing, Laura said, more joking than serious, "Well, he's a handsome rascal. You two could give us some great-looking grandkids."

They both giggled.

"Lori," Laura said, turning serious while she studied the coffee mug, before looking at her daughter.

"Daddy—he's very worried about you, and your knowing so much about these…these strange things going on."

Lori knew it was true. She and her father were close. Always had been. She was worried about him, too, but didn't talk about it much, even with her mother. He had always been a strong male presence in her life, protective, yet at the same time totally loving. Not like so many fathers of the service brats she had known over the years.

Their fathers were usually heavily into drink. By the time their children were teenagers, they had hardly known their dads. Something about the military drove families apart. Probably the fact that military needs always came first, no matter what.

But her dad—he had never let anything stand between himself and her. Between himself and her mother.

The serious drinking had really just begun about six months ago, which she now knew was the time when the nightmares, or whatever they were, began for him.

"He's sleeping in today?" Lori said.

"Oh, you know better than that. He's been up and gone since six."

* * *

All sorties had been cancelled for the day. And, there were no classroom or simulator trainings scheduled. Student pilots and instructors were given a day of R & R, thanks to the President of the United States.

James Morgan strode into the wing commander's office, his angry thoughts trained on a purpose that assured confrontation. He had always been able to talk with Col. Ervin Beery, the wing commander for the T-37, T-38 and T-39 Air Training Command missions assigned to Randolph.

They—whomever "they" were, exactly—had overstepped bounds. Boundaries that he had always maintained around his wife and daughter. His rage had been building since Sunday afternoon, when he had been lectured like a junior high schoolboy in the principal's office. There would be the devil to pay for their interloping.

"Hello, Kelli," James said to Beery's secretary, a WAF lieutenant younger than his own daughter.

"Colonel," she said, sitting more erect, seeing the angry determination in his manner. He had sounded upset when he had phoned 30 minutes earlier for an appointment.

"Sir, I'm sorry, but Col. Beery had to leave...an emergency," she lied, and knew that he knew. "I...I couldn't reach you in time, sir."

"Where is he?" he said, undeterred.

"Actually, sir, there is someone who wants to see you in his office," the young woman said, looking sheepishly toward the door marked "Col. Ervin Beery" in black letters on its frosted glass top half.

She pushed an intercom button. "Sir. The colonel is here."

The door opened, and Robert Cooper stood, smiling, and offering his hand.

"Col. Morgan. James. Nice to see you again," the deputy director of Covert Operations for the U.S. Defense Department said, shaking James' hand, then guiding him inside Beery's office by his elbow.

"Colonel, I know you're somewhat unhappy with us...with me..." Cooper took his seat behind Beery's desk, and sat stiffly upright in the brown leather chair. He fidgeted with the cuffs of the starched white shirt sticking from each sleeve of the dark blue suit.

"I'll tell you, Mr. Director," James said, standing with his fingertips supporting his upper body on the desktop. "I'm through with this cat and mouse game about the Roswell thing," he said, his face reddened with anger.

Cooper said nothing, but sat farther back in Beery's big chair, continuing to tug at the shirtsleeves and play with the expensive cufflinks.

"As soon as I talk to Col. Beery, I'm blowing the top completely off this insanity," James said between clenched teeth.

Robert Cooper's broad face, surrounding the silver-gray eyebrows and icy blue eyes, showed no emotion whatever. The fact angered James even more.

"You will not invade my life any more. Leave my wife and daughter out of this. And, just to make sure, I'm telling the world what I know, Mr. Director!"

Cooper stood from the chair and walked slowly about the room. He moved to the big window and spread the blinds to look out. He then faced James.

Cooper stared for a moment, sizing up the man in front of him.

"No one will believe you, Colonel," he said, seeming to say it as a probing debate point rather than to make an absolute statement of fact.

"If you think that's the case, why all the secrecy, Mr. Director? Why not just leave me alone, and let me shout it at the top of my lungs to all who will listen?"

The stocky man again was silent for a few moments.

"You will put your personal life above the nation's security? That breaks your oath to service, Colonel."

"No, sir! I didn't take the commission to put my wife and daughter in danger."

"They're not in danger, James. All we ask is that they allow us to ensure their security. They won't even know our people are anywhere around."

"No, Mr. Cooper. That's not America. That's just another form of gulag," James said. "They aren't in the Air Force. I am."

"And, why come to Col. Beery?"

James watched the emotionless face to try to analyze the scope of the question.

"He's my wing commander. We've been close…"

"He already knows, Colonel," Cooper interrupted. "I've informed him."

"Then, you won't mind if I discuss the matter with him," James shot back before Cooper's words had gotten out of his mouth.

"No, not at all, Col. Morgan."

Cooper moved to behind the desk, and was again seated. He leaned forward, resting his elbows on the desktop.

"As a matter of fact, he wants to talk with you about the whole matter. He asked that I tell you that he's on the flight line, getting ready to test-flight an aircraft. Wants you to meet him over there.

At the T-38 section, I think he said."

James turned toward the door, stopped, and then half-turned to look at the deputy director, who sat looking at him, the gray-blue eyes masking any emotion he might have. The man was perfect for his freedom-destroying work, James thought.

"What about my wife and daughter? Will you leave them out of it?" James said, his tone a bit less hostile.

"We have no intention of interfering in your..." Cooper searched for and found the right word. "...of interfering further in your life."

Chapter 7

We've got to talk," Mark Lansing said, holding the phone receiver to his right ear and pacing as far as the cord would allow.

"Is something wrong?" Lori, who had decided to get another hour of sleep, said, coming to a new level of alertness from her drowsiness.

"I don't know," he said, looking around the area surrounding the several pay phones against the hangar building's outer wall.

"My orders have been changed. I'll have to leave soon."

Lori sat up in the middle of the bed, trying to clear her mind so as to better understand. The first thing that entered her reviving brain was Vietnam.

"Southeast Asia?" she asked.

"No. It's not a combat assignment. If it were Vietnam, that wouldn't surprise me. This is, well, I don't think we should talk now. I'll be at the snack bar. The one where you found me the other morning."

* * *

Col. Ervin Beery stood going through the checklist for the T-38 he was about to test fly. He then sat behind the line chief's desk and sipped the coffee the chief master sergeant had offered him a few seconds earlier. He continued to flip the pages laminated in clear plastic.

Gunthaar Helstrom drank from the mug of just-made coffee and thumbed through the aircraft's loose-leaf form.

"She's ready whenever you are, Colonel," Helstrom said, letting the form plop on the desk within Beery's reach.

"The bird looks good to go, Swede," Beery said, addressing the T-38 line chief by his nickname.

"Any sign of Morgan yet?" Beery looked out the window of the hangar office to see two men preparing the T-38 he would fly.

"No."

"Good thing the President got out of here early," the colonel said.

"Why's that?"

"I've got a granddaughter's birthday party to attend this afternoon. His going back to DC early cleared the way for me to get in these flying hours, and do you guys a favor at the same time."

"Yes, sir. The President was very thoughtful to leave early," Helstrom said in his raspy voice, chuckling.

Beery grinned, and stood from the desk chair. "There he is!" the wing commander said, seeing James Morgan come through the doorway.

Both men greeted James, who only wanted to talk about matters involved in his troubled thoughts.

"Sir, I was talking to Deputy Director Cooper. He said you are aware of the things…the things that have been happening."

"Yes, James," Beery said, pouring himself another cup of coffee from the big coffee maker against one wall.

"You feel like flying?" Beery said as he drank from the mug.

Surprise flashed across Morgan's face, then he understood that the wing commander wanted to discuss the matter while in flight.

"Yes, sir. I'm always ready to fly," James said.

"I just happen to have a flightsuit and all the fixings in your size," the colonel said with a wry smile.

The wing commander had planned it. Planned for the two of them to make the test flight. And talk about the…problem…while in the air, putting the Talon through its paces.

* * *

Mark was standing just outside the door to the snack bar when Lori pulled the TR-5 into the parking lot. They embraced, and kissed, then he took her hand and walked away from the overhanging, weather-shielded area surrounding the snack bar's front door.

"Let's talk in the car," he said, opening the passenger-side door for Lori, then walking around the front of the car and sitting behind the wheel. He reached beneath the seat to trip the lever that allowed the seat to slide backward for legroom.

"What's going on, Mark?"

"Like I said, orders were issued that change everything, I guess," he said, handing several sheets of papers to her.

Lori looked them over, seeing that his new assignment was Andrews Air Force Base, Washington, D.C.

"When?" she asked, further scanning the pages.

She saw the date of assignment at the same time he said, "Says 'immediately.'"

"You report tomorrow?" Her question was put with exasperation. "What's going on?!"

"It's weird. And getting weirder."

She could see in his face that he was not just being dramatic. He looked uneasy, she thought.

"Mark, what is it? Can you tell me? I mean, it's not classified, is it?"

"It is, but, you know what, that's another thing that's so strange. They told me it's…that it has top security classification, but that it's okay for me to tell you. Have you ever heard of that in the military? Something is top secret, but it's okay for a civilian to know about it?"

"Who? Who told you that you could tell me?"

"One of the top guys at the Defense Department."

She was silent, trying to make sense of his words.

"That's not the half of it, Lori. The President, himself, met with me personally. Told me I am to do something, perform special service for the country."

"The President? President Johnson?"

"I know, I know. Unreal, right?"

She said nothing, looking again at the orders.

"After the President told me that, the deputy director of Covert Operations for the Department of Defense—name's Robert Cooper—he came up to me, and said I am to work on a special project assigned to me by President Johnson, himself. He then mentioned you, by name, Lori. Said to make sure I let you know."

"Me? What do I have to do with it?"

"That's what worries me," he interrupted her. "Why do they want you involved?"

Both sat in silence, considering the meaning of it all.

Mark said, then, "I'm leaving this afternoon."

* * *

Ervin Beery was a concern to many of those involved with flying, both those at Randolph, and those who called him their friend.

He had problems, the rumor went, and they involved personal matters. His drinking, as a result, had become much worse over the past months, the rumor mill claimed.

The thoughts ran through James' mind, while the two men pre-flighted the T-38. Laura had more than once mentioned the talk among flight officers' wives that Col. Beery's wings might soon be clipped. He would be taken from flight status. Not a good position for a wing commander. A man couldn't fly without wings…

"Looks good to go," Ervin Beery said, closing the preflight book and putting his right foot on the bottom rung of the ladder. "That nose strut could use a shot of air, but I don't see that we have a problem there," the full bird colonel said, climbing toward the front cockpit.

James looked at the front strut, and mentally measured the allowable tolerance between the top and the bottom. He agreed. It wasn't a problem.

"Chief," he said to the crew chief who followed Beery up the ladder, and prepared to hand the wing commander his helmet, which had hung on the iron hook jutting from the side of the ladder. "Maybe you'd better take a good look at the nose wheel strut when we get back. Looks like it might need a shot of air."

"Yes, sir," the young man said, helping Beery to straighten the harness straps.

The flight was to last no more than 40 minutes. Just enough time to make sure the new engines were okay to begin a schedule of sorties. He hoped those forty minutes would relax him a bit. Despite the discussion he and the wing commander would have about the things troubling him.

To some it would seem ridiculous, flying a complex, high-performance fighter-trainer, and at the same time trying to carry on a conversation on other matters. Not to the fighter pilots, for whom handling the birds was as natural as walking. The whole thing would be cathartic. Like a conversation while walking down a country lane would be for some.

The crew chief held up his right hand after the plush unit had done its starting work, and both engines were running smoothly.

The man at the rear of the plane manning the unit quickly disconnected the hose and buttoned the panel against the T-38's bottom. The crew chief motioned the jet from where it had sat for more than an hour, and soon it pointed southward down the runway.

After trimming the bird for take-off, Beery released the brakes by taking pressure off the top of the rudder pedals, and pushed both throttles fully forward, igniting the afterburners. The sleek fighter-trainer quickly picked up speed, its afterburners' blue-white flames thundering behind.

Beery kept the plane on the concrete until the last possible second, and then pulled the stick back. The T-38 shot almost straight up.

The maneuver was prohibited, but Ervin Beery rarely paid attention to such regs when flying his test-flights. James wouldn't tell on him, he thought, enjoying the ride.

"Go, baby!" Beery said from the front seat, watching the altimeter spin. James watched the other gauges. All seemed to be working perfectly.

The colonel's breathing was heavy over the intercom, his excitement raging. After 30-plus years of flying, the old man still loved every second of it. The wing commander leveled the T-38 at 40,000 feet, and put it into a series of rolls, coming again to level flight.

"She's as smooth as a baby's butt," he said.

"Let's give the ABs a going over," he said. He pulled the throttles back to 90 percent, to 70 percent, and then jammed the throttles fully forward. The plane shot forward, the increased thrust pushing the flyers back against their parachutes.

After repeating the test several times, Beery throttled the aircraft to cruising speed, and said, "What about these nightmares, James?"

The abruptness of the question's timing took James aback.

"I've had them since the Roswell experience," James said, cutting through to the heart of the matter.

"Yeah. I've been clued in to all of that stuff," Beery said, jockeying the throttles slightly back and forth. "You really think you saw a UFO?"

"I know I did, Colonel. Two over New Mexico, and one over Israel in '48."

"You think these vision things are part of that?"

"Yes, sir. I do."

"Now you're upset with the D.C. bunch?"

"It goes much deeper, Colonel..." James paused to gather his explanation. "They are playing with my mind, and not only mine, but with that of Mark Lansing. Capt. Mark Lansing, a marine F-4 pilot, the son of the man who was my friend. The guy who disappeared that day in '47."

"You think they're doing something to affect your brain?" Beery said, matter-of-factly.

"Yes, sir. I know that somebody is doing it. And now they said they are going to bring my daughter into this thing. I figure the only way to deal with it, and at the same time get back my sanity, is to go to the media, I guess."

There was silence for 20 seconds, before Beery said, "Well, James, you're one of mine. I'll back you all the way, if that's what you're determined to do."

James was stunned, having thought that Cooper, or someone within the D.C. group who knew about his sleepwalking and about his UFO encounter at Roswell, would have told Beery to talk sense to him, talk him out of spilling his guts.

"They gave me a story that you've about lost it, James. I didn't believe them for a second."

James was touched. He had always liked the old man, except when the colonel had been drinking. Beery was known as a commander who would go to bat for his men, no matter the consequences. Now, he knew it was true.

The T-38 flew at 45,000 feet, outrunning the sound of the J-85s roaring behind.

"Let's take this baby home," Col. Beery said, banking a steep left and turning for Randolph's east runway more than 100 miles away.

Without warning, the plane shuddered. An unforeseen thunderstorm held them in its grip.

Impossible! The skies had been clear for as far as could be seen, Morgan thought. Not possible!

"Colonel," James said. No response.

"Col. Beery," he repeated. Still no response. Ervin Beery's helmeted head, James could see through the wind-screen separating the back cockpit from the front, was fixed in a straight-ahead position.

"Colonel!"

James heard a deep growl come over the intercom's earpieces within his helmet. It sounded like the audiotape he had given Mark Lansing to decipher.

The growling words continued, and grew louder. Were they Beery's words? They had to be his words!

"Colonel...Colonel!"

In the front seat, Beery's eyes were transfixed, his pupils dilated. He neither heard his co-pilot's calls to him, nor his own muttered words.

The black swirling grew worse around the T-38, and caused it to shudder again. Ervin Beery pushed fully forward on both of the throttles, and, at the same time, pushed the stick forward.

The bird nose-dived in full afterburners, rocketing ever faster downward through the black, boiling turbulence.

James tried to grab the throttles, the stick. He couldn't move. Try as he did, with all of his strength, he couldn't move!

* * *

Laura shivered, a sudden chill tingling her spine. She walked among the small appliances at the Base Exchange, searching the shelves for a certain brand of toaster. It would be a wedding gift for a major's daughter.

The shiver struck again, and she wished for a jacket, or sweater...something to warm her.

While she was at the BX, she would also find something for Rev. Banyon and his fiancée, Susie. She mused while she shopped. When would their Lori become a bride? Would it be Mark Lansing? Lori would be a beautiful bride. Beautiful, and brilliant! She had finished high school a year ahead of schedule. Undergraduate work a year ahead of schedule. She would finish her graduate studies in molecular biology in just two years...

Brilliant—and—beautiful. Mark Lansing, if he were the one,

would be a lucky fellow.

She daydreamed while her eyes scanned the stacks of every conceivable small appliance. A nice, chrome coffeepot would be just right. But did he and Susie even like coffee? Just because she loved it, didn't mean they did. No, a coffee pot was definitely out...at least until she could find out if they liked coffee.

Rev. Banyon. Why was he suddenly preaching Bible prophecy? Nothing else, just prophecy.

Why was it so much on her mind? Must be because the pastor preached it so much, she thought, picking up a small toaster and examining it. She put it back and moved a bit farther along the aisle.

Did the fallen angels really come to earth? Intervene in the affairs of human beings, the women of the times just before the Flood? Was there really a flood that covered the whole earth? Rev. Banyon thought so, with all his heart...

Again the shiver of a chill.

Laura hoped she wasn't coming down with something.

"Will Mrs. Laura Morgan please come to the front?"

The Base Exchange's loudspeakers crackled her name. "Mrs. Laura Morgan. Come to the front, please."

She saw an officer in dress blues standing, his service hat in hand, a solemn look on his face. It was Col. Carl George, an adjutant to Gen. Matsen, the base commander.

She knew before he spoke. Something was terribly wrong.

* * *

Mark had said his goodbyes to Lori. He had kissed her and promised to call every day they were apart, no matter where he was when it came time to call.

Her tears were almost more than he could stand. He fought now to choke back his own emotions. A combat pilot, an F-4 fighter pilot. How would that look? A United States fighter pilot— a Marine—showing emotion because he had to leave his...what was she to him? His girlfriend? She was no mere girl. She was a beautiful woman.

Whatever was going on with the trances, the weird things happening, he had to follow orders. He wanted to talk to Lori's father before he left, but they wanted him to leave now. Said to contact no one other than Lori. He hadn't yet told her, asked her. But, she was as good as his soon-to-be wife, in his mind—which should now be concerned with getting this bird pre-flighted.

The thoughts ran swiftly while he knelt to look upward beneath the aircraft. He rubbed his right fingertips along one panel.

No. Only clear liquid, not red fluid. Just moisture collected from the humidity. Not hydraulic fluid as it had first appeared.

After satisfying himself that all looked good on the F-4's belly, he stood and flipped the page of the pre-flight book. He would next check the horizontal stabilizer on the aircraft's left side.

Why had they ordered him directly to Andrews, rather than to his home base? He supposed someone would fly the F-4 back to Egland from Andrews.

Why the hurry? His things at Egland would be gathered and sent to him at D.C. Why the hurry...?

"Sir." A transit sergeant dressed in a white jumpsuit approached him while he stood by the drooping, camouflaged horizontal stabilizer.

"I'm sorry, Captain, but flying has been temporarily suspended," the non-com said. "Maybe we can resume in about two hours, they tell us."

"What's the problem?"

"A T-38 went down south of here. Rumor has it that it was a test flight being flown by Col. Beery."

"The wing commander?" Mark said.

"Yes, sir. They say it flew straight into the ground," the sergeant said, shaking his head. "Col. Beery was a good guy."

"Didn't make it out, huh?" Mark said.

"No, sir. Some think it might have been a heart attack."

With his take-off delayed, his order to take time to talk to no one but Lori was, at least in his mind, no longer valid.

He had cleared things with Base Ops. He could be reached in the little snack bar.

He removed his g-suit and stowed it in the cockpit while standing on the ladder. He would call Lori. Hopefully, she would hurry to him, and they could spend at least an hour and fifteen minutes or so together, before he would have to again put on the g-suit.

He walked quickly to the several pay phones around the corner from the snack bar, searched for change in the flight suit's zippered pockets, and dialed.

The phone rang five times, and he slammed the receiver in its cradle. He searched his mental files of phone numbers she had given him where she might be reached if she were not at her parents' apartment. He recalled a couple of the numbers and dialed them. No luck. Lori wasn't there.

Mark walked back to in front of Base Ops, surveyed the vast, almost empty flight line, and wondered what to do next.

Where was she?

He looked to his left to see his F-4C being buttoned up by the transit crew chief and two other men. Civilians, he surmised.

"Mark!"

Lori's voice! He turned to see her hurrying toward him, her arms outstretched.

"Oh, Mark!"

She was crying. Not sad tears of having to part, but tears that gushed as if her heart were being torn out.

"Lori, what's wrong?" He held her close.

"They say…they say Daddy was killed today!"

Chapter 8

"I was just thinking about calling you," the deep voice said, after answering the phone.

"Oh?" Christopher Banyon was surprised. The two men hadn't talked in nearly a month. "I was thinking about driving over for— to get some thoughts from you," Christopher said.

"And, I was just thinking about inviting you," the man continued the banter, glad to hear from his friend again.

An hour later, they sat in Randall Prouse's San Marcos home, in the cluttered office just off Prouse's den. Both were Christians, Christopher Banyon was satisfied, but each came from different doctrinal backgrounds.

Banyon's own denomination paid scant attention to Bible prophecy yet future, to eschatology—the study of end-things from a Biblical perspective, Christopher Banyon thought. His church viewed prophecy as mostly already fulfilled. That which wasn't yet fulfilled was either symbolic, allegorical, or both.

Dr. Randall Prouse believed that the greatest, most profound prophecies in the Bible were yet to be literally fulfilled. Prouse was considered a fanatic by most of Christopher's Reformed Church colleagues—those whose doctrinal views were distinct from Catholic tradition and ritual. The kind of thinking that had got Luther and the others in trouble, and set in motion the reformation. At the same time, the Reform clergy viewed prophecy much as did the Catholic Church they left.

Despite their differences, Christopher considered Prouse a

close friend. This brilliant scholar had influenced his growing disaffection for his own church's refusal to consider the possibility of prophetic things as being literal. Things like rapture, tribulation, Armageddon, and the millennial reign of Christ.

When Banyon brought the subjects up in conversation with colleagues of his denomination, he could count on being subjected to amused, head-wagging condescension.

Prouse who had earned a doctorate in theology, was viewed by most, even non-Reform Protestant ministers in the area who knew him, as a part-time preacher, who only espoused prophecy. These were prophecies that they viewed in most cases as insignificant and irrelevant to the time, or to the future.

"I've got to tell you, Chris, I'm wary of dreams and visions," the San Marcos college professor of archaeology, who also held a Ph. D., said. "Usually it's bad pizza, or spaghetti, or too much sauerkraut. But, I had my own nightmare last night. One that included you."

"Me?" Christopher said with a surprised laugh.

"Yes. You were in a terrible storm. You were cut off from any chance of help. Then, out of the lightning came—I don't know what."

Banyon, who held a cup of tea on a saucer, almost dropped it, spilling some of the cream-laced liquid.

Prouse reached forward to help steady him, seeing the younger man's face go ashen.

"You okay?"

"Yes, yes, thank you. I'll be fine," Christopher said, setting the cup and saucer on one corner of his friend's old desk.

"You don't look okay," Prouse said, getting a roll of paper towels nearby and tearing off a few sheets. He knelt and dabbed at Christopher's pants and shoes.

"Thanks, it will wash out. Hope the carpet's okay."

"It's mostly on you, I'm afraid," his friend said, finishing up mopping the spill.

"Sorry to startle you. This dream of yours must have been

something. When you told me that you were in a storm during your—dream—and that there were creatures struggling outside your window, I had to pay attention."

"Like I said when I called," Christopher said, "this wasn't a dream. It, like your dream, happened during that terrible thunderstorm last night."

"Yes, we had a really strong one, too," Randall Prouse said, resettling himself in the chair across from his friend. "I think that's what set me to dreaming. About the storm. I don't know what brought you into it, but it was one of the most realistic nightmares I've ever had."

Christopher felt still shaken by his friend's revelation. He started to tell his experience during the storm, but his words spilled out in the form of a question.

"Do you know much about the...*bene elohim*?"

"The *bene elohim* means the 'sons of God,' or the 'sons of the mighty.' They are the angels, created directly by God. They are most referenced in the Biblical books of Genesis and Job as the angels that left their first estate, their given habitation," Prouse said after a momentary pause for recall. He said, then, "They apparently were part of the angelic creation that followed Lucifer in his rebellion."

"Yes. That was my findings," Christopher said, his eyes narrowing, his brows wrinkling in a frown of agreement, remembering his brief time of research.

"What's this about, Chris? You went ghost-white when I mentioned the nightmare."

Christopher said quietly, "Randy, it was just like you described. I saw a dark, human-like thing in the rain, by the big tree. It started for me. But this glowing figure, pulsing with light and energy of some kind, it intercepted the dark form."

"And, you say this thing, this experience, wasn't a dream. You believe it really happened?"

"It was real, Randy. As real as me sitting here now, talking with you," Christopher said.

"What happened next?"

"I looked away. It was so bright when they, they locked up."

"They fought?"

"Yes. They fought, and they—their surroundings got so bright that I had to look away. When I looked again, they were both gone."

"And that's it? The thing didn't come back?" Prouse said, watching Christopher's face while the minister concentrated.

"No. There's more. The phone, which had been totally knocked out by the storm, rang. I answered it. After a few second of the line being dead, there was this voice…"

"Whose?"

"I have no idea. It was deep, strange…"

"What did it say?"

"It said that I am *'to watch…to watch for the bene elohim.'* It said, *'As in the days of Noah, so it shall be. Watchman. Watch, therefore, for the bene elohim…'*"

The phone on Prouse's desk rang, causing the young minister to jump. Prouse answered.

"Hello. Yes, he's here," he said, then handed the receiver to his guest. "It's for you."

After listening, a grim look on his face, Christopher said, "Yes. Okay. I'll be there in about 45 minutes."

"A problem?" Randall Prouse said, standing with his guest.

"There's been a crash. An aircraft from Randolph. The wing commander was killed. They think that the husband of one of my parishioners might have been on board, too."

* * *

Transit flying, as well as all other flying, was cancelled until 6 a.m. Tuesday. Randolph was in a near lock-down mode because of Col. Ervin Beery's death in the crashed T-38.

Rumors flew that he was drunk when he took the aircraft on the test run. Others said that he committed suicide. There was also the growing rumor that there was another pilot in the plane when the ranchers saw it nose earthward in full afterburners.

The crater was more than 30 feet deep in the rough, barren land populated only by rattlers, horned toads and jackrabbits. The T-38 was in thousands of pieces, few of them larger than the size of a half-dollar.

Pieces of the titanium tail cone and the main landing gear stainless steel struts were the only identifiable parts of the plane.

The pilot's lap belt clasps had been found, still together. The only thing of the pilot that was even slightly identifiable was two teeth, the end of one thumb, and an eyeball.

Rescue workers and investigators poured over the wreckage site, putting down red markers and yellow markers when things of interest to the investigation were found.

Maj. Herman Roarke looked into the deep crater, seeing charred wreckage and blackened earth, from which smoke continued to rise. "Well, now we know what happens when one goes straight in doing almost mach two," he said.

Maj. Red Germand only grunted. Ervin Beery had been his immediate superior, and love him or hate him the colonel had been a force in his younger days. Germand had found him a fair superior, always ready to back his people. Red Germand admired loyalty in any officer. He tried to be that kind of officer.

"Won't be much we can do piecing this one together, Red," Maj. Roarke said, watching workers picking up tiny fragments in preparation for tagging, then piecing the jigsaw together in a hangar on the west side of Randolph. The retrieval would go on 24 hours a day until every piece of the aircraft that was recovered was tagged.

"The eyewitnesses said they will swear the bird was in afterburners," Red Germand said, disbelief in his voice. "Why?"

"If the colonel had a heart attack, he could have jammed the throttles fully-forward, and fallen forward on the stick. That could account for it," Roarke said.

Germand shook his head no. "Very unlikely. The inertia reel

would keep him and the chute pulled back against the seat. It would take a conscious effort, not an accidental push, to put that bird into burners."

Herman Roarke was in no position to argue. He had no wings. He was one of the few officers assigned to aircraft crash investigations who had not been a flyer.

"What about the rancher who saw the crash? You've talked to him," Germand said. "Did he say anything to you about seeing some sort of object near the 38 just before it went in?"

Roarke said after a few seconds of thinking about Germand's question, "This is secondhand. I haven't talked with him at length. But, the rancher…and, actually one of his ranch hands, out looking for a cow or something, saw something, according to Col. Buford. They both told him that it was shiny, like a bright star, only much bigger—and it just seemed to hang there, while the bird nose-dived. I don't know this for sure, but I would have to guess that they forgot about it with the sight of the T-38 nose-diving in afterburner. When they again thought to look, the object, whatever it was, apparently was no longer there."

* * *

"Are you sure you don't want someone from the base, a counselor, or someone, to stay close by tonight?" the Air Force Protestant chaplain stood in the foyer, holding his service hat, his tone subdued.

"Thank you, chaplain. My pastor will be here soon. And, thank you for calling him," Laura said, wiping her cheeks with a tissue.

The captain left after again offering his condolences and assuring that he wanted to help in any way he or the Air Force could.

Mark sat close to Lori on the sofa, while she, like her mother, continued to mop tears from her face.

"Why was he not listed on the flight?" James Morgan's daughter said, half-sobbing through her question. "How do we even know he was on that plane?" Her words, were, Mark realized, meant to give herself and her mother hope. Hope that wasn't there. He decided that it was best to just say it to establish the fact that her husband, and his father, was gone. It would be best to end the doubt.

"Lori, I talked to the line chief, Chief Master Sgt. Helstrom. He said that Col. Beery didn't want to go to the trouble of officially listing your dad as part of the flight. It was, for some reason, something he just didn't want made official. Probably just forgot about it, and when Col. Morgan showed up, didn't want to take time to do it right."

"He was upset when he left this morning," Laura said. "He said he was going to talk it over with Col. Beery. He had high regard for him."

Laura broke down, but pulled herself together by sniffing, straightening her shoulders, and taking a deep breath. "They both just probably wanted to discuss things on that test flight. James always felt more relaxed on one of those silly airplanes than he did down here with the rest of us."

Mark knew the feeling. But, he didn't say so, feeling Lori convulse while he held her close.

"I'm glad you're here, Mark. Thanks for caring," Laura sniffed. "It means a lot to Lori and me."

"I got permission to wait until 1100 hours to take off," he said. "Wish I could stay longer. I don't know why this change of assignment." He fell silent, thinking that they didn't need to hear his thoughts on the matter.

"Have you thought any more about that thing the other night? The voice that told you that you would be contacted?"

Lori's question seemed to give her strength to pull away from her heavy grieving. Maybe it would help to talk about it, Mark considered.

"Oh, I've thought about it. It's hard not to think about it. The weird human-like thing in the dream, or whatever, saying he was Dad. Then, the change of orders, the President, the deputy director.

How can you get that off your mind?"

"Do you think Dad's...his..." Lori couldn't bring herself to mention the word "death" in trying to ask if Mark thought her father's crash in the T-38 was a part of the things involved with the night visions.

Mark, reading her unspoken thought, intervened. "I'm going to find out. I promise, I won't stop until I get answers," he said.

"It does have something to do with everything, you know," Laura said, in an unemotional tone that said there were no more tears to be cried. "All of the things he went through—that we've all been through, they're not coincidence."

The three of them sat silently for a moment, each reflecting upon the way their lives had changed and now would be changing even more.

"I've decided not to do the summer program at Austin," Lori said. "You're going to need me with you," she said, going from the sofa to bend over the chair where Laura sat and hug her.

Laura wouldn't, couldn't, argue the point. She did need Lori right now. Very much.

"Will you stay with us tonight, Mark?" Laura asked. "We would like that."

Lori looked at him, pleading through swollen, reddened eyes.

"My things are packed up in the F-4," Mark said. "I'm officially out of officer's quarters. And, I've got my flightsuit on. I'll stay, if it will help."

The doorbell rang and Mark could see in their expressions that Lori and her mother were, without saying it, asking him to answer.

"Christopher Banyon," the man said, looking upward at the taller man who opened the door.

"I'm Mark Lansing," he said, offering his right hand. "You're Mrs. Morgan's pastor?"

"Yes," Banyon said, craning his neck to look around Mark. "And, this is Susie." He turned to the young woman who smiled. "My fiancé," Banyon said.

After greetings and introductions, Laura said, "Pastor, one thing I'm learning. You think you know how someone feels who's lost somebody…" She started to choke on emotion, but caught herself. "Well, let me tell you…" She let the thought go unspoken.

Rev. Banyon held Laura's hand, patting it. "There's no way to know unless you've been there," he said.

"There have just been so many strange things happening lately," Laura said, still trying to regain control. "It seems like the world is crashing right now."

The minister said nothing, but continued to pat her hand while she talked. "Do you believe that Satan actually punishes people?" Laura's words made her daughter uncomfortable, and Mark felt her body tighten when her mother asked the question.

"With the things that have been happening, Rev. Banyon, it's almost like the things you've been talking about are happening to my family."

"Oh? What things? I mean, what have I been talking about that makes you think that Satan might be responsible?" Banyon asked.

"The, what do you call them? The fallen angels. The ones you said you believe have returned to doing the same things they did during times just before the Great Flood in Noah's time."

The pastor raised his eyebrows with Laura's words. She sensed his surprise, wondering why it would startle him.

He had to know more.

"Mrs. Morgan, Laura. I'm sorry if I've said something that adds to your suffering at this time."

"Oh, no. The things you've been saying are things we—I, at least—need," she said, her voice more in charge of her emotions. "The things you've been saying make me wonder…" she hesitated, thinking that perhaps she shouldn't go on with the thought.

"Tell me about it, Laura. Believe me, I want to hear about it," he said, more for himself than to comfort her, he considered, feeling a twinge of guilt.

Laura didn't know if she should say more. Others were

involved. Lori and, especially Mark, were involved.

She looked at Lori and Mark, who sat on the sofa close to each other. Laura saw on her daughter's face the look that said, "Dad wouldn't like you telling this." Mark's expression was one of curiosity, wondering what she would say next.

Her husband, Lori's father, was gone. She had to tell her pastor. Susie was a sweet little girl, and would never betray the trust of her husband-to-be in hurtful gossip.

"James had been having nightmares, I guess they were. He had had them for years, ever since a strange accident in 1947. Only, it wasn't an accident."

Laura looked at Mark, who knew what was coming next.

"My husband and..." she nodded toward Mark. "...Mark's father, Clark Lansing, were flying in a small plane in New Mexico. James and Clark saw some UFOs, two flying saucer-type craft."

She felt the pastor's hand grip hers more tightly.

"Clark just, just vanished from the back seat of that little plane that day. He's never been seen again. At least, not as he was before that day."

"What do you mean, Laura?" Banyon's words were strident, anxious.

"She means that I believe I've had contact with my father since...just the other night," Mark said.

"What kind of...what was this contact?" the minister said, the pitch of his voice raised.

Mark could see that Banyon's interest went further than mere curiosity. The preacher looked panicked.

"At the time, I swore it was a real experience. That my dad really did come into my bedroom, while I was in the BQ for officers on Randolph. But, now I don't know. Maybe it was a nightmare."

"Tell me, Mark, about this visitation," the pastor said, having released Laura's hand and moved to sit on the sofa with Lori and Mark.

"I...I'm sorry. I don't mean to seem crass or interfering. But, I would like to know all about this," he said.

"This whatever it was appeared in the middle of the room, near the end of the bed. It seemed to be made of a black, boiling cloud. Its form was human-like. You know, it had a head, arms, legs—like a boiling cloud-man of some kind."

"And it sparked with electricity. It looked menacing, and it had no facial features," Banyon interrupted Mark's description, finishing it for him.

Everyone sat in stunned silence. The pastor's face paled, his eyes wide, his mouth open.

"How did you know that?" asked Mark, voicing Lori and Laura's thoughts.

"What did this…this being say to you?" Banyon said.

"He said he was my father. He told me that I would be contacted. The thing said I was to do what they told me to do. He said he was alive and well, and that we would be together again soon."

"What is it, Pastor? What is this about? Do you know?" Laura asked.

"A watchman watches," Christopher Banyon said in a whisper, to no one in particular.

* * *

Laura had taken the two sedatives just before Christopher Banyon arrived. The Air Force doctor had given her the sleeping pills after she learned James had died with Ervin Beery in the crash. They were powerful, overcoming the high emotional state she was in now, as the drowsiness overtook her.

Lori helped her mother to the bedroom and saw to it that she was dressed for bed and tucked in. Lori kissed her mom on the cheek and shut off the light. "I think maybe she can sleep," Lori said, shutting the bedroom door and walking to sit near Mark.

"How about you?" Mark said, holding her hands in his while they sat on the sofa.

"I'll try," she said, smiling through her tears.

He dabbed them away with a tissue. "We'll both try," he said, rising from the sofa. "Unless you need me to talk to for awhile."

She shook her head. "No. You have a flight tomorrow. Don't want to lose you, too," she said, her voice cracking with emotion.

He pulled her to her feet, and after a light kiss, embraced her. "You're not going to lose me. You couldn't get rid of me if you tried. Remember, I love you, Lori Morgan," he said.

"I love you, Mark Lansing," Lori responded. She wondered fleetingly how someone could know so much anguish, and, at the same time, so much happiness.

* * *

Christopher had left Susie's front door at 10:45. It was later than they usually stayed out together, even on dates.

He was grateful that she had been with him while he tried to console Laura Morgan and her daughter. Susie would be a valuable asset to any husband. But, she would be an asset beyond value to a minister.

Why had she picked him, of all the men she could have chosen? She told him it was "God-ordained," using the vernacular she knew he would appreciate.

She had laughed softly when she said it, her way of self-deprecation that she knew he would understand, and that would make him laugh. How on earth did the Lord ever find in him anything that made him worthy of her?

He drove now toward the church building, his blue Volkswagen moving through the empty streets bordered by closed businesses and houses whose occupants slept. It was 1:45 a.m., and he was wide-awake.

He needed the books and study materials in order to prepare for Sunday's sermon. Might as well put the time of insomnia to good use. He would pick up the things and take them home. By then, he would be sleepy, he hoped, but the study materials would be there, and he could study at home when he awoke.

He would get the book on the nephilim, by—he couldn't

remember whom. He knew right where to find it. Third shelf, about four or five books from the left corner. Randy Prouse recommended it highly. Christopher had purchased it upon his friend's recommendation, but had never cracked it open.

The nephilim had something to do with the angels who rebelled. Something, therefore, to do with the *bene elohim.*

He must get back to Randall Prouse as soon as possible. He could talk to him about these matters without betraying pastor-parishioner confidentiality. Laura hadn't told him not to discuss the strange things, the death of her husband. He would have to make sure he didn't mention names. But, when he talked about a crash—And, Randy already knew that he had been called away from their conversation to go to a church member who had lost her husband in the T-38 crash at Randolph. Most likely, his friend had already put two and two together. Keeping the matter confidential was already out the window, he thought, pulling the VW into the long drive running alongside the building. He would simply talk to Laura before going to see Randy. He would ask her permission to discuss these things.

Christopher fumbled for the keys. Got to get rid of some of these. Too many, he thought. But which? They all still served a purpose. Maybe break them up into several rings of keys. There! He found the right one, and inserted the key. He twisted it, turned the knob and switched on the wall switch once he was fully inside. He walked the series of smaller hallways that ran through the complex of class-rooms and staff offices behind the sanctuary. He switched on the top lights of his study, and began going through several stacks of unfinished business.

He picked up a book, with a note-paper clipped to the cover. It was from the church secretary: "A friend said give this to you."

He read from the cover: "*Our Struggle* by Randall Prouse." Subtitle: "A life-long battle for the soul of man."

He opened the hardback and saw the personally inscribed words: "To a brother and friend of like mind–Randy"

He turned to the next page and read the only words printed

there.

"For we wrestle not against flesh and blood, but against principalities, against powers, against the rulers of the darkness of this world, against spiritual wickedness in high places"–Ephesians 6:12.

He reread the words, a warm wash of inward prompting spreading throughout his spirit. "A watchman watches," the inner voice said in a wind-like whisper.

* * *

The clock against the wall of the darkened living room chimed two o'clock. Laura turned in her bed, her arm stretching, her hand reaching to find her husband. She felt only the empty place left there by the crash.

A tear rolled down her cheek, even though the sedatives would not let her come to consciousness. But she fought hard to find a rational thought, and finally she sat up in the bed, trying to clear her eyes and her brain.

Daylight. She looked at the clock on the nightstand. No. It wasn't daytime, not unless it was two in the afternoon. And she knew she hadn't slept that long.

She rubbed her eyes.

There was no sunlight coming in through the bedroom window.

Sitting on the side of the bed, she felt with her feet for the soft slippers. When she stood, she collapsed back to a sitting position on the bed's edge. Her head whirled, and she sat for a moment before trying to rise.

She managed, with struggle, to stand again, then shuffled slowly to the bedroom door and opened it. Bright light pierced her eyes, and made her shut them and shield them with her right hand.

Sun? Not sun, but a brilliant white light coming from somewhere she couldn't determine.

She walked a short way into the living room, hearing a low, humming sound. The hum grew louder, and turned into a growl that sounded at first like a large, angry dog. But, she realized, the more alert her senses became, she was hearing words. Words spoken by at least two voices.

The words intermingled, as if in an echo chamber, in a language she hadn't heard.

The French doors—they were open! Who had opened them? From where, from whom were these words coming?

She walked to the doors. They were open wide, the balcony filled with the bright, white light. She saw them, then.

Her daughter, in her nightgown, stared into the sky. Mark stood beside her in only his briefs, also staring skyward.

They held hands, while their mouths moved in unison. The strange, indecipherable words came in deep incantations that ripped Laura from her grogginess.

She looked upward, to the source of the light, her eyes growing wide. She tried to scream, but couldn't, just before everything went black.

* * *

"What happened?"

Christopher Banyon hurried toward Mark, who sat in the waiting-room chair against one wall.

"We don't know," he said, while the minister stood above him.

"I found her about five this morning, lying on the living room floor. It looked like she had fallen, maybe knocked herself out."

Banyon had rushed to Brooke General after learning through Mark's phone call that Laura was in a coma. He sat beside the Marine and looked around the waiting area.

"Is Lori with her mother?"

"Yes. She's been with her the whole time."

"You say she hit her head?" Banyon said.

"No. We don't know. That was just a guess. She was totally out when we put her in bed, so she couldn't tell us anything. They haven't found any marks on her, so far as I know. Of course, there could be a bruise on her head they haven't found yet...I just don't know."

Mark stood and began pacing, looking down one hallway, then another. He glanced at his watch.

"8:59."

"Will you still be flying out this morning?" Banyon said.

"Yes. At 11," he answered.

The minister knew the fact that the pilot had to leave frustrated him. "You don't have to worry about them, Mark," he said, trying to put the Marine at ease. "I'll stay with them."

Mark said nothing, but smiled his appreciation. Still no sign of the doctor, or Lori, or anyone who could clue him in on Laura's progress.

Mark determined that it was time for him to seek someone out. He had to leave now, drive to Randolph, check in with Base Ops and Transit, then pre-flight the bird.

Lori entered the hallway from a room far down the corridor and hurried in his direction when she saw him.

A voice called to him from the opposite direction—the direction of the elevators.

"Capt. Lansing!"

He turned from watching Lori walking toward him, to see the impeccably dressed man with two younger men following him.

Robert Cooper held out his right hand and shook Mark's.

"Good morning, Captain," he said with a tight smile. He reached to take Lori's hand, clasping both of his around hers.

"I'm Robert Cooper. How is your mother, my dear?" Cooper said, trying to sound paternal and concerned.

"The doctors aren't sure of her condition yet," she answered, casting a questioning look in Mark's direction.

"Lori, this is Deputy Director Cooper of the Defense Department," Mark said.

Lori said nothing, but nodded in the direction of the stocky man in the perfectly tailored navy pinstriped suit.

"And these gentlemen," Cooper said, motioning to the men, who nodded to Lori, "are from the Treasury Department."

"We are very sorry to hear of your mother's accident, Miss Morgan. We can't do much to help the doctors at this point, but, I do think we'll be able to help in a way that will improve things for you," Cooper looked up at Mark, "and for you, Captain."

Christopher Banyon had stood, and walked to a table full of magazines. He pretended to be interested in one of them, but listened while the deputy director talked.

"So, you don't know what happened last night? I mean, what happened when Mrs. Morgan fell?"

"No. Mark woke up around five, and found her in the middle of the living room floor."

"Well, let's pray that she recovers very quickly," Cooper said, taking her right hand again, and patting it.

"Thank you," she said with a slight smile, thinking she didn't like this man with the strong personality. He had bullied her father. But, he seemed genuine in his effort to console her.

Why was he, a man of such high rank in government, bothering with her? With the problem of her mother?

"Now!" Cooper's tone became upbeat, his smile stretching in a straight, taut line across large, but barely exposed teeth. "There's something your government wants to do for you."

"Shall we be seated?" He motioned for them to take their seats.

"First, Mark, I've some good news. You are on a week's leave as of this moment. You don't have to report at Andrews until next Tuesday."

The words brought an instant smile to Lori's face. Mark was pleased, but at the same time, questions raked at his thoughts. The same questions as always…

What was it all about? Why the special attention? Why was the President of the United States so interested in an F-4 pilot?

The deputy director seemed to have a prescient understanding of Mark's unspoken questions.

"Ah, yes, why the special treatment? What's our interest? Right?"

Cooper laughed. "Well, put your mind at ease, Captain. We've found a way for you to pay us back for our generosity!"

Chapter 9

The funeral had no body, so there was no casket on display. In a way, it was best. If there was no casket, the absence could provide the illusion, at least, that there was no death.

It was more a memorial service than a funeral, and that's the way Lori wanted it. Her mother was still in a coma, although the doctors at Wilford Hall, to which she had been transferred, said her responses to neuro-sensitivity tests showed improvement.

Christopher Banyon sat near the back of the chapel's little sanctuary, listening along with the 75 or so others who came to memorialize Lt. Col. James Masterson Morgan. He watched Lori and Mark from his distant seat, then cut his eyes to Robert Cooper, who sat far to their right, flanked by the Secret Service agents that had been with him in Brooke General at Fort Sam Houston two days before.

Lori had explained to Rev. Banyon that despite the fact that he was her mother's pastor, Laura would want Father Joseph Malhooney, the base chaplain, to perform the ceremony.

Her father had become good friends with the lieutenant colonel / chaplain since coming to Randolph as an instructor pilot. They hadn't talked much about matters of religious value, according to her dad, but he had enjoyed their socializing at the Officer's Club.

Father Malhooney was wrapping it up now, 15 minutes after the services began with three short testimonies to the quality and good character of Lt. Col. James M. Morgan. They all sang "Amazing

Grace," leaving Father Malhooney a little less than seven minutes to complete the memorial service.

All in all, it was a very depressing service, Christopher Banyon thought while Malhooney spoke the closing words.

"He lives on, in our hearts. And, he lives with our memories as a great pilot, an excellent officer, a good husband, a good father, and a terrific friend. Sleep well, James Morgan."

The priest then offered in an authoritative tone, "Amen, and Amen."

Banyon started to go to Mark and Lori, but saw that Cooper and the agents were already surrounding them, the deputy director of covert operations for the defense department holding Lori's hand in both of his and giving her words of condolence. Before Banyon could make his way to Lori, he saw Cooper and the agents hustle both her and Mark Lansing out a side door.

He hurried to the door, and arrived outside into the overcast day just in time to see them leave in a long, dark car...the personal limousine of Robert Cooper.

* * *

Christopher pulled into the parking lot of the 12-story apartment building an hour and a half later. Lori's little TR-5 was in its parking place.

He signed the guest register at the lobby desk under the watchful gaze of a uniformed guard. Two minutes later he pushed the doorbell on Laura's apartment door.

He turned an ear toward the door, hearing thumping, like the sound of someone pounding. Momentarily, the door opened, and he stood face to face with a man dressed in a white jumpsuit. The man had a hammer in one hand.

"Yes?" the man said.

"Isn't this the Morgans' apartment?" he asked with puzzlement in his voice.

"Was," the maintenance man said. "I guess that was the name.

Don't really know."

"What? What happened? Where are the Morgans?" The minister looked around inside. The apartment had no furniture. Two men in jumpsuits similar to the one this man wore painted the walls.

"We're getting this fixed up for the next tenant," he said. "I really don't know about the folks who lived here. You'll have to check with management, downstairs."

"Thank you," Banyon said after a few seconds, turning away with a perplexed expression.

He looked for Lori's sport car upon leaving the building. It was gone.

He stood in a phone booth several minutes later, thumbing through the San Antonio phone book attached to the booth by a steel mesh-covered cord. Traffic whisked by less than 100 feet away, along Loop 410. He closed the folding door, and the noise lessened to a tolerable level.

He had talked to the apartment building's assistant manager, who told him the Morgans had left no forwarding address.

He found the number of Wilford Hall's Admissions Office, and dialed after inserting the required coinage.

"No, sir. We don't show a Mrs. Laura Morgan. There's been no such person admitted that I've found."

The woman had taken several minutes to check admissions records, and Banyon was certain that Wilford Hall—the admission's office, at least—had no record of Laura having been there.

* * *

The gleaming C-141 settled onto the east runway. It came between sorties that were fully up to schedule at Randolph Air Force Base. The crash investigation involving Col. Beery's downed T-38 continued. But, Lt. Gen. Sam Maddox ruled that the critical mission of getting fighter pilots ready for advanced fighter-combat training, then on to Vietnam, took precedence over the crash incident.

Mark admired the huge, chrome-like 141 while it rolled up from the south end. This was all for him, Laura, and her mother. They—the Department of Defense, he guessed—sent this gigantic bird just for them.

Why? He wondered now, seeing the stainless steel-appearing Starlifter pull ever closer. Something clawed at the back of his mind, seeing the monster turn off the taxiway and head for the parking area where Lyndon Johnson's plane had sat the weekend past.

It was the markings. It had no discernable markings other than an American flag on the tall vertical stabilizer beneath the horizontal stabilizer affixed to the top.

Robert Cooper had told him little. Just that the President had taken a special interest in the situation. Cooper didn't know the full scope of the matter, he had explained.

Mark didn't believe him. Deputy Director Robert Cooper was not someone in whom he would put his full confidence.

But the President of the United States—and it could have been no other. There was only one such man. He had told him to not let the President or the nation down. Most likely, only President Johnson, himself, could have ordered this special aircraft—from what Air Command, he didn't know—to airlift three insignificant people, two of them civilians, to he didn't know where.

"Arrangements have been made, Captain," Robert Cooper shouted to be heard above the Starlifter's many engines while it rolled to a stop less than 80 feet from them.

"The F-4 will be sent for by your colleagues at Egland. And, we got your things from the seat box. One of my people will see to it they are put on the plane."

No sooner had the C-141 shut down than the rearmost portion opened up, a big ramp whirring to a rest on the tarmac.

"I know you have questions, lots of them, Captain, and they will be answered—at least partially—in the very near future."

They watched as a white ambulance with blue Air Force

markings rolled to the base of the ramp leading up to the Starlifter's belly.

When the ambulance was aboard, they watched Lori's TR-5, driven by an enlisted man in an Air Force uniform, pull to the base of the ramp and stop.

"Miss Morgan said that we had no deal if we didn't bring that car," Cooper said with a grunt-like laugh. "So it's coming, too."

"The expense of all this. What's so important that you would lay out this much expense?"

Mark's words were incredulous, spilling out without his meaning to say them aloud. The cost for just the flying time, alone, was staggering for an aircraft this size.

"At 26, you're awfully concerned about your government's spending habits," Cooper said, Mark thought, with an edge of abrasiveness in his tone. "Your service to your country will more than pay for it," Cooper then said with a laugh, slapping Mark on the back, taking the Marine's arm in his hand, and starting to walk toward the awaiting mammoth silver Starlifter.

* * *

Lori wiped her mother's forehead with a smooth, damp cloth. She dabbed a bit of water on another cloth and applied it carefully and slowly to Laura's mouth. When she smoothed on Laura's parched lips a thin film of the ointment the doctors had given her, her mother's lips again took on a healthy look.

Lori sat with Laura in the ambulance, beside the stretcher that had transported her mother from Wilford Hall on the other side of San Antonio earlier that day. Laura's eyes were sometimes open, but stared straight ahead, seeing nothing.

Her mother had passed every neurological test the Wilford Hall specialists could think to give her.

"It will just take time," they had reassured before packing them into the ambulance for the ride to Randolph and the rendezvous with the Air Force transport.

Lori was worried that they had misdiagnosed her mother's condition. The woman she knew as vibrant and livelier than anyone of her acquaintance looked now like an old woman struggling for life.

"She will begin to rally quickly, once recovery begins to set in," they had told her. "There's no reason, physically, that she shouldn't recover," they had assured.

It was the word "physically" that bothered her. Was she to infer that neurologically, or psychologically, she might suffer irreversible mental health problems? She had studied a great deal in brain physiology, as well as other things having to do with brain functioning. The fixed, dilated pupils worried her.

She hadn't had time to consider the decision so hastily made—the decision to completely leave everything behind. To pull up all ties to Austin and the University of Texas. Pull out of the Ph.D. program for advanced molecular biology. For what? To take a job with a program that Robert Cooper promised would make the doctorate program at any university in the world seem kindergarten stuff by comparison.

"The people who know have analyzed every part of your potential, Lori."

Robert Cooper's words traversed her memory, while she continued to tend to her mother's needs.

"The President himself approved the new position they've created for your special gifts and talents," Cooper had said with praise in his inflection.

It wasn't the ego massage that convinced her to agree. It was the fact that her mother would be given the most advanced medical attention and care, free of charge, that did the trick.

No. There was another consideration at least as important.

"You and Mark will be working very closely together in this special assignment," Cooper had said, clinching the deal.

But what exactly was the deal? For some reason the question kept returning, and burning into her mind. She should be ecstatic. She was promised security in a government job, working in her area of what some called her "genius." Cooper guaranteed her a Ph.D. from the school of her choice—including the University of Texas—within a year of completed work for her government.

But, the worry was there. All Robert Cooper would—"could"—tell her was that it was a cutting-edge project involving molecular science. It had both civilian and military implications. There were reasons that both she and Mark had unique qualifications for the work.

"How is she?"

Mark bent forward through the door's opening.

"I don't know. She's so sick, she looks so old."

"They said she would come out of it quickly, once the recovery begins," Mark said.

"I guess a lot of it is that she's not wearing make-up," Lori said, applying more ointment to her mom's lips.

Lori looked into Mark's eyes, seeing in them the strength she needed at this moment.

"Are we doing the right thing, Mark? Did we make the right decision?"

"We'll be together," he said with confidence, but felt his own apprehension welling.

* * *

The tall, aristocratic-looking chief master sergeant looked at the papers the Secret Service agent had handed him a moment before.

He went to his desk and phoned the T-39 section's commanding officer.

"Major. We've got a guy here says he's got orders to take one of my birds to D.C. You know anything about that?"

The voice on the other line responded, and T-39 Line Chief Stephen Sullivan listened impatiently.

"So, you're telling me you've already approved it?"

He waited to hear the major's explanation of why the chief

wasn't informed as soon as the orders came down.

"Yeah, I know that your staff is limited, sir. But, how the…" He calmed, and spoke with controlled anger. "Major, how do you expect us to provide VIP service with all these training sorties going on, without giving a little warning?"

Sullivan's complexion returned to normal, his less reddened, Irish-German bald head displaying his calming demeanor.

He slammed the receiver on its cradle and said in a booming voice to his assistant, a tech sergeant sitting at a desk in the next room, "How long will it take you to get a bird ready to fly to Washington?"

The sergeant appeared in the doorway. "We've got one that can be ready in about 30 minutes. It needs a top off, and quick clean-up."

"Do it."

Robert Cooper waited, watching the gray, white and black T-39 being prepared for his flight. He looked northward and saw the C-41 taxi from its position less than a hundred yards from Base Ops. He sat in the long limo, the dark-tinted windows shading him from the Texas sun that had broken out in full glory an hour before. Even with the darkened interior, and the air-conditioner on maximum cool, the deputy director of covert operations for the Department of Defense sweated beads of perspiration just below his almost non-existent hairline.

He removed the white, silk handkerchief from the coat pocket of the dark suit and mopped the perspiration.

How he did hate Texas. D.C. was humid, but there, he would secret himself away in the bowels of the Pentagon, locked in the absolute cool comfort of his plush office.

He always hated to come to Texas. He hoped this would be his last mission for the men he didn't like, including Lyndon Johnson. Soon he would be director.

Texas was his least favorite place. He would rather follow the Starlifter to New Mexico than stay here. He wasn't that crazy about New Mexico, but at least it didn't have this humidity.

How would his young converts take to the operation in the barren places outside Taos? Were they really converted to the government's designs for them at this point? They knew only the basics. That the project was a very important one involving molecular science experimentation. They had been—he smiled—pre-conditioned. But, was that enough?

Fewer than 3 minutes later, he watched the glinting C-141 leap from the concrete after a short take-off roll. The huge aircraft climbed, like most of the transport aircraft in the inventory, maintaining a near-level position as it lifted. The Starlifter continued to ascend, and began a slow turn to the right.

Cooper returned his gaze to the T-39 and watched the crew while they pumped JP-4 into it through the long, thick black hose running from the yellow fuel truck. He wiped his face with the silk handkerchief. He would be glad to get out of Texas.

* * *

Twilight displayed its final colors, the Texas spring sunset beautiful in Christopher's rear view mirror. He drove his VW bug eastward on I-35 toward San Marcos. Randall Prouse had said he wanted to discuss the happenings of recent days…the things that had somehow drawn Laura and Lori Morgan, as well as Mark Lansing, and him, Christopher Banyon, together.

It was as if they had vanished from the earth, he thought, glancing again at the magnificent lavenders, pinks, yellows and reds of the quickly fading sunset. He had tried the apartment manager's office, the hospitals, Randolph Air Force Base. They were nowhere to be found. It was eerie. His spirit told him it had something to do with the figure that he and Mark Lansing had seen in their … What were they? Their dreams?

His own had not been a dream, not a nightmare. It was real. Mark believed his encounter with the thing was real.

The encounters, Col. Morgan's death in the T-38, Laura's inexplicable coma—they must be related in some macabre way, his innermost being said as he turned down Randall Prouse's street.

"Lord, if it's important to you...please provide the way to the answers."

The minister said the prayer silently while he pulled the Volkswagen into Prouse's driveway.

Before Banyon could push the headlight switch "off" and shut down the engine, Randall Prouse had opened the side door of his home and moved down the few steps. Prouse motioned to him, mouthing words Banyon couldn't hear because of the engine noise.

The archaeologist motioned him to hurry. "Chris! I've found something! You've got to see this!"

Banyon followed Prouse through the doorway and down the short hallway to Prouse's book and paper-cluttered study.

Prouse rifled through the mess on his desk.

"Here. You've got to see this!"

Prouse turned to the page he had marked only a few minutes earlier. "This is by Julius Barnard, Dr. Julius Barnard. You remember him. He's the guy who did those studies in the occult, about spiritism, both heavenly and demonic. The book's title is *'Angelic Visitations'*—a secular work."

Christopher searched his mental files. "No...I don't recall a book by that title," he said. "I do remember the name, though. Julius Barnard. He was the scientist who disappeared, according to his wife, wasn't he? About 1960 or '61, somewhere in there?"

"That's right. The police, the prosecutors. Remember? It was a national story. They all believed his wife murdered him, or had him murdered. There was never a body," Prouse said, continuing to look for the exact passages he wanted. "He worked in particle physics, remember?"

Christopher smiled, and shook his head. "No, Randy, my head doesn't get up into that stratosphere. I just remember it was a big flap. But, she was exonerated, wasn't she?"

"Yes. She swore that he just vanished right in front of her eyes one night while they were walking. She claimed there was a bright light, and the good doctor just wasn't … Like Enoch in Genesis 5."

Prouse picked the book up from the desk and held it open at the chosen place. "This is a book I bought back in 1959. '*Angelic Visitations*'…"

Prouse sat in one of the two chairs in the small study. Christopher sat in the other.

"Listen to this, Chris. It might strike a familiar chord."

Prouse checked once more to make sure he had the right spot to begin reading.

'*The pathway exists upon which both the spiritual and the physical can walk together. My attempts to bring both worlds, or, if you will, dimensions, into a common field, if for a brief moment, seems to offer promise.*

Here is a timeline record of a degree of accomplishment in this endeavor.

June 6, 1957: While attempting to open my mind to the vastness of space I meditated upon, more than one light appeared to me. They seemed at first friendly enough. They seemed to hover over me. This was not a dream, or trance-like state. The lights were real, but at the same time, did not consist of matter, so far as I could discern.

I became frightened, when they seemed to draw my thoughts, or my actual, physical self–I could not be certain—to themselves. I resisted their allure. The brightness grew to the extent I had to close my eyes. The brightness was unbearable, even with my hands covering my eyes.

When next I opened my eyes, the lights–the bright, hovering lights were gone. My pained eyes than beheld a dark, boiling mass. From it sparked flecks of lightning-like eruptions. The boiling, rolling mass took on the form of a human.

It stood perhaps 10 feet from me, and spoke. It said that it was my father. It beckoned me to join its mass. It told me I could be part of changing the Earth. It told me that soon would come the taking away, and that the Earth must be prepared for that quantum moment.

I struggled hard against its pull. I was terribly affrighted. When the struggle of wills ended, the thing was gone.'

Christopher sat forward. It was a stunning revelation. This man, who, himself, had disappeared in front of his wife, according to her, had described precisely the creature he, Christopher Banyon, saw that stormy night.

"He said the thing spoke to him in both Hebrew and Greek, Chris. Barnard is—was—a top-notch scholar in both Hebrew and Greek."

Banyon got to his feet, and paced. "The Marine pilot, Mark Lansing, he and Lori, Laura Morgan's daughter, said the recording they made of James, Laura's husband, was in both Hebrew and Greek. They told me that James' words on the tape were deep, and guttural–not at all like his voice. The professor who translated the taped words said that James, in that unearthly voice, said something about the 'taking away.' That it would be soon…"

Both men were silent for a few seconds, reflecting on the meaning of the experiences, identical to that of Julius Barnard.

"Did you get the books I had delivered to your church?"

Banyon, still deep in thought about what he had just heard, snapped his attention to his friend's question. "Oh, yes. I did."

"Did you read the Scripture on the first page of my book, '*Our Struggle?*'"

The minister diverted his mind from the things that had been read to him, to the book in question.

Randall Prouse said, before Christopher could answer, "For we wrestle not against flesh and blood, but against principalities, against powers, against the rulers of the darkness of this world, against spiritual wickedness in high places."

Banyon considered those words of Ephesians 6:12. He

remembered the words on the phone that night when the phone was out of service because of the violent storm.

"*Watch for the bene elohim.*"

"We're dealing here with the Biblical sons of God?" he said, quietly.

"'As it was in the days of Noah, so shall it be in the days of the coming of the son of man,'" Prouse said, in a tone that said he measured carefully the gravity of the words before uttering them.

"The Lord obviously wants you involved in opposing this end-time intrusion, this invasion," Randall Prouse said. "Don't you sense that?"

The minister didn't know what to say. He looked with a dazed expression to Prouse for answers.

"Whatever God allows in our lives, He gives us the tools or weapons necessary to deal with it, Chris," the bigger man said, giving his guest a brief hug. "You and I have got to work on this project—together, if you'll have me as a partner."

Banyon said nothing, but wondered, after a smiling nod of approval, what sort of weapon would be required to deal with such an enemy.

* * *

Susie just smiled when he told her. He saw no anger, no tears, no rebellion. She just smiled, her pretty, oval-shaped face, inset with the most wonderful brown eyes God ever made, taking on the shy look of a teenager about to go on her first date.

He had just explained to her that he had decided to resign as pastor of St. Paul Presbyterian Church. He and Dr. Randall Prouse would be devoting themselves to following the strange intrusions into his life, and the lives of the others, to whatever destination waited at the end. He wanted her with him, and could provide for them by assisting Randy in archaeological digs, and other ways the professor had in mind to support them during their quest.

Then, too, there was the matter of the inheritance left him by his great aunt that would soon be available. He didn't know what that might amount to, but it could be considerable, his mother had told him.

Most importantly, he had prayed much about it, and was convinced that he must do it.

"I...I'm sorry, Susie. I realize we've waited this long to get our house ready."

Christopher held her small hands in his and kissed her cheek, then her lips.

"It's as if the Lord himself has a grip on my spirit, my soul. I know now. This is what I was put here to do," he said, looking into the eyes that looked softly into his.

"Whither thou goest, I will go; and where thou lodgest, I will lodge," Susie responded with her characteristic tenderness. It was the part of her he loved most, expressing her total love for him with the Biblical words from Ruth 1:16.

He knew that this would be her response. Knew she would accept whatever came, so long as they were together. But, her loving acquiescence to his sudden and unexpected —even outrageous— action, brought relief to his many troubled thoughts.

Her faith in his decision, her unquestioning love, gave him the confidence and the strength he needed to do what must be done.

* * *

01:40 MST, the Friday following the crash

Maj. Red Germand looked over the hangar floor while standing high upon a mobile scaffold. Debris from the T-38 crash covered the hangar's smooth concrete floor, laid out in a tight configuration that approximated the shape of the destroyed talon.

Lt. Col. Larry Cox, head of the investigation for the Air Force, climbed the grated metal steps and joined Germand, who continued to study the debris.

It was late, and it had been a long day for Germand. For some reason, he just couldn't leave the hangar. Something raked his thoughts. Thoughts that had at their top position the fact that after combing through every centimeter of the 30-foot crater and the surrounding area for 200 yards in all directions, there was evidence of only one pilot who had been in the bird.

"Why don't you get some rest, Red," Cox said, patting him on the shoulder.

"Yeah, I guess there's not much I can do, standing up here studying this heap of metal."

"There's still no evidence of Morgan?" the lieutenant colonel said.

Red Germand shook his head, and sighed. "No, Larry, I just can't figure. Every crash I've ever been involved with has produced at least a shred of every person aboard. I just can't figure."

"They've found several parts of Beery's helmet, they tell me."

"And, just an hour or so ago, they found part of his 'chute," Germand said. "They've still found nothing of the colonel's body but that tooth, the end of his right thumb, an eye, and a rib, I think. But they have an accumulation of things that were on his person."

"But, not one scrap of evidence that James Morgan was ever on that aircraft." Cox's assessment was offered in a frustrated, questioning tone.

"What percentage of the bird have they recovered? Anyone given an estimate, yet?"

"It's just decimated," Maj. Germand answered. "Most crashes just don't happen like this one—full burners, straight in."

"I guess we're lucky to get something that looks even that... helpful," Cox said, scanning the floor below, evaluating the debris jigsaw in the process of being assembled.

"Yeah, I guess," said Germand.

Chapter 10

***Washington, D.C., the White House Oval Office,
May 31, 1967***

Lyndon Johnson was in a burning rage. Vietnam consumed his every waking hour. The press was making life miserable, as were the hippy "make love not war" protestors. Now, the Israelis strained at the US leash wanting to get at the Arabs threatening them.

He wasn't one to hide his wrath, and those around him always stepped lightly when he used unabandoned foul language. It wasn't typical of such a master politician as Johnson to swear, taking the Lord's name in vain, with so many present. He was no typical politician.

He was settling down into bubbling anger, able again to control his temper.

"Listen to what Nasser said on the 27th," the President said in the Texas drawl familiar throughout the world. "'Our basic objective will be the destruction of Israel. The Arab people want to fight.'"

Johnson threw the briefing the CIA had prepared for him onto the big desk's top, then leaned back in the tan-leather high-back chair. He pulled the glasses from his nose, and rubbed the sore places they caused.

"You told me these boys wanted to start talking peace, Buddy," the President said, looking to George Grayhouse, whose nickname was "Buddy".

The CIA deputy director reddened a bit. "Mr. President, that was our assessment, based upon intelligence from our Turkish allies. They assured that the threat to close the Tehran Straits was just a threat."

"Listen here what else he said," Johnson interrupted, after leaning forward to pick the briefing paper from the desk. "He said the very next day, May 28th," Johnson said, adjusting the reading glasses and peering down his nose to see the print. "'We will not accept any coexistence with Israel. Today the issue is not the establishment of peace between the Arab states and Israel...The war with Israel is in effect since 1948.'"

Johnson lowered his face, looking, with his forehead wrinkling, over the glasses at Grayhouse. "Listen to what this other guy," Johnson paused to scan up and down the page, and lift one page from another to find the name. "This guy, President Abdur Rahman Aref of Iraq... 'The existence of Israel is an error which must be rectified. This is our opportunity to wipe out the ignominy that has been with us since 1948. Our goal is clear—to wipe Israel off the map.'"

Johnson again plopped the briefing pages on the desk and leaned back in the big chair.

"These Arabs say a lot of things, Mr. President. They feed off of each other's big talk," Grayhouse said.

"Yeah, well, this big talk might just bring us into a...situation with the Soviets." Johnson leaned forward, picked up the papers and thumbed through them.

"Eganberg says we're covered in this covert operations thing. Do you concur?" the President asked, looking over the glasses at Grayhouse.

"Yes, sir. We've kept the F-4 under wraps. Very high security," the CIA man said, nodding affirmatively.

"And the Israelis...they know not to do anything until we say so? Unless they're attacked?" Johnson said.

"They won't do anything until they get the word from CIA,

Mr. President."

"Tell you what worries me, boys, "Lyndon Johnson said. "That those Jews will blow hell out of those ragheads, before they are attacked. Breshnev would then be under pressure to unruffle his hawks' feathers by direct intervention."

* * *

Taos, New Mexico June 1, 1967

Dr. Edward Teller moved slowly among the small group of scientists. He wore the slightest of smiles while he shook hands, and spoke approving words. His bushy eyebrows and harsh-featured face had been world famous since the hydrogen bomb test at the Bikini Islands in the 1950s.

All present tried to engage the great man in conversation about the science they loved and shared in common with Teller. But, it was Lori he chose for conversation, his dark, somewhat ominous eyes seeming to brighten as they talked.

"We have been watching you," he said to Lori in Hungarian-accented English, which, nonetheless, she had no problem understanding.

"You are becoming a star among the stellar bodies of molecular manipulators," the renowned scientist said with a quick smile.

Lori nodded a confident smile of appreciation. "There is just so much to learn…"

Her answer seemed to please him.

"We are all still learning, Lori."

Teller held her hands in his while he talked. "You are so young to have come so far. And, there is no limit on your possibilities, here, my dear, except those you impose upon yourself."

Lori listened intently, but said nothing.

"I shall be observing your progress. You will be working with Gerhardt Frobe, it is my understanding."

"Yes, sir."

"There is none more qualified. I will have a special word to him about you."

Teller held her hands to his lips and brushed them with a kiss.

"Please call on me when I can be of any help to you."

"Thank you, Dr. Teller, that's very sweet," she said, not knowing what else to say.

"Ah! That's me—sweet!" he said with a hearty laugh, and a quick glance around at the other scientists and the entourage that followed him through the underground complex.

Everyone laughed. Teller patted her hands and moved along.

"Dr. Teller is the one who got you assigned to Dr. Frobe," the man in the white smock said—with snooty condescension, Lori thought.

"Oh?" she said, startled by the man's sudden words. She hadn't seen him before.

"He sort of likes the ladies, if you know what I mean," the man said in a high voice tinged with an irritating whine.

Lori was incensed, and her face reddened. "Better he likes ladies than gentlemen, if you know what I mean," she said, then slightly cocked her head, and set her chin in a way that said she was prepared for verbal combat, if he wished to continue.

He didn't, saying nothing, but looking down the long, thin nose, his lips pursed tightly. He said, then, "Well, I must stay close. He often calls on me for assistance when he's in the molehole."

Lori turned abruptly, leaving the man standing, while she walked away in the opposite direction of Teller's entourage. The term "molehole" stuck with her. She had been told that it was the pet name for the molecular biology lab section of the complex.

Her time in the vast complex had been exciting. But, if not for Mark's being nearby, she could see how the sequestered work-life here could be hard to abide for long stretches of time.

She hurried through the door marked "The Waste of Time Room –Female." The eccentric attempts at humor in this scientific community beneath the New Mexico desert-like land both amused her and irritated her, she thought while she washed her hands and studied her face in the mirror. Perhaps it was just that everything irritated her in these tombs, despite the ultra-modern technologies and comforts.

Her face was as pale as she had ever seen it. *The lack of sun can't be good,* she thought, pinching her cheeks, hoping to see a bit of color.

She walked to the elevators after leaving the Ladies' Room. Less than two minutes later, she entered the hospital area.

"How's Mom?" she said to the nurse who had just finished talking with another nurse.

"She's about the same. But Dr. Spillane says it seems she improves a degree or two about every two days."

"Thanks," Lori said, pushing through the double doors and, moments later, walking into her mother's room.

"Mom, I'm here. It's Lori," she said, picking up her mother's right hand and kissing it, then rubbing it while she talked.

"I'm really liking the work, Mother. I've only just got acquainted with people, and with the facility. We'll start on the project tomorrow. At least, that's when I'll get involved. It's been going on for several years, actually."

A tear trickled from one of Lori's eyes. She missed her mother so much. But, the doctors said to keep talking, keep carrying on conversation with her as much as possible. They still believed she would eventually pull out of the comatose state.

"Mark is involved in the thought-helmet project. He likes the work, but I can tell that he's ready to get back to his precious F-4s. Was Daddy ever like that? Did he ever seem to love those stupid planes more than he loved us?"

"Miss Morgan."

Lori turned to see a man dressed in a suit and tie.

"Dr. Frobe would like to talk with you, when your visit is finished," the man she hadn't seen before said.

"I'll be with you in a second," she said, and then turned back to Laura, still holding her hand in both of hers.

"I'll be back in an hour or two, Mom. I love you—more than

anything."

She kissed her mother's forehead, and left, wiping her tears with the sleeve of her smock.

"Sorry to keep you waiting, Miss Morgan," the man of about 50 said, walking through the doorway behind Lori.

She stood and turned to meet him. He shook her hand.

"I am Gerhardt Frobe."

"Nice to meet you, Dr. Frobe," she said, taking his offered hand.

"And, are you somewhat at home here, now?" he asked in a mild German accent.

"I'm getting there," Lori said.

"Good, good. Lori—may I call you Lori?"

"Sure."

"Lori, Edward—Dr. Teller—has the utmost confidence in you. This is amazing, for one so young," the scientist said, holding her forearm and gesturing for her to be seated with the other hand. "I cannot tell you what his recommendation means."

"I don't know what I've done to deserve such…"

Frobe held up his hand for silence. "I did not mean that you were unworthy otherwise. It's just that I have never had anyone added who comes to us with such a pedigree of higher-ups who recommend them. Do you realize that the President of the United States, himself, suggested you for this project?"

"No, sir. I had no idea."

She knew that the President had spoken to Mark. She didn't know the "deal," as Robert Cooper called it, had included the President recommending her. She felt honored, but more than a little unsettled by what it all might mean.

"Other than maintaining a 4.0 grade point throughout my academic career, I can't think of what might qualify me—"

Again Frobe through up his hand for quiet.

"Your value as a bright student is quite important, Lori, please let that be understood." Frobe fidgeted with a pencil he held in his fingers, pausing in order to think about how to best phrase his words. "However, it is your… genetic resume with which we are most intrigued."

* * *

"There will be no pain, Captain. This involves sound wave technology that has no adverse effects."

Dr. Gessel Kirban adjusted the helmet on Mark Lansing's head, standing in front of the pilot, his bespectacled eyes going over every centimeter of the metal and plastic headgear device.

"Is that comfortable?" he asked, making one more adjustment.

"It's a little tighter than I'm used to," Mark said. "But, it's not uncomfortable."

"Yes, well, over a period of several hours, it will become unbearable," Kirban said, removing the helmet, and adjusting the interior's elastic straps.

He put it on the pilot's head and again began the process of adjustments, rocking the gold-colored helmet from side to side.

"There. Better?"

"Yes. Much better," Mark said, seeing the pleased look cross the professor's age-creased face.

"As I was saying, this inflicts no pain. It is based upon low-frequency sound wave technology."

Dr. Kirban stepped back, folded his arms across his chest, and began kneading his upper lip with his right thumb and index finger while he studied the device. "You will be the first to put this into practical use, actual use," he said in an Israeli accent, then scratched the top of his head. The frown of concentration told Mark the Ph.D. in cellular biology and other things beyond Mark's pay grade to know about was trying to think of how best to explain…

"You will use this … first in a number of practice sorties, as they say."

The Israeli scientist went into an adjoining room, and returned several seconds later with a sleek, diamond-shaped black object. It looked to Mark to be about the size of a football, but much slimmer in configuration.

"This is the Audiodyne Cognightor," the professor said, handing it to Mark, who turned it in every way he could. There were no seams to be found.

"This instrument is ensconced within the lower part of the aircraft. It is what gives the technology its capability to anticipate what action you must take next. It gives the one wearing the precognition neuro-diviner its oneupsmanship on the enemy."

"The precognition what?" Mark asked, amused with the jargon.

"The precognition neuro-diviner…" Kirban said. "The helmet you are wearing."

"Mind if I just call it a helmet?"

The professor looked at him for a second, not understanding. Then laughed. "Yes, yes. Let us keep it simple, at least in terminology."

Kirban, with great care, lifted the helmet from Mark's head while he talked.

"But it is a most complex instrument, Captain. It lives up to its high-sounding name, I assure you."

"Exactly what does it do?"

"Only your using it will tell you that. You must experience for yourself its unique power to…perform," Kirban said, placing the helmet on a velvet cloth draping over a nearby pedestal.

"Mark." He turned, removed his glasses, folded them and put them in the pocket of the white smock he wore. "You have the clearance now, so I will tell you more, since you will be actually flying 'under the influence,' as I like to say."

The professor pulled a tall stool from a drawing board and seated himself atop its rounded seat.

"We don't yet know just what the system will do, at least not under actual flying conditions. To be honest, we could use none of our other test subjects—pilots—because they didn't have the precise genetic confirmation that the tests show that you have. Our data shows that the pilot who uses this technology must possess certain—how shall I explain?—certain genetic anomalies. Unusual biological qualities and characteristics, combined with some peculiar cerebral disposition."

"You mean I'm a little bit odd? A little funny in the head?" Mark said with a grin.

"Well, uniquely qualified for this instrumentality, I would rather put it," the Israeli scientist said without changing expression.

"I've never heard of anything even close to this technology, Dr. Kirban," Mark said. "Did you develop this precognition thingamajig?"

"Let's just say the technology has come out of close association with those with special gifts and talents for advancing mankind's lot for the better," Kirban said. "I'm privileged to have been put on the front lines in this particular technological breakthrough."

Kirban stood to begin an inspection of Mark's scalp. He parted the hair at several points around the crown of the head.

"Yes, yes. These have healed nicely, Captain," he said, feeling the soft filaments at each location on the pilot's head.

"The technology is only as proficient as its user, no matter of what that technology consists, young man. This instrument's ultimate capabilities are geared to your own, unique potential. You will become one with the helmet, as you wish to call it. You will determine how far and how fast we can go with it into the future."

"When do we start?" Mark said, like any good Marine, ready for the challenge.

"We've already begun. But, there is one way to give it the ultimate test right away. Are you up to it?"

Kirban looked at Mark, awaiting an answer.

"Whatever you think best. That's why I agreed to join the helmet project," Mark answered.

"This must be between you and myself only, Mark. At least for the time being. Will you trust me with a decision I've made?"

"Yes, sir," Mark said with questioning obedience in his tone.

"Are you up to a bit of limited combat—actual combat?" Kirban asked, with hesitation.

"Vietnam?" Mark said.

"Israel," Dr. Kirban said.

* * *

Washington D.C., the Pentagon

Robert Cooper sat in the burgundy leather judgeback chair in his plush semi-darkened office. He brooded over having to play second fiddle to Director Daniel Eganberg, who was chosen by Defense Secretary Robert McNamara to brief the President on the Taos project.

The underground operation that lay between Taos and Santa Fe was his own baby, and they all knew it. Cooper grinned. Neither Eganberg, McNamara, nor the President knew the whole story, however.

Not about "Dark Dimension." Not about RAPTURE, and all it entailed.

The director would brief Johnson, but be able to tell him nothing of consequence, so far as the real scope of the operation was concerned. The truth, the whole truth, was known by fewer than a handful. The truth that had been a growing, clandestine reality since Roswell. It was a reality that the President would learn at the same time the rest of the world learned.

Johnson was kept too busy with Vietnam, the Soviets, and now the Arabs and Jews, to even lightly pursue learning details residing within the papers on Majestic and Project Jehovah—documents he had demanded to see.

"Mr. Director."

Cooper looked to the side door of his oak-paneled Pentagon basement office.

"Mrs. Eganberg is here," Lucy Holland announced.

"Yes. Send her in," Cooper said, rising from his chair and making his way around the massive, hand-carved oak desk.

The tall, exquisite-looking woman walked into the office upon being summoned by the secretary.

"Thank you, Miss Holland. No phone calls, please."

The young woman smiled and shut the door quietly behind her when she left.

"It was the same last night," Gwendolyn Eganberg said, standing face to face with Cooper, who glared at her.

"Tell me about it," he said in a detached tone.

She gave him the report, her inflection indicating she was suppressing her emotions.

"They came to him, just as you said. He talked with them. As usual, I couldn't understand a thing he said. Of course, I heard nothing at all from them."

"And, were you frightened?"

"How can one keep from being frightened?"

Both were silent for a second before she spoke.

"Bob, who are they? What are those things?" Her questions came in a breathless burst.

"They—are friends. They are going to make this nation the absolute authority over all who would oppose…"

Cooper caught his fiery euphoric climb, and quenched it.

"And I—we, dearest Gwendolyn, will see to it that that power is implemented correctly."

"But, they are intimidating. So unsettling."

"They are with us," he interrupted.

"What is happening to Dan? What are they doing?"

"Just a little pre-conditioning. Nothing to be concerned about," Cooper said.

"What's it all about, Bobby?" She wrapped her arms around him and pressed against him. Their lips locked, their passions rising with each lust-driven kiss. Cooper pulled away.

"There will be time for us, Gwendolyn," he said, his eyes

taking on a faraway look. He turned from her to let his innermost thoughts pierce into one dark corner of the office. He said, "The time is quite near. I can feel it in my bones."

* * *

The minister writhed on the bed, wrestling with the pillow and the sheet that covered him. The air conditioner was out, and it was sweltering, the humidity at its highest point of the spring.

Christopher Banyon emerged from sleep, and sat on the edge of the bed. He got up and went to the kitchen to retrieve a cold pitcher of tea from the refrigerator. He leaned inside the box, enjoying the cold air. He wished the church would fix the blasted thing, but he had no right to say anything about the problem, other than to report it broken, which he had done.

They had been very kind to him. When he announced his resignation, they insisted that he live in the church-owned home until he and Susie were married in two days, on June 6. The new bride and groom would then go on a brief honeymoon to the south, to Padre Island, and return to live in an apartment, which Randall Prouse had arranged only yesterday.

It would be nice to have the air conditioner working, he thought, sipping from the pitcher.

He hoped—prayed—that he hadn't made a terrible mistake leaving the church. Was it really God's will? Or was it just a lust for some sort of weird adventure? Where to begin?

He put some ice cubes in a glass and moved with the pitcher and the glass to the little kitchen table.

Had he let Randall Prouse talk him into it? Into leaving the pulpit to pursue...what?

Bene elohim? Fallen angels? Was he nuts? Was he really going to take his sweet, loving bride on a hunt for demons?

No question that it seemed ridiculous at this moment. Three-thirty on a humidity-soaked, air-conditionless Texas morning, sitting sipping iced tea and thinking about chasing spiritual beings.

But, this was the first time he had had serious second thoughts. The mission had been clear in his mind. He and Randall had discussed it at length on many occasions. Susie—sweet, loving Susie—trusted him completely to make the right choices.

Why had they left without a trace? Laura, Lori, and Mark Lansing? Why had they not contacted him? Didn't Laura need her pastor to at least help them comfort her and Lori?

But, he was no longer a pastor.

"*Feed my sheep.*" The voice played again in his mind, the wind-like voice that said, "*Feed my sheep.*"

"*A watchman watches; watch, therefore for the bene elohim,*" he heard again within his mind the words spoken over a telephone line that was out of commission.

Christopher bowed his head. "Oh, Lord," he said in prayer, "please guide. Help me to trust in you with all my heart, to lean not unto my own understanding. Help me to acknowledge you in all my ways. And, dear Lord, please direct my—our—paths."

The ringing telephone shattered his meditation.

"Oh! Not another call on the phone, dear Lord," he said, smiling at his own words.

"Hello," he said, halfway expecting to hear the wind-driven voice on the line.

"Chris!"

"Randy—"

"I know, it's three thirty. Sorry to call at this hour. But, I can't keep this to myself."

"What's wrong?" Christopher said, his heart racing. It must indeed be important for Randall Prouse to call at this hour.

"They've found something in the scrolls!"

"The scrolls? What scrolls?"

"The Dead Sea Scrolls, the ones found at Khirbet Qumran in 1947!" Prouse exclaimed.

"What have they found?"

"Get Susie packed, Chris. We're off to Israel!"

Chapter 11

A song played, almost inaudible, but growing in volume.

> *Jesus loves the little children,*
> *all the children of the world.*
> *Red and yellow, black and white,*
> *they are precious in his sight,*
> *Jesus loves the little children of the world...*

Lori breathed deeply, taking in the salty sea air that seemed to bring to her ears the music of her young childhood. She looked into the Gulf of Mexico while she stood on the orange sand of South Padre Island. The blue-green Gulf water turned gray with the opaque mist that coagulated somewhere off shore and moved toward the beach.

She shut her eyes, trying somehow to cause the oncoming fog to dissipate. It worked! When she again opened her eyes, she now faced the University of Texas Tower, its top almost engulfed, shrouded by the same gray mist that had before rolled across the water.

The music began again, but the song was another.

> *Jesus loves me, this I know,*
> *for the Bible tells me so.*
> *Little ones to Him belong,*
> *They are weak, but He is strong...*

The song's volume increased, and echoed, as if sung within an empty 50-gallon drum. Her eyes were drawn upward toward the façade of the tower. To a large window, where a dark figure glared down at her, a hulking man with huge binoculars held to his eyes.

She tried to break free from a strange, vacuuming wind that sucked her toward the dark giant with the binoculars.

Again surroundings changed, and the music grew deafening before it suddenly stopped. Small gray humanoid figures surrounded her bed and grasped at her, and she sat in the bed pulling her hands and nightgown from them while they reached toward the center of the bed to snatch at her with thin, tentacle-like fingers.

Lori awoke, startled, her eyes opened wide, the vividness of the nightmare still reverberating throughout her gathering consciousness.

She was alone. She turned the small stem of the nightstand lamp, and was reassured to confirm that there were no small, gray beings. She smiled slightly. The man with the binoculars was gone; the gray creatures were gone. But, while she turned off the lamp and settled back to the pillow, the remembered songs replayed in her head, and they brought pleasant memories of her few visits to Sunday school years before.

> *Jesus loves the little children,*
> *all the children of the world...*

* * *

Taos underground complex, June 2, 1967

Gessel Kirban flipped on the light switches in his spacious laboratory. The hour was late, depending on whether one considered 3 in the morning late or early, he thought while picking up a clipboard and lifting pages to look at the statistics his lab assistants had left for him. He ran through in his mind again and again the conversation with his friend in Texas. He hoped he wasn't leading Randall Prouse astray with the information he had relayed.

Yadin had made a discovery that he hadn't revealed to anyone. It was just too shocking. So shocking, it couldn't be legitimate. But, it was real. Kirban could feel it in his core being.

A very fragile fragment, but more legible than most all of the fragments found from Yadin De Vaux's excavations. Plainly in ancient Hebrew, the words: *"War in heavens and on earth shall begin the consummation when first scroll words shall be found."*

There was more, but Kirban couldn't remember. Didn't want to strain to do so at the moment. It had been a long day.

The fragment—a prediction? A prophecy? It was a question for the scholars, for the archaeologists and further digs to determine, perhaps.

Yadin depicted the fragment with the words as separate from the Hebrew texts that proved the authenticity of the Old Testament—at least to many scholars' satisfaction. Of course, there would always be the Allegros of the world who wouldn't believe, no matter the proof dug up.

The prophesied words, Yadin assured, were in reference to the first discoveries in the cave at Khirbet Qumran in February, 1947. But did it mean that the writer predicted the discovery would unleash the wind-up of the great battle between good and evil? Between God and the Devil?

The secret discovery excited Randall Prouse. There was indeed something in the words on the fragment that evoked exhilaration for his archaeologist-friend.

He had called Randy at the request of Yadin. Yadin said Dr. Prouse was needed to help him confirm something or the other. The three of them had been friends from the old days in Jerusalem, and Gessel Kirban was the first person the Arab thought of when the need to try to contact Randall Prouse came up.

The fluorescent lights in the ceiling of the lab flickered.

Unusual. There was never a power problem here, in perhaps the most advanced laboratory in the world.

Kirban shrugged it off, and again began examining the data on the clipboard. After a few seconds, there began a vibration—no, a hum. A low noise. It grew into a distinct droning sound that vibrated the air around him. He had heard many strange noises from time to time in the complex. But never this one.

The scientist turned his head one way, then the other, trying to determine the direction from which the source of the noise was coming.

Kirban walked from the laboratory and into the long hallway off of which other labs, like his, were located. The corridor, bathed in dim light, disappeared into the distant darkness.

He turned in the opposite direction, seeing that the corridor that way was brighter. The hum, still at a low decibel, but growing louder, seemed to emanate from the darkened direction.

The directive had been that everyone be alerted when one of the experimental molecular technology labs was in use after hours. For security reasons, only those with clearance for the particular lab to be used were to be allowed in the complex during after-hours usage.

He had received no such alert. He had not been denied access when he came to his own lab for after hours work. Had there been an oversight? Not likely. There had never been an oversight, to his knowledge. This complex was probably among the top three most secure complexes in the world.

He walked the corridor, his movement eerily silent, except for the rustle of his lab coat. The darkness grew thicker, the farther he progressed, and he wished for the small pen light attached to his key chain—the keys left behind in a drawer in his office two floors above.

He felt the bones of his nasal passages vibrating now, engendering the need to sneeze. The hum was much more pronounced, and grew louder while he walked. Still, there was a hint of light, and he peered hard through its strange, misty, iridescence. Movement in the distance stopped him cold.

He blinked, unable to convince himself he had seen the black, human-like form pass from one wall, move across the corridor, then move through the other wall. A chill traversed his spine from top to bottom, and rose again to ripple across his scalp.

His imagination? Too many hours in this people-consuming place?

Kirban began walking again, watching for the emergence of another form. He stopped to examine the walls through which the thing had passed seconds before. Nothing unusual. Solid walls. His imagination; had to be...

Within moments, he arrived at a double-doored laboratory. He tried, but couldn't make out the lab's title on the piece of black plastic. Too dark.

The weird sound, the hum—no doubt about it. It originated from regions beyond these doors.

No need to try putting his card key in the slot. He didn't have access to this end of the building. He knew few who did have access to the area.

He started to turn to begin walking up the corridor toward his own laboratory. Almost at the same time he did so, he gave the door device a push with his right thumb.

To his great surprise, the door wasn't locked.

He stuck his head inside, and found the area better lit than the hallway.

"Hello...anyone?" Kirban said above the loud hum, which, once he was fully inside, became an annoying whine.

He maneuvered through several short hallways that branched in many directions, toward the whining hum that now sounded as if it had a heartbeat. The last corridor he entered was even darker than the others, and he felt his way along the right wall with the back of his right hand.

Whatever was making the sound must be expending tremendous energy, Kirban thought, the very air surrounding him seeming to pulse in a strange, rhythmic beat. He was in forbidden regions of the complex, but he couldn't make himself turn and leave. It was as if the source of the pulsing energy that hummed and whined in the unfamiliar reaches of darkness just ahead was possessed of a vortex that sucked him along, mesmerizing him, drawing him deeper, ever deeper toward its ominous center.

The scientist heard voices. One male, the other female. A shadow-blackened niche in the right wall allowed him to slip unseen into it and press hard against its recesses. Just in time for the two to pass by him in the corridor.

"You say neither of them will remember any of this?" the man said to the woman walking beside him.

They stopped, and faced each other, the woman checking a clipboard she held.

"That's right," she said, continuing to thumb through the pages. "The girl will remember only the work she was doing earlier this evening, the work on the RAPTURE."

"What about the Dimensionals? They insist upon entering the other subject."

"They are just determining whether the genetic predisposition is as we calculated," the woman said. "So far, our estimations have been even more accurate than we could have hoped for."

"Of course, you had the Dimensionals' work, up front, to make certain."

"Yes. It's doubtful they would have insisted on the entries if their calculations and preparations weren't first figured in. It would be too risky for the subject."

"It's my understanding," the man said while the woman continued checking data on the board, "that the precognition neuro-diviner helped them to prepare the way for testing their... their indwelling."

"The device opens the mind, especially the cognitive process, to transference of thought that involves decision making based upon surrounding factors of influence."

"You mean it allows for ideas and decisional thinking—other than the subject's own thinking—to influence directly?"

"Totally influence," the woman scientist affirmed. "But, it is as if the thoughts are his alone, based upon factors influencing his decisions."

"In theological circles, that would amount to possession,

wouldn't it?" the man said.

"Why, Doctor! I didn't know you could even think in such terms," the woman said with a stifled laugh.

"Yes, well, my Catholic upbringing, I guess."

"The Dimensionals are a bit spiritual, I suppose," the woman said. "But, if it gives us the advantage, I'll—we'll—take the help of the Devil, himself."

A terrible chill of understanding ran through Gessel Kirban's thoughts, while he watched the two move on down the corridor and turn the corner in the semi-darkness. His own project was but a ruse, designed to cause him and others to miss the real intentions involved.

These non-material beings, the dark, human-like forms that moved through solid walls. What were they? The scientists called them "Dimensionals." Kirban's thirst for knowing more overrode his fear, and he moved from the niche, and farther down the dark corridor.

His heart thumped hard in his chest, keeping pace with the beat within the darkness. He had arrived at the very core source of the palpitating machinery.

He tried the door, thumbing the latch of the door's handle. Open!

Kirban moved in total darkness, which he welcomed as an accomplice to get near his objective. The area just ahead, within which lay the source of the mystery he was determined to solve.

Two steel doors, having no visible handles for entry, had at eye level a series of small, rectangular clear-glass windows. They were arranged horizontally.

The scientist peered carefully from one corner of the end window on the right. His eyes were drawn to the two people standing at the center of the room with rounded walls. Lights of every color sparked and blinked and strobed outward from their inset positions within the walls.

When his eyes had adjusted to the vision-obscuring brightness, he saw a number of people sitting in chrome-like, glinting booths.

They all wore precognition neuro-diviners upon their heads. All faced the two people standing upon a stainless steel platform. They, too, wore the helmets.

Several men and an equal number of women performed checks and did other work, moving as they did so throughout the half-spherical chamber. Kirban saw them, then. Perhaps ten dark figures, shaped like humans, but far from being human. They walked through the walls that contained the lights, arose from and descended through the solid tile floors, and emerged from, and ascended through the solid material that made up the room's ceiling.

The human subjects at the room's center, almost naked, were young. They faced each other while standing on the gleaming stainless steel platform, reaching to touch each other with fingertips at various points on their faces and necks. One short, bald man in a white smock apparently gave them instructions on where and when to touch. He then marked on the clipboard he held.

The droning heartbeat sound suddenly stopped. The couple on the platform let their hands drop to their sides. They remained motionless, as the scientist instructing them turned to his left.

A large black being materialized, as if from nothingness, in front of the human with the clipboard.

Kirban could hear nothing spoken by the dark creature. But it obviously said something, or implanted the thought, or whatever it did, Kirban observed, because the scientist nodded, and gave orders in compliance.

"Let us begin," the man said.

As one, the people wearing the helmets and encircling the two young people at the room's center began to speak. They spoke the same words. Gessel Kirban, an Israeli, recognized the words as spoken in Hebrew.

But, the words were as if growled from something other than human voice boxes.

"*The taking away will come,*" the words began in Hebrew. "*All must be ready. All must speak as one...*"

Kirban felt the vibrations assaulting his senses, as if surrounding and engulfing his thoughts.

"We shall speak as one...When the moment comes...We shall speak as one..."

Kirban's brain filled with terrors. He had to get as far from the facility as possible—leave this hell of darkness and unbearable vibrating noises.

He held his palms over his ears while he stumbled from the big, steel doors. He frantically searched the hallway.

Which to take? So many, so many directions!

When he lurched toward the hallway he chose, his eyes widened. Horror sucked the breath from him.

Two dark human-shaped forms stepped from within the solid walls and blocked his path. Huge, and terrifying, each stood stiffly, faceless heads gray-black and seeming to boil atop thick necks and wide shoulders. Pain burned within his cranium, as if flames would at any moment shoot from the crown of his head, from his nostrils, from his eyes and ears. *The pain—the unbearable, searing pain!*

* * *

Over the Atlantic, June 3, 1967

Randall Prouse was a man of high energy and quick movement, possessed of a hyperactive physiology usually reserved for much smaller men. He plopped into the seat next to Christopher Banyon, and took several seconds to settle in.

"Word is, it's going to happen, maybe before we land," Prouse said, without looking at Christopher.

"War is that inevitable?" Banyon asked, while Susie listened from the seat on her husband's right.

"Yeah. All of that wrangling I had to do with State and with the committee was taken care of just in time. Glad I started on it the second I received word from Gessel."

"Your committee of support didn't want to fund you on this?"

the minister asked.

"Oh, no. They're great. They've got my digs funded for five years or longer. They didn't want me to go because of the dangers. Or their perceived dangers of the Israeli-Arab thing."

"And, you're not worried?"

"I'm sort of sorry we're bringing Susie along," Prouse looked across Banyon to let his eyes meet those of Susie Banyon.

"I only mean, Sweetheart, that I don't want to put you in harm's way even for a second," he said.

She smiled, knowing Christopher's friend meant his tender words. Not an easy thing for a man of such powerful, adventurous drive to express.

"Don't mind putting you in harm's way, though," Prouse said, grabbing Christopher's leg just above the knee and squeezing it with his fingertips and thumb.

"Yes, well, I'll try to remember to duck," the minister said with a subdued laugh.

"I was talking to a State Department guy up there in First Class," Prouse said. "He's a guy I went to school with at Georgetown. He says the Arabs are amassed in every direction you look from Jerusalem."

"You have chums from schools all over the country," Christopher said.

"And it's a blessing in this business of antiquities digs. Guess I've got so many contacts because I could never settle down in whatever I'm doing. Drives Ruthie nuts."

"So what do you think we should expect?" Christopher said.

"If I know anything at all about the IDF, they won't let things stay like this very long."

"IDF?"

"The Israeli Defense Forces," Prouse said, leaning his head into the aisle of the 707 to see his State Department friend, Clarence Trowell, part the curtain and make his way toward them.

"Welcome to the commoners' humble abode," Randall said to the solemn-faced Trowell when he arrived.

"Yes, well, some of us have to sop the gravy," he said, a brief smile crossing his lips.

"They've locked down Ben Gurion, Randy. I probably shouldn't be telling you, but I believe it's important for you to know. We'll be the last plane permitted to land for the foreseeable future, other than Israeli government and military aircraft."

"What does it mean for our getting into Jerusalem?" Prouse said, a frown of frustration crossing his face.

"Don't know," the diplomat said. "Maybe, just maybe, I can bring you along with me."

* * *

"They brought him in this morning. The maid found him in his bed, and thought he was dead. She called the service she works for, and they called a hospital, and they learned he worked here, and called us."

The doctor looked to Mark Lansing, then to Lori, both of whom stood near the nurses' station in the dispensary of the vast Taos underground complex.

"What's wrong with him?" Mark said, his thoughts on the fact that his newly found friend and instructor had been in good health and spirits when he last had seen him.

"We just don't know. Preliminary tests show neurological functioning is nearly normal. But we won't be able to know any more without further tests."

"Sound's like Mom's case," Lori said, frustration in her voice.

The doctor lowered her eyes, concentrating on when she first got involved with the Laura Morgan case.

"As a matter of fact, Lori, Dr. Kirban's case is very similar to your mother's. We've put him in a room next to hers, because of that."

"He's in a coma?" Mark asked.

"Yes. And, with the almost-normal brain activity going on,

that's hard to figure," the doctor said. "You may visit him for a few minutes, if you wish."

Mark and Lori stood moments later beside Gessel Kirban, whose body was attached to IVs similar to those hooked to Lori's mother.

"Dr. Kirban? It's Mark, Mark Lansing."

He put his hand on Kirban's arm and gripped it gently.

"Lori and I are here for you, Dr. Kirban. You have friends," Mark said, continuing to grip his scientist-mentor's arm.

"You need to get well, Dr. Kirban. They tell us you have every sign of being able to get better soon."

Tears came to Lori's eyes. They were more for her mother than for this man, but the thought he had no one, no family to be with him now, saddened her.

"Too bad about Dr. Kirban."

Mark and Lori turned, startled to hear the familiar, disconcerting voice. "He's in the finest facility in the world for getting help," Robert Cooper said, before smiling a tight-lipped smile and reaching his right hand to Mark.

"Lori, are you getting settled in here at our little complex?"

"About like expected," Lori answered, an ominous flush of uneasiness coming over her.

"And you, Captain. I've heard praise reports about you!"

"Oh? We were just getting started. I didn't know we had accomplished that much."

"Oh, you've accomplished a great deal with the project, I'm told," Cooper said with exuberance. "And things must go on, even with Dr. Kirban's sad...setback."

"He's being replaced? Already?" Lori said.

"Unfortunately, we are at a critical time in these projects. We can't, I'm sorry to say, always put individuals ahead of our efforts. And, Mark, it is about our moving on in this project we need to explore. It seems the opportunity to put the project to practical use is upon us—more quickly than we might have wished."

Cooper squinted and looked into the younger man's eyes, a

look of important things on his mind.

"Your President sent me, personally, to ask if you are up to a very special mission for him, and for your country."

* * *

Washington, D.C. 2:15 p.m.

The thunderstorm was sudden, and violent. Wind and rain buffeted the windows of the apartment high above the city's streets. Fractured streaks of lightning lit the darkened bedroom, where the director of Covert Operations for the United States Department of Defense lay naked beneath the single sheet.

Daniel Eganberg waited impatiently for his wife to come to bed.

He looked to the nightstand to his right, and picked up his wristwatch. He had an appointment at 3:45 with Bob McNamara, and he must not be tardy.

He put the watch back on the stand and sat upright in the bed, looking toward the master bathroom where Gwendolyn had walked nearly 10 minutes before.

"Gwendolyn!"

There was no answer to his shout. "Gwen!"

He lay back. Surely she would emerge from...whatever she was doing within a minute or two.

A tremendous streak of lightning seemed to hit the building itself, and the director jumped with a start. The resounding thunderclap reverberated for what seemed to be seconds, and the rain and wind blew harder than ever against the glass-paneled double doors to the balcony.

Eganberg thought he saw something in front of the intermittent flashes. He strained hard to see if his eyes were playing tricks.

The lightning again illuminated the balcony, giving the director an instantaneous still-frame moment of realization.

A darkly clad person looked to be standing, looking in at him.

"Who is it?!"

His shout was drowned out by yet another thunderous blast of sound that rumbled on for several seconds.

"Who are you?!" he screamed, his fear rising. Was it someone—an assassin—sent to murder him?

He pulled the drawer of the nightstand open, and grabbed the Walther PPK 7.65 millimeter pistol.

Panic-filled remembrances of an assassination attempt ran through his mind: the one in Sophia, Bulgaria, five years earlier. He had killed that man—he would kill this one!

Eganberg pointed the semiautomatic at the intruder, who stood motionless, dark and featureless in the blowing wind and rain just outside the French doors.

He felt suddenly paralyzed, unable to move even his fingertip, which was all he needed to move in order to dispatch his would-be murderer.

His eyes became fixed, the pupils dilated.

A slow gurgle came from his voice box. He tried to speak, but couldn't. He could only sit, staring. Transfixed.

His wife had heard his scream. She peered from the bathroom door, which she opened no more than 2 inches.

She started to scream, but stuffed her mouth with the bath towel she held. Her mind filled with terror, while she watched the horrifying scene in the bedroom.

Her husband sat holding the Walther at arm's length, unable to move even the trigger with his index finger. The thing—she saw it step through the closed door and walk, almost glide, to the end of the big bed.

The boiling human-shaped mass walked through the mattress and box springs until it reached Daniel Eganberg. She saw it enter her husband's nude body. Her terror grew while she watched the thing turn and assume the shape of the man. Eganberg, with the dark form assuming his shape to the extent it could no longer be determined to be separate from his body, stood from the bed and walked to the balcony doors. He dropped the Walther and opened both doors, so that the fierce wind and rain blew hard into the bedroom.

The director walked across the balcony, jogged a few paces, running into the railing. His upper body doubled forward over the railing, then the legs followed in a somersaulting plunge 17 floors to his death.

* * *

Approaching the Middle East, June 4, 1967

Mark Lansing sat looking out the small porthole of the KC-135, his mind back at the Taos complex with Lori. He was the only passenger on the refueling aircraft, besides a crew of six.

The cobalt blue Aegean crawled far below, the Cyclade chain of islands stretching in spine-like fashion north and south.

The parting had been one during which he had put up his bravest front. He would be back in no time. They would be together again. Then, they would discuss their future together in a serious way.

Lori made no pretense. Her tears couldn't be contained, and she exposed her deepest fears to him. She told him about the recurring nightmares –the man with the binoculars. The dream that haunted her over and over since the incident on the University of Texas campus. The ongoing nightmares involving the small, hideous gray creatures with the bulging black eyes that hovered around her bed like giant insects –trying to tear at her.

He would be getting into something neither of them knew much about. She didn't trust Robert Cooper. Then, there were the strange cases of her mother and Gessel Kirban that raked at her emotions, if not her rationale.

Lori had kissed him, apologized a dozen times that she was sending him off with such a "downer" farewell. She would try to do better. Try to be strong, to concentrate on the work they had given her, whatever that would be.

She was still not sure of the particulars of her assigned duties, but was promised by Gerherdt Frobe to find out the very afternoon that Mark left for Israel.

Burning at the back of her mind, and his, if he had been honest with her, were the matters involved in the weird dreams and visions or visitations or whatever they were. He was told by the—thing—that said it was his own father, Clark Lansing, that he should do whatever he was told. That they would be together again.

But, it was not his father in appearance or in voice, as he remembered from all those years ago. The thing was monstrous. Dark, boiling. Sinister.

Or, was it just a nightmare? The food he had stuffed himself with at the restaurant that evening?

No. The minister, Christopher Banyon—he had seen the monster. Or another monster of the same family of monsters?

Mark smiled at his own ruminations, as if going over a nightmarish Saturday matinee he and one of his buddies had seen back in the 1950s. Maybe "The Creature from the Black Lagoon," with the hideous half-man, half-fish creature that almost got the woman in the white, skin-tight bathing suit.

Lori was not just morose over his leaving. She was fearful, for some reason she couldn't pinpoint.

He had tried to assure her that if the President of the United States had personally gotten them both placed in the complex to do whatever they were to do for the country, it must be acceptable.

She had reminded him that his father was gone. Disappeared from the backseat of her own father's plane. Her dad was dead in a strange crash in which the T-38 was seen plunging nose down into the earth. Her mother was in a coma that was medically inexplicable, as was his scientist-mentor, Dr. Gessel Kirban.

Lori, beautiful Lori. His whole being ached for her now. But, he must be a big soldier, as his mother used to say when he was a little boy. He had duty to perform...but he still didn't know its nature.

"Captain."

The KC-135's co-pilot eased himself into one of the few seats available in the Boeing 707 constructed for carrying jet fuel.

"Our ETA is about 10," the Air Force captain said.

"Got some stimulant," he said, pouring coffee from a Thermos into a paper cup, then handing it to the Marine pilot.

"Thanks."

"You must be something special," the officer said, pouring himself a plastic cup full of coffee.

Mark said nothing, but raised his eyebrows while sipping the hot liquid.

"Yeah. We were told that we are to get you to Ben Gurion, no matter what happens. We thought it was the fuel for the Israeli Air Force that was the critical mission. But, we were told, in no uncertain terms, that you are the mission."

Mark looked surprised. He thought that, if anything, Cooper, or whomever was ultimately in charge—the President, maybe—would want his mission kept low key.

"There's nothing special about me," he said, with a slight laugh.

"Right," the co-pilot said with a smirking grin.

"Look out that window, about two o'clock."

Mark glanced out, his eyes locking onto a desert camouflaged Super-Mirage. Its fuselage was marked with a bright blue Star of David.

"Just joined us," the captain said. "There's one on the other side, too."

"Makes sense," Mark said. "War's brewing. Israel needs refueling capability. Why shouldn't they send a couple of escorts for your bird?"

"That just ain't how it works here, my friend," the co-pilot said. "The IDF doesn't just send escort for refuelers. It's got to be because you're on board."

"Then I suppose I'm flattered," Mark said, taking another swig of the coffee.

A little more than an hour later the fuel-laden 135 sat down, Mark thought just a bit hard, on the runway at Ben Gurion. The airport he remembered as usually bustling with aircraft and vehicular traffic servicing aircraft looked vacant, eerie. There were aircraft of the military sort, but not many civilian planes that he could determine from his vantage, while the big jet rolled out its landing and began its turn from the runway.

When the engines whined to silence, an enlisted crewmember opened the forward-most hatch on the left side of the fuselage. Before Mark could stand after unbuckling the seatbelt, several uniformed men entered the aircraft.

They swept the interior with their eyes, their glares affixing on the Marine captain, who looked in mild amazement at the swiftness of their actions.

"We are here to take you to your assignment," an Israeli officer dressed in desert fatigues and dark blue beret said.

Three other dressed similar to the officer maneuvered into positions behind Mark and the man who had spoken. They carried machine guns slung from their shoulders by leather straps.

"Where are we going?" Mark said, being whisked toward the opened hatch.

"Not now," the man said in accented English. "You will be briefed soon enough."

The KC-135 co-pilot watched the entourage leave his plane. He grinned at Mark as he passed. "Good luck, Captain," he said.

"I've got to get my things before we leave. The package they put aboard, the reason I'm here," Mark said, trying to slow the four men from hustling him away from the aircraft.

"It's taken care of, Captain. Everything's already aboard the chopper," the Israeli officer in charge said.

* * *

Randall Prouse's buddy from the State Department had parted from them with the admonition, "You would be better off in the hotel room, until we see which way this thing is going to go."

Trowell laughed, and said, "But I know you better than that, Prouse. If there's something to be dug up out there, there's nothing, not even an Arab-Israeli war, that's going to stop you."

"Yeah, well, that's what I'm about, Trowell, just like you've got to stick your nose in everybody's business around the world—invited or not."

They hugged, both laughing, promising to get together before they left Jerusalem.

Randall Prouse became serious, then. "Thanks, my friend, for getting us out of Ben Gurion. I'm very grateful."

Forty-five minutes later Randall Prouse turned one way, then the other, sighed, and rolled his eyes toward the ceiling. Finally, his lack of patience was rewarded.

"So sorry for the delay, Dr. Prouse," the voice, in broken English, said in his ear. "I believe we have your party, now."

"Yes, thanks."

Prouse's eyes narrowed in concentration, awaiting the connection he had been trying to complete for a half-hour.

"Randy?"

"Ruthie!" he said, a wide smile betraying the fact his mood had brightened.

"Are you safe?" There was anxiety in Ruth Prouse's voice.

"We're all fine, Sweetie. Just having trouble with these infernal connections to the States."

Christopher and Susie Banyon looked at maps spread on the hotel bed. Susie smiled when she knew Ruth had at last heard from her husband.

"Ackmid is coming by for us. He's taking us to Yadin, to examine the piece of the scroll from cave 11," Prouse said with joy in his voice.

Susie glanced at the archaeologist, thinking of his anxious wife on the other end. Ruth Prouse just wanted to talk about them being together again, and Randy was expressing his elation over his work. Such, Susie thought, is the plight of wives tethered to men of such boldness. She herself must be such a woman. She was here, in Jerusalem, at the worst possible time.

"The kids? Giving you any trouble?" Prouse said. "Yeah. You tell him I'll deal with him when I get home."

Prouse let his eyes wander the room, seeing nothing, listening to his wife's domestic talk. A knock on the hotel room's door caused him to interrupt her.

"Yeah. Well, Ruthie, I gotta get off now. Everything's fine here. I'll let you know when we'll be coming home. Love ya, Babe!"

While Prouse hung the receiver on its cradle, Christopher reached for the door.

"Hold it, Chris! Never open your door here, unless you're absolutely clear who's on the other side," the archaeologist said, pulling aside the small security viewing hole's cover.

"Akmid?"

"Yes, Randy. It is I…" the high-pitched voice came from the other side. Prouse recognized it as Akmid Jepha, a Palestinian Arab he had known for five years.

Greetings and introductions made, Prouse looked into the Arab's dark eyes, totally absorbed in the man's words.

"The piece is about so…"

Akmid held his hands about 12 inches apart, indicating the size of the piece of scroll in question.

"However, although it is in ancient Hebrew, it is not a part of the Isaiah text itself. It is—how do you say? A supplement, apparently, according to Yadin."

"Where is Yadin?" Prouse asked, while rising from sitting on the edge of one of the beds and walking to the window. He pulled the blinds apart and peered out to see the Dome of the Rock's rounded top shimmering in the Jerusalem sun.

"He awaits at the Museum of Antiquities," Akmid said. "We'd better make tracks while we can," Prouse said. "They might lock this old town down at any second."

* * *

All of the Taos scientists sat around the huge mahogany conference table. They had just been told the status of the major projects in which the secretive complex was involved.

People on the outside had complained of a troubling hum coming from the areas surrounding Taos and Santa Fe for years. The government had always denied the existence of any military or any other research and development that would cause the low throbbing noise that plagued the ears and brains of some people in the region.

The Cold War and the arms and space races with the Soviet Union made the lies to the public justifiable. Government spokesmen automatically branded anyone who tried to investigate the "hum" as being of the "UFO kook" mindset. Media, for the most part, agreed. Even presidents stayed away from the uncomfortable subject of the Taos hum, except for Lyndon Johnson.

But, this President was too involved in Vietnam, and now the brewing problems about to explode between Israel and its enemies, to pay attention to details.

Robert Cooper was glad of the fact. Johnson was just the sort of powerful man—from his days of almost absolute sway over Congress, as Senate majority leader, to be put off, if he truly set his mind to get involved.

Johnson trusted Daniel Eganberg—under the supervision and oversight of Robert S. McNamara—to carry on with the Taos underground research and development. He was promised "great things" from the facility. Both the President and the Secretary of Defense bought the package Eganberg sold them.

It was he, Robert Cooper, who had assured Eganberg that the venture would "be successful beyond our wildest dreams."

But none of them—not the President of the United States; not the Secretary of Defense; not his superior, Eganberg—knew the whole truth. They were in the dark, he thought, with an inward smirk, about Dark dimension. About RAPTURE, the acronym for the Rapid Atomic Particle Transmolecular Unification Reassembly Energizer. They knew about the precognition neuro-diviner device—but not what it was actually designed to do. They knew nothing about the RAPTURE—or about the Dimensionals...

Cooper smiled to himself, knowing what the young man with

the somber look was going to tell him. The Secret Service agent, especially chosen to also represent the NSA, CIA, and FBI so all clandestine possibilities were covered, approached his boss, who sat talking to Gerhardt Frobe.

The agent bent to whisper in the deputy director's ear. Cooper, a grim look on his face, stood and walked to the podium at the top end of the conference table.

"Pardon me, ladies and gentlemen," he said into the microphone attached to the lectern's top.

"I've some tragic news to report."

All voices co-mingled in surprise and he waited for the rumble to subside.

"I've just been informed that Director of Covert Operations for the Department of Defense, Daniel Eganberg, was killed when he fell from his apartment's balcony."

Chapter 12

June 4, 1967 – 1:50 p.m. Jerusalem time

E ast Jerusalem was in turmoil. The crowds of mostly Arab inhabitants hurried to get their essential marketing needs completed. War was imminent.

The brilliant sky caused the new and ancient structures to cast shadows of flickered darkness, then brightness upon them. Randall Prouse, Christopher and Susie Banyon, victims of Akmid Jepha's driving, negotiated the narrow streets.

The World War II vintage Jeep felt as if it would rattle apart with each pocked area Akmid couldn't seem to avoid.

Hostile looks met them around every corner, the hatred glaring mostly from young Arabs in native dress. Randall Prouse wouldn't say it aloud, but it was the first time in years he had felt so threatened while traversing the old city.

His worries stemmed from the fact Susie was with them. If they were attacked, he would, without hesitation, cover her, get her to any shelter he could manage. Maybe it would have been better to have waited until this thing blew over to meet with Yadin.

No…it was critical that they examine the find.

Once the fighting began, there was no telling where it would end. Many thought it would end only with the final battle of the prophesied war called Armageddon. It would end at Armageddon, of course. But how near was that war to end all wars?

Christopher Banyon felt the tension in Randall, saw the intense concentration in his eyes. Not concentration on the buildings in order to get to the Antiquities Museum as quickly as possible, but concentration upon each group of Arab men they approached.

Pressed against his friend while the Jeep jostled them, he felt the tautness of the archaeologist's muscular body ripple with each gathering they passed.

Susie felt every bump and shake while the Jeep rattled onward, and she did her best to just hang on, and not let the men know that the ride was almost painful. It was all worth it, though, she thought, hanging on to the side of the Jeep. The words kept running through her mind, *"Whither thou goest, I will go..."*

Akmid showed no concern while he herded the Jeep down one narrow roadway, then another. If there was one good thing about their situation, running the hostile streets of east Jerusalem, it was that their driver was an Arab, known by all other Arabs.

The Palestinian Antiquities Museum was a welcome sight to the archaeologist, who quickly jumped from the Jeep and offered his hand to the tiny hand of Christopher Banyon's new bride. She had a problem extricating herself from the seat, so he lifted her by her waist and deposited her on the stone surface that fronted the ancient building.

Christopher lifted the big map case from between the seats and the rear of the Jeep, then followed his wife, Prouse, and Akmid into the museum.

Musty smells and dank odors assaulted their nostrils. Randall Prouse didn't notice, while he quickly led the way in the direction of the basement steps, toward the oldest area of the structure. He knew that Yadin would be waiting there for them.

"Friend, Randy!" the small man said with a toothy smile peeking out from between the opening in his graying beard. The two men embraced.

"Too long, my great friend, Yadin," Prouse said continuing to hold onto the Arab.

"Too long, Randy," Yadin said, his eyes glistening with

emotional tears of reunion.

"You are most welcome," Yadin said, after Prouse had made the introductions. "Although it is a most troubled time," he added.

"What do you think will come of this...trouble?" Prouse asked, glancing around the room, trying to see the object of his visit.

"Only God knows," Yadin said, shaking his head and lifting his clasped hands toward the basement's ceiling.

"Will you and your family be okay?" Randall asked, looking into the dark eyes.

"We shall take precautions, until this is settled."

"Good. That's good," said Prouse, his mind on Yadin's wife, Mary, and their large family. He knew them all, had spent time as their guest on many occasions, some of those occasions under threats by Yadin's own hate-filled Arab brothers.

"Now. You must see this, Randy!"

Yadin looked around the bulky archaeologist to Christopher Banyon. "Your friend—does he know the possible significance?"

"Believe me, Yadin, he knows."

"Come, then—come, see what we have discovered. It is truly phenomenal," the Arab said, moving into an adjoining room.

He led them to a large table covered with felt. Christopher thought it looked like it could once have been a pool table.

A large, flat portfolio-type case lay atop the green felt.

Yadin unzipped the case and carefully moved that half to one side. Another felt cloth, this one earth-brown, covered the object of their trip.

When the Arab archaeologist removed the cloth, Randall Prouse stepped closer for a better look, his pulse rate increasing.

"This fragment was part of the same scroll, but in a place that indicated it was an adjunct to the scroll. It isn't part of the Scriptures. But, see here—the one who wrote the Scriptures, wrote this also."

Randall Prouse accepted from Yadin a large magnifying glass and moved it over the Hebrew letters.

"Yes. It is the same hand, no question."

"And, see what it says. It is fantastic!"

Randall Prouse read with slow deliberation, emphasizing each word as he read from right to left.

"*War in heavens and on earth shall begin the consummation when first scroll words shall be found.*"

The Arab said with excitement, "And now, the part broken off of that fragment." Yadin unfolded another cloth from the second, smaller fragment.

Prouse again ran the glass over the Hebrew writing. Christopher Banyon moved closer, to look at the fragment of text, while Prouse read.

"*Watch for the bene elohim...The bene elohim deludes when approaches the great taking away.*"

Christopher Banyon felt a rush of strange emotion hearing the words.

"You okay, buddy?" Prouse said, seeing the minister's dazed expression.

"What does it mean, Randy?" Christopher said, but knowing Prouse had no answer. "What in the Lord's holy name does this mean?"

* * *

Robert Cooper sat in Gerhardt Frobe's office. He stared straight ahead while he sat behind the scientist's desk, its top cluttered with papers and devices of experimental science. He listened to the phone's receiver. It was Gwendolyn Eganberg, and her voice was filled with panic.

"Bobby, you've just got to come back here. I can't stand another minute of this interrogation! If you were here, they would leave me alone. But, they act like I had something to do with him falling from—"

Cooper heard her sob, then regain control.

"Bobby, should I tell them about...about the thing I saw, you know, when it entered Dan's body?"

Cooper blinked, his mind snapping back to the conversation, from almost total immersion in thought about the certainty that he would be receiving another phone call at any moment.

"What...? No, No!" he said, cursing.

"You say nothing. They'll think you're completely crazy if you tell them something like that. They will take you in for interrogation like you do not want, Gwendolyn. Do you hear me? Do you understand?"

There was more sobbing on the other end of the line.

"Listen, Gwen. You had absolutely nothing to do with Daniel's death, except a husband-wife argument over sex. You were in the bathroom, and he was depressed because you and he weren't getting along. You had cut him off from sex..."

He paused, to hear that her sobs had quieted.

"Remember, that's the story. He was under stress because of his heavy responsibilities at work, and depressed because you and he had had an argument, and he just, he decided to end his problems."

Gwendolyn Eganberg sighed, sniffled a couple of times, and wiped at her nose with a tissue.

"Do you hear me, Gwen? That's all you have to say, okay?"

"Okay," she said, trying to regain composure.

"I'll see to it that the whole thing is taken care of—the funeral, everything."

Frobe's office door opened a crack, and the scientist stuck his head inside. "Bob. It's the Secretary of Defense on that line that's blinking."

"Gotta' go, Gwendolyn. I'll be back in D.C. on the 6th. I'll take care of everything. Relax, get some rest."

When he hung up, he took a deep breath and pushed the blinking button, the second from the left along the bottom of the phone's plastic console.

"Hello, Mr. Secretary," Cooper said through a tight-lipped smile.

"You probably have some idea of what this call is about, Bob," the voice at the other end said.

"Sir, not for sure," the deputy director lied, his eyes slits of concentration as he stared into the shadows of Frobe's office.

"I have someone here who I think you'll want to speak with," Robert McNamara said. A second later, a familiar voice was on the line from D.C.

"Bob? How are things down Taos way?"

"Fine, Mr. President," said Cooper, sitting a bit more erect in Gerhardt's desk chair.

"We've got to move on with the project, don't you agree?" Lyndon Johnson drawled.

"Yes, sir. It's crucial."

"You're our boy, Bob," Johnson interrupted. "Your nation needs you. I need you to carry on."

"Yes, sir. I'll do my best, Mr. President."

"I've named you acting director of Covert Operations at Defense. I know I can count on you. We can make it permanent when I've had a chance to talk to my national security people."

It was a done deal, Robert Cooper told himself with a satisfied smile. No one dared buck Lyndon B. Johnson, not even Wilbur Mills or the other powerhouses. Acting director, director, it was all the same. The deal was done.

"I don't know what to say, Mr. President. I'm humbled."

"Just get in there and pitch, partner. Like Dan did. You'll do a great job."

"Thanks, Mr. President, I will try."

"He's gone, Bob," the Secretary of Defense said, having taken over the conversation from Johnson.

"I understand you're making all the arrangements for the funeral."

"Yes, sir. I'll take care of everything," Cooper said.

"Great. Keep us informed."

"Yes, Mr. Secretary, will do," the newly designated acting director of Covert Operations for the Defense Department said, his heart racing with the thrill of conquest.

* * *

Taos underground complex—Late evening, June 4

The nursing station was vacant just outside the room where Laura Morgan lay comatose. Those nurses assigned to both Laura and Dr. Gessel Kirban were permitted 30 minutes every 2 hours to break for personal reasons. Usually, the nurse on the 11 p.m. shift took only 15-minute breaks, preferring to take 15 minutes per hour.

This evening she had dimmed the main lights to zero by turning the rheostat switch on the wall near her booth-like office space. The only lights remaining were one 50-watt bulb in a glass-enclosed covering above the cabinet where typing and other office supplies were kept and a red light above the door that was the exit from the suite that contained the four private rooms.

Julia Rameriz, a nurse who had been in the employ of the federal government since 1958, stuck her head in from a door that led to a hallway. She didn't see her friend, so figured she had left for a snack break. She would go to the small snack bar several corridors away.

A second thought struck. She had better first look into the patients' rooms. Perhaps her friend was in one of the rooms.

She walked past the nurses' station and looked first into the room where Gessel Kirban lay, his body attached to several intravenous tubes.

She then moved the few feet to the door where Laura Morgan lay unmoving, like Kirban, hooked to several tubes and monitoring wires.

The nurse started to turn to leave, but caught out of the corner of her right eye a dark, moving shadow that seemed to emerge from the cream-colored wall.

Her eyes widened, her mouth opened to scream, while her hands shot to her mouth in terror.

The black, boiling mass stepped the rest of the way through the wall, peering at the nurse, who could neither scream nor move.

The thing's head, she could see through her own transfixed stare, glared at her, two slits widening to reveal eyes that glowed like red-hot embers. The being sparked small flickers of what looked to be electrical energy, and it towered almost to the ceiling while it looked at the woman.

She then relaxed, her hands moving from her mouth to her sides, her demeanor displaying that she was completely oblivious to the creature's presence.

The black, whirling mass shaped like the human form moved toward the bed and Laura. It moved through the mattress, then began to lie precisely as Laura lay, placing its back upon her full-length.

When its back had entered no more than an inch through Laura's flesh, a tremendous flash of light, accompanied by crashing, crackling sounds, lit the room brightly.

The nurse stared at the scene, through eyes whose pupils were opened to full dilation.

The dark form spasmed, going from lying atop the comatose woman to standing in a crouched-for-battle position near the wall it had entered. Its long, vortex-like arms thrust forward. Its lengthy, stiletto-like fingers clenched and opened, then clenched again. Its entire black, boiling body began to pulse with flickers of light.

The room's darkness burst with light. The air about the nurse's head crackled and popped with energy, and a supernatural wind blew from the light's center.

The dark form had escaped through the same wall it had entered. The light grew in brilliance until nothing was visible to Julia Rameriz's eyes. Then the light began retracting, until it formed a single ball of sun-like light while it hovered at Laura's bedside.

The nurse's body seemed to again become supple, unleashed from the paralyzed state it had endured since the moment the dark form had emerged from the wall. Still, she seemed to have no will of her own. She stared straight ahead, while she walked slowly, almost robotically, to the side of Laura's bed where were connected all of the medical support wires and tubes.

The glowing ball of light pulsed, all the rainbow seemingly wrapped around its core, while it urged the nurse to do its bidding. Julia carefully, methodically, removed the intravenous tubes, and then detached the monitors from Laura's thin, dissipated body. The coma had done its debilitating work, and Laura's muscles had already atrophied to the point the doctors questioned whether she would ever regain their usage to any extent. Certainly not to the normal range of use, they had determined.

The nurse finished her task, and moved near the doorway. She stared at the ball of light, which glided above Laura Morgan. A million laser-like beams of lights of every color streamed from the sphere into her body at every point of her flesh.

Even in her transfixed state, Julia knew at this moment she didn't want to leave. But she did leave, and forgot all she had seen.

* * *

Israel, the same hour

Mark pulled the form-fitting G-suit to his thighs, then struggled against the material of his desert-camo flight suit to tug the expandable material to his waist. He sat on the wooden bench in front of the locker he had been temporarily assigned the day before.

His stomach crawled. The bench, the locker, even the smell. They evoked vivid memories of the Friday nights before high school games. Recollection of getting ready for the annual rivalries that were part of New Mexico football seasons.

But this was more akin to the championship game, the one in which he had scored the final touchdown. It was in a losing cause, he remembered with pain. 34 to 7... He hoped today would not turn out to be like that championship game nine years earlier. He pulled one boot on and began lacing it up, then reached for the other. He looked up, when the Israeli officer's voice caught his ear.

"We are scheduled for takeoff at 6:50," the Israeli major, dressed in flight gear similar to Mark's, said.

Mark looked at his watch. It read "05:10."

"Nervous, Captain?" the major said.

"I would be nuts if I weren't," Mark said.

"Good! Glad to know I'm not riding with a crazy man today," the major said solemnly in accented English.

He had heard of the Israeli military's dark humor and their penchant for understatement about the fortunes of battle. About the probability of death in war. The stories were true.

It was eat, drink and be merry, for tomorrow we might die—but so will four times as many of the enemy.

"Shall we give you a look at our bird?" Maj. David Rashfer said.

Moments later, both men stood beside the especially equipped F-4, the word "Moshi" painted on the aircraft's nose.

"Moshi?" Mark said, looking closely at the fiery red word against the sand-colored paint.

"Moses," Rashfer said. "He was the Deliverer. This Moshi will be a deliverer, also—the deliverer of judgment and destruction on Israel's enemies."

Mark, following the major around the aircraft as they pre-flighted it, looked at the windows completely encircling the hangar at the ceiling level. They were covered in black, so that not even a single ray of sunlight could shine through.

"I've never seen a hangar so secured," he said, scanning the vast space to see armed guards at every door. "Not even at Andrews where the President's fleet is kept."

"Perhaps you and I will know, before this day is out, why this hangar, with this one bird, is so secure," the Israeli pilot said, bending to inspect the F-4s wheelwell.

* * *

Through a swirling mist of smoke, they came at him. Many of them. Their eyes burning, glowing embers set in ovaled blackness.

They reached for him, tore at his face, his clothing, and his body. He ran naked, his bare feet burning with each strike of his feet upon the lava flow that stretched in the distance as far as he could see. He ran, his knees slowing in their pumping action, as if they had become bogged in a river of thick petroleum. His arms, too, slowed in their pumping, so that his progress was almost at a standstill.

His pursuers raged just behind, overtaking him. Their long, black, human-like arms outstretched, the tentacle-like fingers reaching, trying to grab him.

He felt their fiery, sulphurous breath on the back of his neck. A ringing sound caused his eyes to pop open, and he sat up on his side of the bed.

Christopher Banyon blinked, trying to separate nightmare from reality. The phone rang again, and Susie stirred from her sleep, while she lay beside him.

"Hello...Yes?" Christopher stammered into the phone receiver's mouthpiece, still trying to regain sensibility.

But, he thought, he was still in the nightmare. The voice—not possible.

"Pastor Chris..." The voice, familiar, yet not possible.

"Is that you, Pastor Chris?"

Yes! It was Laura Morgan.

"Laura?"

"Pastor, I haven't much time. You've got to listen."

"Laura? What happened?"

"A miracle. Two miracles. There's no time," Laura Morgan's voice said.

"Laura, is that really you? How did you get me here?"

Susie sat up part way, leaning on elbows, and looked sleepily at her husband.

"Listen, Pastor. God is at work. Please do what He has told me to tell you."

"Yes, okay, Laura; of course..."

She interrupted him, giving the instruction in an almost robotic fashion. "You must go to the Mount of Olives. To a spot you will be shown. There, pray, until you know the Lord's will is done."

Christopher Banyon was stunned. The woman he thought was near death sounding strong, confident, as if she had a message directly from the Almighty.

"Laura—how?"

"God is moving, Pastor Chris. You will know soon. You will know." Laura Morgan said, and then the minister heard only the steady dial tone.

Randall Prouse was already awake and dressed. He checked maps and several books that dealt with the history of the scrolls.

Something was in the air. He knew it. Jerusalem had an indefinable, but undeniable life force. It pulsed with excitement, and the archaeologist, who felt at one with this ancient place, sensed it now as never before. Something was definitely up.

The phone rang twice, and he lifted the receiver from its console, which sat atop a small nightstand.

"Randall Prouse," the archaeologist said, in the manner he always answered a phone call.

"Randy. It is Gessel. Please listen carefully. There is limited time," the Israeli scientist said in his familiar accent, causing Prouse's eyebrows to raise with surprise.

"Gessel! How did you track me down?"

"Please, Randy. There is no time. Listen carefully. The Lord God is at work this day."

Prouse thought his friend's voice sounded stiff, unnatural. "Are you okay?"

"I am better than at any time before. Now. I must tell you of matters of profound importance. Please listen."

"Yeah, sure," the archaeologist said with puzzlement in his voice.

"They are here, just as the fragments foretell. The...the things are here. I have seen them, have experienced them."

"What things? What is here?"

"The Dimensionals."

"Dimensionals?" Randall said, his eyes narrowing in concentration while his brain ran quickly through its files for a connection.

"I have been told to instruct that you take the preacher, Christopher Banyon, to Mount Olivet. You must go now."

"The Mount of Olives? Why? Who told you?"

"The Lord, Randy. The Lord told me!" Gessel Kirban said with, Prouse perceived, glee in his voice.

"Laura Morgan and I—we are instructed by the Lord to go to where the Dimensionals do their last days evil."

"Are you on something?" Prouse said, still trying to make the connection to the term "Dimensionals" in his convoluting mind.

"No, friend Randy, I am not on something. Rather, I am onto something!"

"Laura Morgan? Has she come out of her coma?"

"More than that. She and I are on our way to investigate what God has to show us."

"Why does—the Lord—want me to take Chris to the Mount of Olives?"

"You will see. Just obey, my friend. There are things, marvelous things the Lord wants you to see!"

* * *

Several men pushed the huge hangar doors so that they rolled steadily on their tracks until the opening was wide enough for at least two F-4 fighters to pass through. A couple of Israeli Air Force troopers brought the yellow tug with a tow bar through the opening. They wasted no time in hooking the bar to the bird's nosewheel, then backed the tug into place so that the circle connector could be placed over the hitch on the back of the tug.

Mark and Maj. David Rashfer pulled open the heavy, steel

door that separated the hangar from the flight offices. When they entered the briefing room, two men in uniform stopped their conversation to look at the pilots.

"Gentlemen," the Israeli colonel said, a solemn expression on his well-worn face. "Please meet Gen. Mordecai Hod," he said.

Mark saw all of the stars, but knew nothing about the officer. He knew, from Rashfer's sudden stiff posture, that the Israeli general was a man of importance. How important, he would soon learn.

"Capt. Lansing, General Hod is Commander of Israeli Forces," the colonel said matter-of-factly, without aggrandizement in his tone.

"Just call me Motti," the man with all the stars said, reaching his hand to take Mark's.

"Maybe you had best call me General Motti, major," the general said with a grin, taking the Israeli pilot's hand and shaking it vigorously. "We must preserve the privilege of rank."

"I shall call you 'sir,' if you don't object," Rashner said, returning the banter.

"As will I, sir, if you don't mind," Mark said, liking the informality he sensed in this, one of Israel's great heroes of battle.

"As you wish, young man," Hod said, turning back to the colonel. "Up to this point, you have been kept in the dark on the mission. And, I'm afraid you will have to remain in the dark to some aspects," the colonel said. "However, it is time to reveal what can be revealed."

"Capt. Lansing…" the general said, his gray-blue eyes piercing into the American's eyes, so that Mark felt that the officer was searching his soul. "The aircraft you and the major will take into this mission has technology that even we who are sending you do not completely comprehend."

Gen. Hod sat on the edge of the colonel's desk on one hip, looking at Mark, then at Rashfer.

"I tell you truly," Hod said in accented English, "Israeli

forces—how do you Americans say it—have our work cut out for us."

He stood and paced slowly while he talked.

"Yesterday, Iraq joined the military alliance with Egypt, Jordan and Syria."

The general stepped in front of a map of the region he was addressing. He circled the area with a gesture of his right hand while he talked.

"Approximately 250,000 Arab troops currently ring the whole of Israel. Nearly half of those forces are in Sinai. They have more than 2,000 tanks and 700 aircraft poised to strike. There is no doubt they shall do so, when their courage is sufficiently bolstered, with the urging of the Soviets."

He was silent for a few seconds, searching Mark's face for signs of concern. He saw none.

"Captain—Major," he said, looking to Mark, then to Rashfer. "The technology you have brought with you from the American scientists had better be the equivalent of what the atomic bomb was to the Allies in August of 1945. The odds are that seriously stacked against us."

"I have to be honest, sir," Mark said. "I didn't have time to do any live practice runs with the helmet. A few hours of simulator practice, but—"

"I am informed that this technology so takes over the pilot's senses that the learning curve is instantaneous," Hod said, interrupting the American.

Mark was amazed at the statement. Gessel Kirban had said nothing about the fact to which the general was privy.

"I and the Israeli government have been assured that this is so. Let us pray it is as they say," Gen. Motti Hod said with clinical assessment.

"At exactly 7:45, you shall be over your target, leading the I F into Egypt in a preemptive strike that, I pray to God, will end this war before it has a chance to get started."

* * *

Gessel Kirban led the way, with Laura Morgan close on his heels. Neither had ever felt physically better, and Kirban was amazed at his own lack of concern about the possibility of being discovered while they moved down the darkened corridor.

Laura depended on the scientist to get them to the secret places in the complex. She knew nothing of Kirban, except the things he told her, upon the glowing sphere hovering over him and awakening him from his comatose condition.

Laura had arisen from her own coma, her muscles' strength and conscious thought miraculously returned to her in an instant. She then was irresistibly drawn by the sphere into the adjoining room. She was, somehow, made to understand that she must remove from the man's body the tubes and wires—the same type of medical devices to which she had been connected.

Kirban told her, after he was again to full health, that he was Mark Lansing's scientist-mentor. The last thing he remembered was investigating the sounds—the almost painful, but low-level hum coming from the forbidden regions of the Taos underground facility.

Laura wondered why she had not asked a thousand questions of him. What had happened to her? What was her daughter, Lori, doing here? What about Mark Lansing?

The last thing she remembered, she had told Kirban, was walking, feeling groggy, into the apartment's living room. She saw a bright light—then, nothing.

There was no time for further discussion. The glowing light, its warmth and intense, yet comforting, electrical-like stimulation had overcome their fears. The glow had grown, divided, and completely engulfed them, individually. Each could see the other, watch the glowing force that flowed over and around the other. The aura grew brighter over each of them, while it changed and intermingled with colors neither had ever seen.

Somehow, the light had permeated even their thoughts. They

knew, at the same time, what they must do. Each must make a phone call to Israel, and the numbers to be given the operator, remained etched in their minds, even now, while they followed the light's innermost directive to go to where Kirban had experienced the unexplainable.

Both Laura and Kirban wore white orderly clothing, which they found in neatly folded piles when Laura looked into a supply closet just outside Kirban's room. Laura let the thought run through her mind now, looking far down the long, dark corridor. Not only the medical clothing fit, even the shoes were the right size.

Her God paid attention to details, Laura mused.

"The hum! Hear the hum?" the Israeli said, stopping, turning his head to better hear.

"Yes. It's like a thumping, an electrical, a buzzing, transformer sound," Laura answered.

"Yes. Exactly," Kirban said, "although it is not as loud, or as irritating as when I last heard it."

They began to move forward again. Kirban stopped abruptly, when he and Laura heard voices at the same instant.

A man and a woman rounded the corner of a corridor leading off of the hallway they walked. Kirban recognized the scientists, who wore long white lab coats. The same man and woman he had seen the night he hid in the shadows...

But, now there was nowhere to hide! They were exposed in the narrow hallway, which now seemed better illuminated than before. They would be found out!

Laura and the scientist moved close to the wall to their right, Gessel wishing they could melt into the very wall itself—step through it, as did the dark, sinister figures from his time before in this corridor.

The man and the woman continued to walk, and talk, headed directly toward the two huddled against the wall.

Why had the pair from the forbidden area not seen them? They seemed not to know the two intruders were only a few feet in front and to the left of them. The man and woman passed them by, the woman gesticulating while she talked.

"All has worked perfectly to this point. This is an excellent test. Our theory will at last become publishable fact," the voices trailed off as the scientists moved farther down the corridor, then turned right onto another hallway.

Kirban and Laura looked into each other's eyes. There was nothing to be said. Neither wanted to question the series of miracles that continued to clear the way while they moved toward the strange regions ahead.

Neither did they now feel the need to travel the corridors in the fashion of thieves. If the Lord had brought them this far, He would finish what He had started, Laura thought. Now, like her companion, she walked with more confidence—without fear.

The ominous hum began to increase in ear-assaulting intensity. Heart-like thumping pulsed more loudly with each step they took toward the area where Kirban had been several nights earlier.

"We are almost there," the Israeli scientist said, searching for the large steel door he had entered before.

What if this door or the others were locked? He had no card. They would be impossible to open if locked—

"There!" he said in an excited whisper. "This is the door through which I entered."

He grabbed the thumb-latch handle he had tried that night. Locked! Now what to do? "We will never get through to the lab I saw unless we can get through this door," he said, his mind racing, trying to concoct another way.

"God will provide," Laura said.

She amazed herself. How did she know—with such certainty— it was God's idea for them to pass through the doorway?

Both stood away from the locked steel door, and looked at the brass latch that was welded on the heavy metal surface of the door's left side. In that moment of helplessness, both sensed something would happen. Something would get them into the secretive areas beyond the doors.

Laura reached to again try the latch. When she pushed

downward on the thumb plate above the handle, the device unlatched. Kirban grabbed the heavy door and helped her pull it open far enough for them both to squeeze through the opening.

Before either could marvel over yet another minor miracle, they found themselves immersed in an invisible sea of vibrations and sounds, undulating sounds that set in motion strange sensations within their brains. Intensive wave-like cerebral convolutions that evoked at the same time great sadness and manic elation.

Laura put her palms over her ears, so painful was the assault. Kirban pulled her to himself and tried to comfort her, while they huddled in the near-darkness.

Just as abruptly as the audible attack on their senses began, it stopped. The familiar thumping, heartbeat-like sound resumed.

"It's this way," the scientist said, sure now that they were very near the oval room he had been drawn to several evenings earlier.

Yes! There they were, the huge double doors. No handles. The long rectangular glass windows at his eye-level.

"This is it, Laura!" he whispered excitedly. "This is where I saw the activity."

"Dear Lord," Laura said, her eyes closed for the brief prayer. "Your will be done," she said, concluding, "in your precious Name, Amen."

"Amen," Kirban agreed.

The Israeli guided her by her right arm, urging her to step up to the narrow windows inset in the doors. He took the right; she took the left.

The room was alive with activity, white-smocked men and women moving quickly about, checking things at various positions along the walls.

Laura saw a dozen people seated at console-like stations, each wearing a gleaming gold-colored helmet. The headgear glinted with the lights of many colors that blinked from their positions along the continuous, rounded wall.

The helmeted people sat erect, staring straight ahead. Shadows within the vast dome-ceilinged room obscured facial features.

Gessel Kirban spoke in a whisper. "That stainless steel platform at the center of the room—that is where I saw the young man and woman. I cannot remember precisely, but something in the back of my mind urges me to believe the young man was Mark Lansing."

"Mark?" Laura said almost at full volume. She then lowered her voice.

"And the girl? Was it Lori?"

"I'm sorry, but I don't know your daughter. She is working with Dr. Gerhardt Frobe—my work rarely crosses paths with his. All I know is what Mark told me."

"And does he—this Gerhardt Frobe—have anything to do with this project?" Laura questioned, hearing the hum and feeling it beginning to increase in vibrating intensity.

"I cannot remember, from that night. But, again, something says to my thoughts that yes, Frobe might very well have been here."

The huge room seemed a living organism. Each thumping beat of the vibrations caused the amber glow to pulse brightly, then subside, before the next pulse again illuminated the group of twelve who sat staring straight ahead beneath their golden helmets.

Voices from behind Laura and the Israeli scientist snapped their attention from activities within the room they viewed through the slotted windows. Someone was approaching, and like in the hallway when the two passed them by, there was no place to hide!

Dr. Gerhardt Frobe, flanked on either side by two men in white lab coats, walked toward Laura and Kirban. No use to run. Impossible to get away, now.

But, the trio of scientists walked past them and pushed the big double doors, then walked into the chamber. The men paid no heed to the intruders, who stood aside, their faces masks of astonishment.

Chapter 13

R andall Prouse drove the Jeep he had talked Akmid into loaning. He swerved to avoid potholes that dotted the narrow roadway leading from east Jerusalem, up toward Moriah and the foot of Mount Olivet.

Christopher held on with all his strength to the top of the Jeep's door, each lurch making him feel as if his skeletal frame would come apart. Susie sat in the rear right seat, fighting, like her husband, to maintain an upright position during the ordeal.

"Sorry," Prouse yelled to be heard above the Jeep's straining engine sounds. He downshifted, then upshifted, while he maneuvered the vehicle over streets built upon 30 layers of previous generations.

"These things don't usually have any springs left," the archaeologist said, again grinding the gears so the engine would be able to pull the grade ahead.

Poor Susie, Christopher thought, looking around to see her struggle against the violent shaking. Always, he thought, she managed to look serene...to remain calm.

He had begged her to stay behind at the hotel. "No," she had told him in a gentle, not rebellious way. "The Lord wants my prayers, too," she had said.

It was her choice, but it was hard on her. Christopher understood why Ruth Prouse as often as not in recent times stayed behind when his friend Randy came to Jerusalem for one archaeological venture or another. As a matter of fact, the minister thought, while Prouse continued to herd the World War II vintage Jeep toward the Mount of Olives, Dr. Randall Prouse's times spent in the Holy Land were known to be adventures, as much as mere ventures.

The weather had cooled significantly in the last ten minutes, since they left the point where Akmid had turned the Jeep over to Prouse. Clouds above the Mount of Olives ahead seemed to be coalescing into a developing storm.

"Uh oh!"

Prouse's exclamation made Christopher scan the roadway and sides of the road ahead. His eyes fell upon a band of six men wearing traditional Arab clothing, all with burnoose headdresses and beards.

Each had an automatic weapon, with ammo belts strapped across their shoulders in bandoleer fashion.

"Better start those prayers, now," Prouse said, eyeing the six men, who stepped into the Jeep's path. They all held the weapons in a posture that threatened.

When the archaeologist brought the Jeep to a stop in the middle of the narrow road, the apparent leader of the Arabs stepped forward. Christopher and Susie took their friend's advice, and silently prayed.

The man with the weapon shouted something in Arabic, but kept the automatic rifle in the order arms position.

Prouse said something back to them, and the leader turned to jabber something to the other men.

"They want to know where we're headed," the archaeologist said, turning only his head so both Christopher and his wife could hear him. "I said that we are looking for a holy man we've heard of, where the woman might be cured with his miracle healing."

The leader of the armed band turned again and spoke in a suspicious tone to Prouse, who responded again in Arabic.

The men looked astonished. They jumped to the side of the road, the angry leader, with urgency, motioning the Jeep and its occupants to pass. He shouted curses at them while they went on their way.

"What on earth did you say to them, Randy?" the minister said, amazed at their response.

"Told 'em she has a rare disease that kills within two days. Said it's one of the most contagious diseases in the world. Said there's no known cure. That this holy man, who we were told we would find near the Mount of Olives, is her only hope. Told them all of us in the Jeep will most likely die, just because we've been this close to her," Prouse explained without breaking a smile. His passengers could not show the same restraint.

"Do you think I sinned, Chris?" the archaeologist said, continuing his deadpan tone and expression. "Do you think God considered it a sure enough lie?"

"I'll have to consult personally with Him on that one, my friend," Christopher said, choking out his words between his laughter.

* * *

The 12 helmeted people sat in a straight, stiff posture behind their waist-level consoles. All stared straight ahead. The walls blinked with points of light that were many colored.

Lab-coated scientists checked the helmets and consoles from time to time, and inspected the many electronic instruments inset within the rounded walls of the gigantic chamber.

Laura Morgan and Gessel Kirban now stood without fear within the room, the colors reflecting off their skin and the white clothing they wore. Laura had never experienced a complete lack of anxiety like she did at this moment. Something within her made her know she was, somehow, stronger than any force of evil this place could bring forth to challenge them.

"They have no idea we're here," she said, looking to Kirban, who, like her, was both fascinated and astounded at their apparent invisibility to all in the chamber.

"See! There!" The scientist pointed to the floor surrounding the gleaming, chrome-like platform.

Dark creatures passed through the floor at several points. They looked somewhat human looking, yet much larger, and not of solid matter. More of them emerged from the floor of the chamber, some walking about, some seeming to float just above the floor. Some entered the bodies of the scientists, then stepped out again. Each time they entered the humans' bodies, they assumed the shape of the person, so that only the human was visible to Laura and Kirban.

"What are they?" Kirban said, as if to himself.

Laura stood mute, watching with amazement while the sinister forms moved to the helmeted humans. The dark beings sat in the console chairs, appearing to take up residence within the sitting people.

Within several seconds, the inhuman forms were no longer visible to Laura and the scientist, who saw, then, the raised metal platform split apart.

Two figures came up from beneath, arising slowly, until the conveyance upon which they stood was level with the platform's surface. Both people who had emerged had their backs to Laura and Kirban. Both wore white lab coats. Laura determined that one of the new arrivals in the chamber was a man, the other a woman. The man reached to remove the other person's lab coat, revealing an almost nude woman, whose slim, straight body told Laura it was a young, though fully developed female.

The platform on which the two stood began a slow rotation, until the girl and her partner faced Laura and Gessel Kirban.

"It's Lori!" Laura shouted, starting to lunge toward Lori and the man who now began attaching electrodes to her body.

Kirban grabbed Laura, restraining her, yet trying to comfort her. "No, Laura. We cannot do anything at the moment. Remember— the Lord is in control, even of this…"

Laura relaxed some, but burned with urge to attack the man touching her daughter.

"What is he doing?" she said.

"Electrodes of some sort. He is attaching electrodes for some reason. I do not think they are dangerous to her."

"How do you know that? How can you say that? How can you be sure?" Laura had panic in her voice.

Kirban gripped her, knowing she would rush the platform if he released her.

"Let us see…the Lord will provide," the scientist said.

Another man in a lab coat approached the two on the platform. He handed the man who had been attaching the electrodes a gleaming, gold-colored helmet, like those worn by the 12 seated around the room.

The scientist placed the helmet upon Lori's head, adjusting it until it was in place. He attached more electrodes—to the helmet first, then to her body. Laura and Gessel Kirban stared in astonishment while a black, cloud-like, human-shaped creature stepped from the body attaching the electrodes to Lori. The thing then stepped into Lori's body, assuming her shape, so that the beast-apparition could no longer be seen.

Laura again struggled to free herself from her friend's grip. She cried tears of frustration, but more so, of anger, while she fought to free herself.

"No, Laura, no—not yet. The Lord will take care of her," Gessel said, restraining her.

With the girl hooked to the ominous electronic machinery, the scientist who had done the attachments stepped from the platform. An amber glow began to grow brighter, and the sounds in the room increased in intensity. The thumping that had ceased earlier now returned, and it felt to Laura and Kirban like their own hearts bumping in their bodies. The pulsing caused their heads to ache with each throb, and both held their ears to try to quell the pain.

The pulsing subsided, and a low, growling sound took its place. The words began as an indecipherable groan. They became the words spoken in the language Gessel Kirban recognized as his own.

"It is Hebrew," he said.

"What are they saying?" Laura said, knowing now that the words were being uttered in unison by everyone who wore the helmets. She could see her daughter's mouth moving, while Lori stared straight ahead, unblinking, as if in a trance.

"*Time has come...the Jew will die...the Jew must die,*" Gessel repeated, translating the menacing Hebrew incantations.

"What does it mean?" Laura said, wiping the tears from her eyes.

"Something to do with our prayer instructions from the light, I imagine," Kirban said, still concentrating on translating the words.

"*Betray the Jews...destroy the Jews,*" Kirban said, repeating the deep, groaning words that seemed to come from something other than the humans uttering them.

* * *

Robert Cooper sat in the darkness, behind Gerhardt Frobe's desk. His face pointed straight ahead, his eyes showing only the whites while they turned upward within their sockets.

His facial features contorted in an expression that was something other than human. The words poured from his mouth in a language he had never learned, while he sat erect in Frobe's chair, his arms outstretched, his palms flat upon the desk.

"Murder them all...kill the Jews," he said in Hebrew, and in a growling voice that vomited from the deepest regions of hell.

* * *

Mark Lansing rode in the rear seat of the F-4E, the golden helmet he wore glinting in the Middle Eastern morning sky. The bird had thundered off the runway only ten minutes earlier, its afterburners glowing in the unusual early morning darkness. They left behind a brewing storm unlike any he had seen. It seemed to have formed, black and ominous over Jerusalem, and over the base from which the flight of Israeli, French-made Super-Mirage fighters, and the single F-4E launched their attack. They were now at 21,000 feet, screaming southward toward Egyptian territory and the bases they, along with other Israeli flights of fighter-bombers, were assigned to destroy.

How would the precognition neuro-diviner perform? The United States Defense Department and the Israeli Defense force had put their complete confidence in the technology, and in his ability to use it.

Yet he had no more than 20 hours of simulator training, no actual practice. Gerhardt Frobe had assured him that the PND would take over, once it was switched on. But, Mark lacked the scientist's absolute confidence now, while he bowed his face to place his eyes upon the soft rubber of the scope's viewfinder.

Gen. Motti Hod had told Mark and his fellow pilot that their bird would make up for the small force of only 200 fighter-bombers Israel could throw into the attack. The F-4, an aircraft heretofore forbidden for sale to Israel—Mark was informed at the last moment before takeoff—was a secret that only Hod, a few other Israeli government officials, and the very top covert operations at the U.S. DOD knew about. The Israeli general told the American pilot-PND operator these facts, Hod had said, only because he wanted to impress upon Mark the absolute necessity of the success of the mission. To fail would mean that Israel might lose all 200 of its fighter-bomber force. The Arabs, particularly the Egyptians, were equipped with Mig 17s and Mig 21s. The Arab forces far outnumbered Israel's Air Force. The French Mirage aircraft, which made up the bulk of the IAF, were formidable. But, without the advantage of surprise, and something other to help balance things a bit, Hod had told the American captain, the probable outcome of even a preemptive strike looked bleak.

The F-4E, equipped with the technology even its operator knew next to nothing about, was meant to be that counter-balance to even things out.

Mark knew the device was linked directly to his thought

processes by the connectors within the PND. He also knew the device would—according to Gerhardt Frobe and the other scientists he had worked with—speed his thinking and reaction time to the point he could almost anticipate a full five seconds in advance of the actions of Arab pilots who would resist the attack.

Mark was puzzled, though, about how the technology was supposed to be effective in a strafing-type run. How would it work? He was certain he could perform what was required in aerial combat. But, how could he contribute to the attack on Arab forces on the ground?

Frobe had told him not to worry, that he would know what to do when the time came. The PND would interact through his subconscious, with technology that was so super-secret, even the operator—Mark Lansing—could not be told about its operations.

The words replayed in his mind now while he looked into the scope, which was lit with an eerie glow, concentric rings encompassing each other that reduced down to a single circle with something akin to crosshairs at its center.

"You will be contacted, son. You must do what they ask," the thing that called itself his father had said that night in a strange language that he had somehow understood.

"You're gonna be asked to do some special things for your country, son. I want you to show 'em you've got what it takes," Lyndon Johnson had said that day on the parking ramp at Randolph Air Force Base.

What would he be asked to do that he didn't yet know about, that he had not been told? Could the device be a nuclear-class weapon? What was the technology that was so clandestine, not even its user was privy to its secrets?

A single F-4E, itself a bird forbidden to interact with the Israeli Air Force, expected to tip the balance in the preemptive strike meant to neuter the Arab's air capabilities. To destroy Nasser's air superiority, in particular…

"Five minutes, Captain," the Israeli pilot said over the intercom.

"Five minutes it is, Major," Mark acknowledged.

Five minutes and he would know the technology's capability, Mark thought, adjusting the scope in the manner he had been taught at Taos.

* * *

They had left the old Jeep at the bottom of the Mount of Olives, Randall Prouse taking care to remove several sparkplug wires. If any of the many unsavory roving bands in this part of Jerusalem wanted to steal the vehicle, they would have to push it.

Christopher Banyon looked upward as they ascended the pathway. The clouds seemed almost to be sitting atop the famous promontory where, nearly two millennia before, Jesus Christ and His disciples sometimes gathered. The spot where Christ ascended into Heaven after giving the disciples the Great Commission.

The mount was now without the dense wooded areas of that earlier time. The trees had been cut for many uses, and, until recently, never been reseeded, or replanted. Yet, there remained ancient, gnarled olive trees and scrub brush at various levels on the rocky hills that comprised the mountain.

A thunderous roar followed brilliant lightning somewhere above the mount's highest point.

"This might not be the best place to be right now," Randall Prouse said, leading the way on the rugged, though often tourist-traveled pathway.

He carried a rolled-up piece of canvas on his right shoulder, in anticipation of heavy rain.

"Where do you suppose we should stop?" the minister asked, shouting to be heard above the almost continuous rumble of thunder.

"Gessel didn't say," Prouse said, turning to look over his left shoulder in order to be heard.

"Neither did Laura," Christopher said.

Susie Banyon, wedged between the two men while the

three trudged upward, said something, but neither man could understand because of the thunder, which increased in volume with each step.

The party stopped.

They both concentrated on what Susie was saying. "I said, Gethsemane. We should go to the Garden of Gethsemane."

"Where Jesus prayed. Of course!" Christopher said.

"Makes sense," Prouse grunted. "We can't be sure it's the exact spot that Christ and the disciples prayed that night Jesus was taken prisoner, but, it's the traditional site that has the approval of many scholars."

Christopher smiled at his friend's clinical analysis, then followed his wife and Prouse as they hurried toward what was considered to be the place Christ had prayed before His crucifixion.

"One thing sure," Prouse said, while veering from the path and stepping onto and over several small boulders. "We're alone up here today, with the war brewing, and this storm."

Susie Banyon thought how very wrong their big friend was. They were not alone...

* * *

Lori's body seemed to glow, while reflecting the amber radiance that filled the room. She stared ahead, unseeing, unaware that her mother stood not 20 feet from her.

Laura Morgan again strained to free herself from Gessel Kirban's grasp.

"No, no, Laura—we must not...the Lord will intervene."

The scientist's words were meant to comfort, but Laura didn't hear them. She saw only her child, being manipulated by the devil's machinery and by the black abomination that had moments before possessed Lori's body.

The things had possessed the bodies of everyone in the room, except the two of them, she thought. She glanced quickly at the faces of the 12 who wore the golden helmets, the mind-controlling headgear like that worn by her daughter.

She watched each mouth move in unison, including Lori's. The mouths repeated the same words over and over, in a growling chant that could not be made by a human being.

"Destroy the Jew...kill them all...Jews must be removed..."

Gessel relaxed his grip on the woman, satisfied that she had calmed. Laura bolted from him, and, when she knew she was free, began to run toward the elevated platform at the center of the room, where her daughter, like the rest, repeated the hate-filled directive.

She would grab Lori, take her from the platform. Jerk from her head the hideous helmet.

Laura suddenly felt frozen in place, and she couldn't speak. She looked downward, able to move only her eyes. She was encapsulated by a bright, glowing mass that was alive with spectacular points of lights of every color. All fear left her in that moment of realization. She knew in that soul-lifting second, her purpose in being there was not to fight them. Her God-ordained reason for existence at that instant of mortal time was to do nothing more or less than pray.

* * *

They descended swiftly from 21,000 feet to just under 2,000. The 15 Israeli Mirage fighters flew their assigned formations, with the F-4E at the center of the flight configuration. The groupings tightened when they reached Egyptian territory, then, three minutes later broke in various directions, so as to approach their assigned targets from many angles. The tactic was one designed to confuse SAM operators who might otherwise more accurately send their deadly missiles to their targets.

The Phantom dropped even lower than the two Mirages that had been flying just off the tips of its wings. The Israeli pilot held the stick in a course aimed straight at the largest of the Egyptian bases. Mark Lansing, his eye sockets pressed hard against the scope's rubber face-rest, watched while the topography in the distance moved quickly toward them. He began the count.

"Switching to PND in five...four...three...two...one!"

He depressed the red button on the side of the scope's encasement, and mentally prepared for the eerie sensations the precognition neuro-diviner initially produced when activated.

The ground moved now in slow motion within the scope's view as he concentrated. Slower than any slow-motion film he had ever seen...

Every stone, each raised point along the desert floor for miles in the distance, presented a vision in different colors that whirred through his brain in kaleidoscopic fashion. He saw the many Migs and other Egyptian aircraft in his increased rate of thought, his brain analyzing the targets and formulating the fail-proof attack the F-4 would make.

Maps, timelines, weapons systems, every conceivable nuance of quality and quantity to do with the Egyptian Air Force meshed with his neuron-to-neuron synapse firing to bring forth the perfect, infallible, preemptive assault.

Then the cerebral perfection began to disintegrate within Mark's wildly swinging thought processes. He heard a distinctive, all-consuming chant filled with hatred, and his brain turned to enraged thoughts that made him know what he must do. He must destroy anything, everything Israeli!

* * *

Billowing storm clouds gathered, rolled, and swept downward toward Mount Moriah, while Randall Prouse led the way up the narrow path on the Mount of Olives. Lightning flickered in jagged streaks above the darkened golden crown of the Dome of the Rock. The wind grew stronger by the second, and the archaeologist, Christopher Banyon, and Susie had to protect their faces from debris that pelted them while they neared the Garden of Gethsemane.

They were forced to turn their backs to the violent, debris-filled wind, pausing, then moving further up the hill during brief lessenings of the storm's assault.

"Somebody up here doesn't like us," the archaeologist said, trying to bolster his own resolve to keep moving.

Christopher held his wife in a firm grip, steadying her in the unpredictable gusts that now included occasional large raindrops. A blinding flash of lightning struck a tree 50 feet upward, causing the woman to scream and the men to jerk with startled convulsions.

"Too close!" Prouse shouted to be heard above the resultant thunderclap. "It's right over there."

He motioned in the direction he wanted them to follow.

Moments later they stood in the center of the spot where tradition had it that Christ had prayed to His father just before His crucifixion.

"Here! Between these rocks!" Prouse yelled, guiding both by their arms toward a boulder that jutted to produce an overhang.

"We'll be more out of the wind, here," he said, kneeling beneath the overhang, then spreading the large canvas over the three of them just as the rain began pelting, driven hard by the wind.

"Now what?" Prouse said. "I know Gessel said to pray—but for what, exactly?"

Susie said without hesitation, "For the peace of Jerusalem."

* * *

Lori's beautiful features were now a hideous mask of hatred beneath the golden helmet. Her mouth spoke words in an animalistic growl that was not hers, but that of the abominable creature occupying her soul.

Her mother, held immobile within the capsule of bursting, colored points of light, could do nothing other. She prayed.

She wanted to pray that Lori be released, that the vile place, the dark forces, be removed from them. But the thoughts in her mind told her otherwise.

"Pray for the peace of Jerusalem," she heard over and over.

Gessel Kirban, like Laura, heard the words, and he prayed for his native land, and for the ancient city where sat the holiest spot on earth for the Jew.

Chanting grew louder within the huge, ovaled chamber, the ambient glow changing from golden amber to ruby red. The helmeted 12 seated around the curved walls began to quiver, their eyes turned upward, so that only the whites were shown.

"All Jews must die!" Gessel Kirban heard the incantations demand in Hebrew. "Israel shall be destroyed!"

He prayed all the harder for the peace of Jerusalem, as did Laura, whose only thought was now directed toward her desire that the perfect will of God be done.

* * *

The American pilot now had complete control of the F4-E. The Israeli major could do nothing but go along for the violent ride, while Mark Lansing maneuvered the aircraft using only his thoughts.

The bird rolled left from the three-plane formation, dove slightly, then shot straight up, its dual afterburners at full thrust. Mark's eyes turned upward so that only the whites were visible. He heard only the words of the incantations, which drove his will to follow the directives from the bowels of the Taos complex.

His Dimensional-controlled brain took the aircraft in an inverted loop. When the bird again leveled off, it trailed the two Mirage fighters who had accompanied the F-4 toward its Egyptian targets.

"What are you doing?!" the Israeli pilot shouted from the front seat. He grabbed the stick, but it moved as if attached to nothing, no longer in commission.

"Get back in formation, Lansing! What are you trying to do?!"

At that moment, the Israeli heard the firing and saw the tracers of the 30-mm DEFA cannon fire strike the Mirage on the right in front of them.

Mark heard nothing, knew nothing, except what the beings directing told him to hear and think.

The Israeli pilot cursed and shouted into the face-mask microphone, but to no avail. He helplessly watched the Mirage, trailing thick, blue-black smoke, dive out of control toward the Egyptian desert.

He looked back toward the flaming carnage as long as he could, hoping, praying to see the ejection seat carrying the Mirage pilot rocket from the cockpit. But, now they were too far removed from where the Israeli jet would hit the earth.

Rashfer grasped for every cockpit control he could think of that might neutralize the madman-traitor's ability to continue his murderous assault.

Nothing. Everything he tried failed. Tears of frustration and outrage filled his eyes, while he continued to look, not for ways to neutralize the American's madness, but to destroy the F-4E, and the two of them with it.

* * *

Lightning crashed around them while they prayed. Their minds and spirits seemed at one with each other, and with a higher power, while they prayed a prayer of singular purpose: that there be peace in Jerusalem, and that God's will be done this moment. While the elements raged above them, a calming, reassuring, though unseen force seemed to engulf the three who huddled beneath the canvas.

Thunder sounded as if it growled words from Satan's own lips, but they prayed on, their deepest desires lifted far above the terrible, raging storm of supernatural conflict. Laura Morgan prayed too, as did the Israeli scientist. They neither heard nor saw the tempest brewing about them, while they appealed to their Deity to fulfill His will in this profound moment of human history.

* * *

Mark Lansing heard a far distant trumpet. Its sound grew louder, overtaking, then overwhelming the chanting that had held him in a trance from which there had been, until now, no escape.

"Lansing! For God's sake, man! Don't do this!"

Mark heard David Rashfer's pleading. He blinked, trying to clear his head.

"Captain! Do you hear me?!" Rashfer screamed.

"Yes...yes, Major...I hear you..."

"Return control to me...Now!" the Israeli demanded.

"What have I done? What's happened?"

"You shot down one of our wingmen, Lansing—you've gone mad!"

An emotional flood of disbelief, then self-hatred overcame him, while he came to his senses.

"Turn the bird over to me, Captain," Major Rashfer again demanded.

Mark reached to comply by pressing the red button on the PND's casing. He froze in place before his right index finger could contact the button. His mind leapt forward, his brain taking on many thoughts at once, knowing, suddenly, and with visceral understanding, the true nature of the conflict he was created to help resolve.

* * *

The acting director of Covert Operations for the U.S. Department of Defense lurched from his stiffened position behind the desk. He batted his eyelids, looking, in confusion, around Gerhardt Frobe's dark office.

Something had gone wrong, terribly wrong, he thought, rising from the swivel chair, and hurrying from the office. He walked down two corridors and into Frobe's laboratory.

Sweat beaded just below his thinning hairline, and on his upper lip. He mopped the perspiration with his suit pocket-handkerchief.

Something had indeed gone wrong!

The deal was made. It depended on the success of the mission. Everything depended upon Lansing carrying out the mission. Without that, the whole thing would collapse, upon one, Robert Cooper's head, he thought, while pushing several buttons on the console before speaking into the phone's mouthpiece.

"What's going on, Frobe? The Dimensional left, and I don't know why."

He listened to the scientist's words, his eyes shifting left and right while he considered what he was hearing.

"They all left their subjects?" he asked with panic in his voice.

"What's happening down there right now?" he demanded, then listened.

"The subjects cannot be allowed to wake up, do you understand, Frobe?! They can't be allowed to come out from under their compliant profile!"

* * *

"The storm's let up," Randall Prouse said, lifting the canvas to see water dripping from the overhang. He removed the canvas covering, folded it, and tossed it aside.

"That wasn't just another storm," Christopher Banyon said.

"Reminded me of the kind of weather we have in Texas, especially in the Panhandle during the spring," the archaeologist said. "Don't see the likes of that one around here at any season."

"It was a struggle…against the prince of the power of the air," Susie Banyon said. "Our prayers, and those of others … ended his storm."

"I believe you're right, Susie, I truly believe you are right,"

Prouse said, peering downward at the place where Solomon's Temple, and later, Herod's Temple once sat. A single, powerful column of sunlight beamed directly upon the center of Mount Moriah.

Chapter 14

Egypt – 7:45 A.M. June 5, 1967

G amul Abdul Nasser's military forces were taken by surprise. Only a few of the Soviet-made Migs ever got off the ground, while Israeli fighters, approaching from every angle of attack, swept in wave after wave, strafing and bombing aircraft and making impassable craters in Egyptian runways.

Mark, oblivious to all but the precognition neuro-diviner technology directing his subconscious, watched everything in super slow motion, while the Mig 17s and 21s blew apart one after another. The fuel-laden jets exploded where they sat, erupting in massive red and yellow fireballs, as did the Tupelov and Ilyushin bombers while they sat in their parking spots.

His companion in the front cockpit rode out the devastating blitz by the F-4E, awestruck at what he witnessed. He said nothing, letting the American pilot do what he came to do—decimate everything they could find that belonged to the Egyptian dictator.

There would be time to find out what went wrong. Why the Mirage was attacked. What happened to its pilot. One thing sure— Maj. David Rashfer thought while he saw Mark destroy with obliterating precision everything he attacked—he had never seen such utter havoc as this single bird of war was wreaking upon the Egyptian Air Force.

"Migs behind you, Moshi!" a voice from a Super Mirage

crackled. But the F-4 had, through the American pilot's oneness with the PND, programmed the maneuvers necessary to position itself behind the Migs, even before the Mirage pilot recognized the danger.

The Phantom's two J79-GE-17 engines went into afterburner, rolling, then looping, following the pilot's thought process, which ran at many times normal speed. The Israeli pilot, unable to do anything other than ride out the maneuvers, anticipated at any moment the firing of 30-mm cannon, or the unleashing of any combination of devastating ordnance. Maybe one or more of the four AIM-7 Sparrow semi-active radar homing air-to-air missiles residing in semi-recessed slots in the fuselage belly... Or maybe one of four AIM-9 Sidewinder infra-red homing air-to-air missiles carried under the wings on the inboard pylons...

To Rashfer's astonishment, the Mig 21s began veering from each other. If it was a defensive move, it was unlike any he had ever seen. The Migs behaved erratically, as if pilotless. No shots had been fired, yet the Russian-made jets were now obviously out of control.

Rashfer could see into the cockpits of both planes. They were empty!

* * *

Chaos raged within the man-made cavern. Laura and Gessel Kirban watched in astonishment when the terrible, black human-forms suddenly left the bodies of the people wearing the PND helmets.

Unearthly shrieks split the air when the Dimensionals departed Lori's body, and those of the people sitting around the room. Excruciating pain raged within Laura's and the scientist's ears while they tried to make sense of the disturbances.

Dark beings evacuated the chamber, the creatures passing through the rounded walls, fleeing through the domed ceiling, through the marble-tiled floor. The huge room glowed red, the many points of light along the walls blinking, the unseen machinery driving the complex humming ever louder, until it seemed the cave-like room would explode from the unbearable noise level.

Laura fought to control her senses through the thumping, whining sound. She squinted through the increasing brightness to see her daughter upon the raised, chrome-like platform at the room's center.

Gessel Kirban held Laura's right arm, and led her toward Lori, who had knelt to one knee and was holding herself up by the fingertips of both hands.

"Oh, my baby!" Laura cried, holding her daughter, while Kirban gently rocked the helmet back and forth until it slipped from Lori's head.

"She will be fine, Mother," the scientist said, his Israeli accented words intending comfort for both mother and daughter.

He helped Laura take her daughter from the platform, then directed them toward the double doors 50 feet in the distance.

Kirban searched their surroundings while he held one of the girl's arms and they shuffled toward the doors. The dark beings attempted to again enter the room through solid walls, ceiling and floor. Each time a Dimensional stepped through the barriers, a brilliant explosion of electric-like static flashed and caused loud popping noises. The beings were opposed while they tried to reenter, as if a supernatural battle raged around the chamber's perimeter.

Smoke from electrical shortages saturated the air, filling their nostrils with the smell of ozone, and creating a Faustian surrealism while they moved closer to the doors. Kirban pushed the thumb latch on one of the gigantic steel doors and struggled to pull it open.

The darkened hallway ahead looked clear, and the scientist tried to hurry the women along. Lori's legs continued to suffer from the effects of the PND-induced trance, and the three of them moved more slowly from the chamber than Kirban wished.

Laura screamed, a huge, human-shaped shadow having

materialized in the hallway, blocking their way. The thing appeared to shrink in size, or dissipate, while they watched.

Where the black entity had appeared, there now stood a man… one of the scientists from the chamber. Gerhardt Frobe!

Frobe's eyes blazed fiery red, his face a gnarled portrait of contorted evil while he stood in the center of the hallway. Smoke escaped from his clothing, from his hair. His mouth spoke, but not with the familiar German accent. The words rumbled from somewhere deep within.

"You must not take our dearest girl from us," the deep voice taunted in a whine, sounding as if it emanated from an echo chamber. "There are big plans for her, big things, indeed!"

The voice was maniacal—the essence of virulent evil…

"He's got a gun!" Laura put herself between her daughter and the German scientist.

"He is indwelt…it will do no good to try to reason," Kirban said, he, too, stepping in front of the girl to protect her.

"What can we do?" Laura said pleadingly, seeing the German's blazing eyes, and hellishly twisted, grinning mouth.

"What is there…to do?" the voice said, followed by a cackling chuckle that thundered somewhere down deep within the scientist. "Just give her to me, and you can be on your way."

"She does not belong with you, whatever you are," the Israeli said. "We are taking her from this devilish place."

The German's face glowed with an amber cast. At the same time, the flesh around his eyes, the hollows of his cheeks, grew shadowy. Almost imperceptible wisps of smoke spiraled from various points along the clothing he wore.

The voice was again whiny, mocking.

"She, like the others, has precisely what we seek. So, you see, she very much belongs here, with us."

"What are you doing here? What kind of unspeakable things are you doing?" Laura's question blurted both with fear and rage, while she huddled with her daughter.

"We shall become one with mankind once again. We shall not

fail this time."

"And, what about this technology in which I was...deceived into believing was for military purposes? The precognition neuro-diviner...What is its true purpose in all of this?" the Israeli scientist asked.

"Ah...don't you love the name?" the thing snickered. "Human science loves such high-sounding phraseology, doesn't it? The precognition neuro-diviner..."

The beast within paused, as if it were reaching for the explanation that most pleased it.

"The PND does have military applications, does it not? You should know, Doctor—you helped develop it with unseen, unsuspected help from we ...Dimensionals, of course."

The vile creature within the German spewed a burst of laughter through the scientist's mouth.

"And the other technologies? The R A P T U R E device ... What is its true purpose?" Kirban asked.

"Enough! That is not to be spoken of!" the voice said with vehemence. "The world will know in time. They will know..." The thing emitted a fading, echoing laugh.

"Now, give me the young woman, if you do not mind."

"Never! You'll have to kill me!" Laura screamed in Frobe's face, starting to lurch toward the scientist. Kirban held out his arm to block her.

Laura's outburst brought thundering laughter from the beast within.

"That, my dear Mommy, can certainly be arranged."

Gerhardt Frobe leveled the pistol at Laura. "One more opportunity—that's all, Mom," the thing said, sounding vicious while its words seethed through the German's teeth. "Give her to me, or I shall off both you, and this Jew."

Frobe pointed the weapon at Laura and reached with his left hand to pull back the receiver, loading a round from the clip, into the chamber in preparation for firing. The German scientist's eyes suddenly bulged as if they would explode from their sockets. A hand reached to grasp the wrist of the hand with the pistol. Frobe fell forward, landing on his face. A gleaming piece of metal protruded from his back.

Laura's eyes widened, seeing their rescuer standing just behind where the German had stood a moment before.

"James," she said meekly, just before everything went black.

Chapter 15

Egyptian air space was secured in the first 30 seconds of the attack. It had been an all-out assault by all Israeli first-line aircraft against what amounted to the major part of Arab air power.

The Israeli forces had destroyed bases in the Sinai and Egyptian territory in a short, efficient, and decisive blow. Hundreds of Egyptian aircraft had been blown to pieces, including bombers, combat planes and helicopters. It had been done in less than 2 hours. The F-4E trailed the KC 135, the same plane Mark had ridden into Ben Gurion. The Phantom was force-fed jet fuel through the probe, to which was attached the long fuel line with its cone-shaped funnel.

With the bird's thirst sated, and the fuel line linkage detached, Rashfer set a course that would soon put them over Syrian air.

Word came that Jordanian and Iraqi, as well as Syrian, aircraft had attacked into Israel. The few Israeli fighters left behind to defend had routed the intruders. A number of Israeli fighter-bombers had then screamed to Jordanian airfields in Oman and Mafrak, and destroyed a major portion of Jordan's Air Force.

Now, several Mirages and the F-4E with the name "Moshi" painted on its nose would deliver knock-out blows to Israel's Syrian and Iraqi tormentors.

"What happened to those Mig pilots?"

The Israeli major's voice crackled with static into Mark Lansing's ears. With the PND turned off for the moment, Mark's concentration was still reeling. He felt as if his mind had been drained of its energy.

"What do you mean? Didn't we get them?" the American asked.

"The birds weren't touched. We fired nothing. But, I saw into the cockpits. The pilots were not there."

"Repeat, please," Mark said, trying to clear both his hearing and his thinking.

"They were not in the cockpits," Rashfer said, repeating each word slowly, and clearly.

"Not there?"

"That's a Roger, Captain. They were not there. The birds crashed on their own, with nothing I could see wrong with them, except they had no pilots."

"And, you say we fired nothing at them? Not the thirtys, not the Sidewinders?"

"As you see—the ordnance is still on board," Rashfer said.

"I don't know, Major, I honestly don't know."

Soon the F-4, accompanied by four Super-Mirage fighter-bombers, swept into Iraqi air territory. They were joined by other IF jets while they engaged and destroyed all opposition in the air, and leveled enemy bases.

Mark again wore the golden PND helmet, his brain at one with the technologies implanted within the bottom of the aircraft's fuselage. While the Mirages fired every weapon they carried, the Phantom did not.

David Rashfer, again sitting with nothing to do in the front seat, wondered with each dumbfounding downing of Mig 21s and Mig 17s by the Phantom, about a weapons system that could make aircraft go down without a shot being fired—could make pilots vanish into thin air...

They attacked airfields in Syria that included Damascus, Damir and Seikel. They decimated Iraq's H-3 airfield in the vicinity of the Jordanian border, eliminating, finally, all Arab opposition air power.

In less than an hour and a half, the mission was done. Even the normally serious-natured Israeli couldn't resist joining the fun.

He, along with the pilots flying the Mirages, performed victory roll after victory roll over Damascus.

* * *

Robert Cooper brooded in Gerhardt Frobe's office, his fears rising. There would be no place to run—not if they truly wanted to get at him.

He paced the room, his anxiety-riddled mind raging. The Dimensionals would not abide this breach of their stronghold. And, they knew his every thought, his every intention. He couldn't get away from them, even in his most private thoughts.

He wasn't at fault. He had no idea what went wrong.

Surely, they couldn't, wouldn't, blame him for…whatever had happened less than two hours earlier. He had no control over whatever had interfered with their activity within the chamber, where the precognition neuro-diviner and R A P T U R E technologies were being used to achieve their purposes—their goals.

Something had short-circuited the channeling efforts, something totally unanticipated. The incantations, the meditation, broken by a force. What force? Whatever it had been, it drove the Dimensionals from the chamber, from within his own mind and body.

But, they were only a dimension away—not extraterrestrial. They could, and would, simply step through the invisible fabric that separated time and space. They would have him by the throat any time they pleased.

Why hadn't they come for him? It would almost be better to confront them now than to stay immersed in fear of the encounter that might lie around the next dark corner. He had made his bargain, agreed to the terms. He was now acting director of Covert Operations for Defense. Soon he would be the fully sanctioned director.

He had not caused the breach. It was not his actions that had put the dark beings from that netherworld to flight, sent them scattering like a flight of blackbirds whose gathering had been suddenly disturbed by shotgun fire...

Cooper's eyes cut in surprise to the phone on Frobe's desk when the ringing shattered his near-panicked introspection.

"Yes?" he said, picking up the receiver.

"Secretary McNamara on the line, sir," the woman's voice said.

"Bob?"

"Yes, sir, Mr. Secretary. Bob Cooper here."

He heard the Secretary of Defense say something to someone in the room back in D.C., then turn again to addressing him.

"Bob. Have you heard the news from Israel?" McNamara said.

"No, sir. Not really. Not the particulars," Cooper said in a sheepish tone.

"Well, it's over. It was over in three hours."

"Oh? Does it look bad?" Cooper asked, dabbing his brow with a handkerchief.

"Bad?!" Robert McNamara said with a laugh. "No! The Arabs were completely routed. It was a resounding success! And it was largely due to you and your project."

"That's terrific, Mr. Secretary, really terrific. Glad to hear that."

"Listen, Bob," McNamara interrupted. "We want you back here tomorrow. I'm sending a plane for you tonight."

"Yes, sir. I will be ready."

"Congratulations, Bob. You are now officially director of Covert Operations for Defense. We want to brief you on your new duties as soon as possible."

"Yes, sir. Thank you. I will look forward to it."

Cooper hung up and grinned with smug self-satisfaction while he peered into the darkness. His government had officially promoted him. He was now more valuable to the Dimensionals than ever. He found strength, even a new force of purpose in the fact. Although the mission was a failure, Robert Cooper's personal fortunes continued to rise…

* * *

June 14, 1967

Israeli Prime Minister Levi Eshkol looked at the result of the war that had lasted only six days. The report was prepared for him in order to address the people of Israel and the world.

He poured over the statistics, a troubled look on his face, despite the staggering victory won against great odds. It ran through his mind how this victory, like the war for independence in 1948, and the battles since—like the attack by Nasser-led forces in 1956—was being proclaimed by religious Jews to be the direct intervention of God. He was not so sure that this was not the case.

Still, the cost was considerable. He let his eyes scan the statistics. In storming the Golan Heights, Israel suffered 115 dead. Altogether, Israel lost 777 dead and 2,586 wounded.

Despite the phenomenal—some claimed miraculous—victory in the brief air war, Israel lost 46 of its 200 aircraft. More than 20 pilots were killed, and a number were captured.

On the positive side, the Prime Minister's people who were supposed to know such things estimated that when the smoke of war finally cleared, Israel would have at least tripled its territorial size. This, of course, Eshkol calculated, meant that it "controlled," not "owned," the freshly won territory. The opinion of the world diplomatic community would be fierce in urging him to return the hard-won land. Already, four days earlier, they had forced a cease-fire.

Still, the added miles were significant—particularly as it concerned buffering for defensive purposes.

He ran his index finger down the page until he found the estimates. The territory had increased from 8,000 to 26,000 square miles. Israeli forces had captured the Sinai, Golan Heights, Gaza Strip, and Judaea and Samaria, which the non-Jewish world called the West Bank.

Levi Eshkol couldn't keep from smiling. The war had given Israel the city of Jerusalem…and the Temple Mount. Maybe not "given" it to Israel, but that great city was now again unified under Israel's control.

The smile was slight, and of brief duration, because Eshkol knew the Arab chieftains would never be content to accept their tremendous losses. There were bleak days ahead, to be sure.

"The call from Washington, Mr. Prime Minister," the woman said in Hebrew, after poking her head through the door opening.

He nodded to her, and picked up the phone, then pushed the button that was lit.

"Hello, Mr. Secretary," he said in accented English. "How are things there?" He listened intently for several minutes before he spoke.

"Thank you, Dean. The aircraft performed flawlessly, except for the shootdown. We just don't know what happened there…"

He listened to the U.S. Secretary of State talk again.

"We put your young Marine on the plane yesterday evening. It was to stop briefly in Paris. He should arrive Washington this afternoon."

He listened again to Dean Rusk before answering. "Yes. The technology performed, I would say, frighteningly well. In every case, the enemy fled as if they had seen a horde of demons."

* * *

It had been nearly impossible to call the States for the past 11 days. Finally, Randall Prouse heard the line ring. He hoped—prayed—that at last a connection could be made.

"Hello," the voice on the other end said, bringing a broad

smile to the archaeologist's face.

"Ruthie!"

"Randy? Are you okay?"

Ruth Prouse's question was blurted, while tears came to her eyes.

"Yes, sweetie...I'm just fine."

Christopher Banyon tried not to listen while he peered between the blinds, looking at the Jerusalem streets below the hotel window. He and Susie had discussed how hard it must be on their friend's wife, not being able to talk with him, except through the few telegrams the Prouses had exchanged over these past days.

Christopher smiled hearing the archaeologist mostly grunt and say "yes" while his wife spilled everything into her husband's ears. Finally, he spoke.

"When did he call?"

Prouse's question was asked with troubling inflection, and the minister looked to see the expression on his friend's face.

"He left his number, didn't he?" Prouse said.

He retrieved a ballpoint pen from the drawer on the nightstand beneath the telephone. "Go ahead. Give me the number."

He wrote on the notepad. "Ruthie, listen carefully. Try to call him back. I'm not sure I can get through. Have him try to get in touch with me, here, at the hotel."

Prouse gave his wife the number, even though he knew she already had it.

"Yes, Sweetie. Everything's going to be okay here. I'll be home next week, God willing."

When he finished talking with his wife, Prouse tore the page from the note pad, picked up the receiver again, and dialed the "0". He gave the operator the number and other required information. He looked briefly at Christopher, then again at the numbers before dialing the final digits.

"Gessel Kirban," he said quickly, then listened to the phone line electronic switches trying to make the connection.

He looked at Christopher again, and spoke while waiting. "He couldn't get me, so called home. I knew he would, eventually."

Prouse's eyes brightened.

"Gessel! Where are you?"

The men talked for the next ten minutes, Prouse doing most of the listening. When they finally hung up, the archaeologist whistled his incredulity.

"You won't believe it, Chris. Laura's husband, James, is alive. They had him in a top-secret area of the complex at Taos, New Mexico."

"Her husband? How? He was killed in the crash…"

"No he wasn't. He's with them now."

"With whom?"

"The three of them—Gessel, Laura, and the Morgans' daughter. Gessel said something else. He said that the Marine pilot's father was in the complex. According to Morgan, he was used, like himself, in channeling thoughts through that weird technology they've been working with."

"Mark Lansing's father?" Christopher said, stunned.

"Yeah. Clark Lansing. That's the name. They wanted to take him, too, but had to leave the complex because a scientist was killed, according to Gessel. James Morgan stabbed him, because the guy was going to shoot Laura, Gessel, and the girl."

What did it mean? The man had disappeared, had been missing since 1947. Had vanished without a trace near the place of the Roswell UFO crash incident.

The thoughts caromed within the minister's mind, interrupted by Prouse's words.

"This is really strange, Chris. Gessel told me some things about the dark human-like things you've been talking about, that you say Morgan and that kid, Lansing, have been seeing in their nightmares, or whatever. He told me the things were everywhere in that laboratory, or whatever it is, the secret technology chamber where they've been doing experiments. He said the experiments have something major to do with why he and Laura called us, asking us to go to Olivet to pray. He said it all involves the Israeli victory against all those Arab forces."

Prouse's expression changed to a frown of puzzlement.

"Gessel said they've got to get out of New Mexico, got to find a place to investigate the technologies he's been working with, but has found out he really knows next to nothing about—says he wants us to work with him on learning the truth about what's really going on with these creatures. These Dimensionals, as he calls them."

"Where can we reach them?" Christopher asked.

"He's looking for somewhere to move his lab equipment. He's set up a laboratory that those at the Taos complex apparently know nothing about. But, he's afraid they're about to catch on to what he's doing. He wants to find another place right away."

Christopher's face brightened. "I know a perfect place, if he doesn't mind cold weather."

* * *

Mark stepped off the bottom rung of the boarding ramp that led upward to the hatch of the Israeli jet that had brought several diplomats, and him, from Paris to Andrews Air Force Base. He had spent five days being debriefed by the Israeli military, and another two days answering questions for Israeli government officials.

He had explained that he remembered nothing of shooting down the Mirage with 30 mm cannon fire that morning of June 5. While he wore the PND, he did only what it programmed him to do. He remembered none of it.

They scolded him, and in the next breath praised him, leaving him as confused as he had been when his co-flyer, Maj. David Rashfer, had first asked why he had shot down the Israeli fighter.

The Mirage pilot was never found. They had made scores of helicopter searches, but to no avail. The jet was found, in a widely scattered pattern on the barren desert floor. There was no sign of the captain who had flown the fighter. It was as if he had vanished, the investigators had said.

He was home now, and that was all that mattered. Home was where Lori was, and that was where he wanted to be more than anything.

"Captain."

Two young men in dark suits approached. Mark put the heavy duffel bag he had carried from the plane on the hot concrete of the parking ramp, and said beneath his breath, "Here we go again."

Both had their IDs in hand and flashed them for him to see by the time they stopped a few feet in front of where he stood.

"We're from Defense," one of them said.

"We've been sent to accompany you from Andrews, Captain," the other man said.

"Why the escort?" he asked, a touch of irritation in his tone.

"We just follow orders, Captain. Will you please come with us?"

* * *

Less than an hour later Mark sat in a small waiting room somewhere in the Pentagon. He thought how easily he had gotten through security at every checkpoint that was designed to prevent intruders from reaching the area where he now sat.

This was not unlike a doctor's waiting room, he thought. The industrial-grade furniture, the indoor/outdoor carpet, the magazines on the small table to his right. He picked up and thumbed through several. *Time*, with Gamul Abdul Nasser's photograph on its cover, The *U.S. News & World Report*, *The New Yorker*...

He glanced at the clock on the wall across from where he sat. 3:15.

"The director will see you now."

A young woman wearing a sharply tailored, though colorful suit, made the announcement with a smile, while holding the door open.

"May I leave my bag here?" Mark said, gesturing toward his Marine Corps-issue duffel bag.

"It will be okay there," she said. "But, if you're concerned, you can bring it here, and I'll keep an eye on it."

He took her up on the offer, lugging it through the doorway and setting it where she directed.

"This way, Captain," she said, leading the way through a series of short corridors. "Right through here," she said, holding the door for him, and standing aside for him to pass into the large conference room.

The room was much different than the areas just outside. The walls were heavily paneled in rich, dark wood, highly polished—as was the huge, coffin-shaped conference table's top.

"Director Cooper will be with you in a moment," she said, looking upward at the Marine's handsome face. "Please, have a seat."

"Capt. Lansing! Mark," Robert Cooper said, bursting through the doorway, his right hand extended.

"Sir," Mark took the offered hand.

"And the flight? Was it smooth today?" Cooper asked, lightly.

"A little rough over the Atlantic in a few places."

"Well, I'm sure you've experienced much rougher, right?" Cooper said, slapping the pilot on his shoulder.

"Yes, sir."

"Like the mission you just completed. I'll bet there were rough moments," Cooper said, in his best ice-breaking tone.

"I was so busy, I didn't notice."

"Right, right! All business when on a mission. And, you took care of business, too, according to every report I've seen. Congratulations, on a terrific job!"

"Thanks, sir."

Cooper's expression became more serious. "Have a seat, Mark."

Cooper pulled the big, high-back chair from the head of the conference table, and was seated. Mark took one of the burgundy leather conference table chairs near where the director sat.

"Guess you're anxious to get back to Miss Morgan?"

Cooper's voice continued to have a friendly tone.

"Yes, sir. I'll be glad to see her, and Mom."

Both men were quiet for several seconds. Cooper's intense, blue-gray eyes narrowed while he looked directly into Mark's eyes.

"You know, Mark, the things you accomplished over there must never go beyond a rather tightly defined circle. They are highly sensitive matters, for a number of reasons. World war or peace might be—" he searched for the word, "—influenced for the worse, should the technology be known by foreign interests. You do understand that, don't you?"

How could he not understand it? He had undergone everything just short of brainwashing to be made to understand the point. He wanted to blurt the thought, but said, "Yes, sir."

"You did everything asked of you. And, I've been authorized by Sec. McNamara, himself, to give you this."

Cooper stood and walked to where Mark sat. The younger man instinctively stood.

"You've earned it, Captain. And, now I must say... Major!"

Cooper reached up to the taller man's neck. He removed the captain bars from Mark's collar, then reached into his suit coat pocket and retrieved a gold-colored oak leaf insignia.

He pinned it where the captain's insignia had been.

"Congratulations, Major Lansing," the director said, taking Mark's hand and pumping it with vigor.

"Thank you, sir," the newly made major said, surprised, despite his accomplishments in the Middle East, to have made the rank so quickly.

"Tell Sec. McNamara, and whoever else is responsible, that I thank them," Mark said.

"I will, I will. But, you are the one who's responsible, young man," Cooper said, returning to the chair at the head of the table.

"Now, Mark, I've got to tell you something, something that I'm afraid will be—that will be a shock."

The Director paused to study the younger man's face. There was no change of expression, although Mark's heart jumped to a faster beat. Was it Lori? Had something happened to Lori?

"You mentioned your mother a moment ago. You said you would be glad to see her again," Cooper again paused, obviously, this time, searching for words.

His mother! Something was wrong. Something had happened to his mother!

"She is remarried, isn't she?" Cooper asked.

He said "is." At least she's alive. The thoughts stumbled through Mark's travel-fatigued mind.

"Yes, sir. She remarried quite some time ago."

"Here's the thing I've got to tell you, son. It's about your father. He's alive."

* * *

Jerusalem, June 16, 1967

Randall Prouse was jubilant. He talked while he and Yadin stood looking at the Temple Mount from across 30 yards of open spaces and badly deteriorated streets.

"This means they should open the digs beneath Moriah, again," he said, while they watched Israeli soldiers and military vehicles move along the streets, and near the Mount.

"I think it wise to withhold too much optimism, Randy," Prouse's Arab-Christian friend said. "The opposition is terrible in its vengeance. There must be some compromise about the holy mountain, or I am afraid the killing will be unlike any we have seen."

"Compromise?" the archaeologist said, his enthusiasm now a bit dampened. Yadin had his finger on the pulse of this city, of the Israeli-Palestinian problems, as few others. Certainly better than many of the diplomats who flew in and out of the region in their futile efforts at peace making.

"If there is not compromise, jihad will almost certainly result," Yadin said, watching a truckload of Israeli troops jump from the back of a big truck and take positions near the Wailing Wall.

"You think Israel will give the Temple Mount back, now that they've won it in war?" Prouse asked, surprise in his voice.

"Maybe not give it back, but at the very least, share its administration with Islam."

"The Islamics aren't interested in sharing," Prouse said.

"Yes, but we live in a strange world, Randy. Pressures on the Jew are never ending—our Bible tells us so," Yadin said, before turning to walk back into the small Arab shop, the place where they had both agreed to meet that morning.

"The soldiers are there today, to assure that the Jews are not hindered from worship at the wall, are they not? All should be worshiping on top of Moriah, but, even with Israel now fully in control of East Jerusalem—of the Mount, the Jews must be protected while they worship at the foot of the mountain."

The Arab examined merchandise while he talked, picking one thing up to look at closely, then another.

"If my Arab brothers heard this from my lips I would be instantly dispatched from this earth," he said seriously, but without fear in his voice. "Nonetheless, what I say is true. The Jews have for too long refused to hearken to Jehovah."

The American archaeologist, always an admirer of this man's courage, never ceased to be amazed by his ability to discern truth. Yadin, a Bethlehem-born Arab, was like the great Jewish king, David—a man after God's own heart.

"I am reminded of the many times the Jewish leaders the Jewish people have refused to listen. I am afraid they will refuse to listen yet again to what God has said, through giving them this great victory," Yadin said.

"Their own prophet Isaiah said, 'But ye are they that forsake the LORD, that forget my holy mountain, that prepare a table for that troop, and that furnish the drink offering unto that number. Therefore will I number you to the sword, and ye shall all bow down to the slaughter: because when I called, ye did not answer; when I spake, ye did not hear; but did evil before mine eyes, and did choose that wherein I delighted not.'"

Prouse was silent, thinking about how easily, how perfectly this son of Ishmael used Scripture that God gave through the Jewish race.

"Friend, Randy," Yadin said softly, looking upward into the much bigger man's eyes. "Until the Jews, all who will believe, recognize their Messiah, and until that king sits on that mountain, in control of everything, there shall be no peace for Jerusalem... for Israel, for my people."

* * *

She had never felt so cold. Laura stood in the night air, listening to the connections being made to Israel. Although mid-June, the high desert nights chilled the bones, the cold made worse by the drastic change from daytime temperatures. Only a few hours earlier, temperatures of more than 100 degrees had baked this desolate place. Now the thermometer struggled to stay in the thirties. A wind, uninhibited by anything but distant, monolithic buttes and expansive plateaus stung the skin without let-up.

Gessel Kirban sat in the Jeep station wagon, behind the steering wheel, watching Laura make the call. He had driven her to the remote gas station to avoid the danger of his own phone line perhaps being tapped. The probability was unlikely, he thought. No one, except certain people within the Israeli government, knew about the private laboratory, which they had funded. It sat beneath a plateau 30 miles from Taos and Santa Fe. It had been well camouflaged by desert experts. Still, the security forces—and who knew who else—would be after him, after the four of them.

Lori had stayed behind with her father, who was far from full recovery. James Morgan did little more than sit, staring into nothingness. His malady was much like that suffered by an aphasic stroke victim. The Israeli scientist let the analogy move through his thoughts, while he saw Laura clench her arms tightly and shuffle her feet, trying to generate warmth while she listened for the overseas connection.

Morgan seemed to respond most to conversation that included Clark Lansing's name. That, and Laura's addressing him as "Smiling Jack."

Kirban wondered if the PND helmet had done cellular damage to Morgan's brain. The low frequency electronic hum the device produced—could it destroy cognitive functioning over time? What other things might they have done to their victims, the ones used to channel whatever they were channeling through the human brains they held captive within the precognition neuro-diviners?

What of the dark beings—how might they affect the brain? What damage, through cellular rearrangements, might they do to the victims?

Kirban saw Laura's mouth moving. She had made the connection, at last.

"Yes. This is Christopher Banyon," Laura heard the minister answer.

"Pastor! Pastor Banyon, is that you?" Laura said, barely able to hear the voice.

"Yes…Laura? It is me, Chris Banyon."

The voice was louder, clearer.

"I've been advised not to talk but a moment, Pastor…Chris," Laura said. "We can't take chances on who might be listening."

"I understand, Laura."

"Do you have the instructions for us?"

"Yes," Christopher said. "Have a pen and paper?"

"Yes," Laura said, pinning the receiver between her cheek and the wool material covering her right shoulder.

"Go to Boothbay," the minister said. "Ask someone to point you to Rutledge Cove Road. There's only two houses there. My mother's home is the saltbox house on the left, the second house. It is painted yellow, with white trim, and a gray roof. You get all that?"

"Yes. Yellow, white trim, gray roof—Rutledge Cove Road," Laura repeated.

"Mother's name is Grace Banyon. She'll be expecting you."

Within ten minutes of ending the phone call with Laura Morgan, Christopher Banyon answered a knock at the hotel room door.

"Yes? Who is it?" he called through the closed door.

"It is I, Ackmid," the Arab said, his familiar high-pitched voice a welcomed signal that his and Susie's ride to the Temple Mount had arrived.

They were halted several times on their way to meet Randall Prouse, like before when they had gone to pray at Mount Olivet. This time, however, the tension was not there. Their road guards were the Israeli military. Rather than feeling danger, they felt relieved that they had armed protectors all the way from the hotel to the small shop, in front of which Ackmid stopped the old Jeep.

Randall joined them, taking the seat beside Ackmid, who drove the Jeep as fast as it would move, his passengers hanging on to whatever they could find. They stopped 50 feet from the Wailing Wall, and Prouse, Christopher and Susie, glad to do so, stepped from the old vehicle onto the broken concrete that separated them from the often-visited shrine of worship.

"Ilusia said he would meet us here," the archaeologist fumed 15 minutes later, while they sat again in the Jeep.

His colleague was notorious for being tardy, and Prouse was more irritated than concerned. Still, there was worry in the back of his mind. Ilusia Karpin had to travel from areas that were reportedly still full of fighting.

Pockets of resistance dotted the Judean hills, and his friend had been wounded twice before by the Palestinian radical thugs, while moving about from dig to dig.

Christopher and Susie watched the black-hatted worshipers at the wall, bowing and chanting while holding the Torah in front of their faces with both hands. Some placed written prayers in cracks along the wall.

"Can we go closer?" Susie asked.

"Not much closer. Not without a hat and shawl," Prouse said. "The Orthodox clergy frown on men approaching the wall without wearing the right get-up."

"What about women?" Susie asked. "Do they have to wear... get-ups?"

"Women always have their heads covered, but it's the men who have to wear the hats and prayer shawls. The reading of the Torah is forbidden, unless one has the hat and shawl," Prouse answered, while again checking his wristwatch.

Several blackhats, deeply in meditation, walked past the Jeep without acknowledging the vehicle's passengers.

Christopher watched the three Orthodox Jews continue toward the wall of prayer, their heads slightly bowed in meditation.

Randall saw it coming. A pick-up truck, its bed covered by a high canvas top, rolled to a quick stop just behind the Jews. Several men, dressed in khaki uniforms, their faces covered by cloth masks, leaped from the truck, brandishing automatic rifles.

The men in the black hats and robes saw them, but it was too late to take cover.

"No! No!" Prouse shouted, but to no avail.

The attackers sprayed the three men with several bursts of automatic fire and jumped into the pick-up, which sped away. Israeli military vehicles immediately took up pursuit, and the staccato firing could be heard while all three vehicles disappeared around a corner in the distance.

Prouse already knelt at the sides of the fallen men. He rushed from victim to victim to determine who should be helped first.

"This one's alive!" he yelled. "Get some medical help over here!"

Susie knelt on both knees beside another man. Christopher sent Ackmid to find a military medic, whom he prayed was somewhere near the contingent of troops assigned to prevent just such an atrocity.

Prouse had torn open the black robe and undergarment, then

placed his handkerchief over the sucking wound in the man's right chest area. The victim's eyes were open wide, and he mouthed words the archaeologist couldn't hear.

"It's okay," he said to the dying man. Then, realizing the wounded man might not speak English, he tried to reassure him in Hebrew.

"I've sent Ackmid. I saw a vehicle with a red cross on it. I hope that's a medic vehicle," Christopher Banyon said, looking into the face of the dying blackhat.

The victim's eyes widened even more when he saw Christopher's face. The man suddenly was possessed of strength, and of full voice. He grabbed the minister with both hands, clutching Christopher's khaki shirt just above both breast pockets. The wounded man pulled Christopher toward him, and spoke in gasps, his dying eyes penetrating, his words spoken with desperation. He blurted in English, "Take the fragment, the piece not of the holy scroll—take it into the cave of first discovery at Qumran…Do not fail!"

He seemed to pause to gain strength, then said, "Old men shall dream dreams…Young men shall see visions."

The man's eyes bulged in his death throes, and he collapsed in Prouse's arms.

* * *

"I'm sorry I had to tell you these things in such an abrupt manner, Mark, but you had to be told. We need your help. Time is critical."

Robert Cooper had told him the day before, but, despite the fact it worried him to the point it kept him awake all night, it hadn't fully sunk into his tired mind. It was all too fast, too much to digest.

His dad, *alive*! Could it be? His father alive. Not a dark, boiling monster, but truly alive?

Lori's mother, out of her coma, for some reason Cooper

couldn't explain. Kirban, too, out of his comatose condition. And, now, for some reason, a fugitive... the new director of Covert Operations for the Department of Defense repeated the events that had taken place at the Taos complex while Mark was fighting with the Israeli Air Force.

"As I told you yesterday, Laura Morgan and Lori were both taken by Gessel Kirban. He's an enemy agent—we don't know who he's working for—but, he must be stopped at any cost."

"But, what does he need with Lori and her mother?" Mark said, pacing to work off anxiety-driven energy.

"Just as hostages, we think," Cooper said, watching Mark walk back and forth on the conference room carpet.

"You say he's an agent. What has he stolen, or whatever you're worried about?"

"He has intimate knowledge of the PND. Like I told you, that technology must, under no circumstances, be discussed, much less displayed outside of security clearance parameters."

"And my dad? If he's really still alive, what does he have to do with the project?" Mark stopped his pacing to put the question.

"Mark, like you were told yesterday, there are things... profound things...that we simply cannot divulge. Suffice it to say that your father was working on some top-secret things in 1947. Things in which people like Einstein, Oppenheimer, and Teller were involved. Things at Alamogordo, White Sands. The bomb projects, other technologies..."

Cooper swiveled in the chair to face Mark, who took a seat to the director's right along the big conference table. "Your father was a top-of-the-line physicist. He was caught up in what the geniuses of such things call a transmolecular accident."

"What does that mean?" Mark asked, his mind running in a thousand directions.

"Again, all I can say is that it has to do with the disassembly and reassembly of the molecular structure of matter," Cooper said.

"It was an accident?" Mark's question was put in a more demanding-to-know tone.

"Yes. Something to do with his genetic profile. And, being in the wrong place at the wrong time. I'm not one of them, the geniuses who study such things—I, therefore, can't explain it."

"When can I see him?"

Cooper said nothing for a few seconds, then spoke in a formal tone, as if, Mark thought, he had been programmed to speak the words.

"You will be reunited with your father in due course. But, first, we have something that must be done for the sake of the security of the nation."

Mark watched the stocky man as he stood from the swivel chair at the head of the conference table, seeing the man's cold, calculating side emerge.

"Our priority for now must be to find them, to bring them in so the things they know can't fall into dangerous hands."

Cooper stood with his right hand resting atop the high back chair. "I'm depending on you to find them, and to bring them to me…to the complex. For their own good, as well as for national security," the director said, looking down at Mark. "Once that's done, we can reunite you with your father."

"How can I find them?" Mark said, anger rising in his thoughts, if not his voice. He felt the pressure of Cooper's words. Extortion. There was no other word for it.

"You know their ways, what their habits are," the director said after sitting again, and leaning back in the chair. He tried to sound consoling.

"Lori…she will move heaven and hell to find you. You're the one thing that's important to her, other than her father and mother."

"I thought they were taken from the complex…forcefully taken by Dr. Kirban. Now you sound as if they're doing all they can to avoid your finding them."

Cooper leaned forward on his elbows again, his eyes narrowing beneath the thick, dark brows in an expression that said he was becoming agitated.

"Whether it is their choice, or whether they've been taken by force, I don't have time to play hide and seek with anyone. The nation's security must take top priority."

He pushed back from the table and stood.

"And, I assure you, it will take precedence. I really hope you will help resolve the matter as quickly, and as incident-free as possible."

Robert Cooper walked to the door leading from the conference room to his office complex. He turned at the last second to glare at Mark, who stood from the chair.

"Let me be perfectly clear. There are others, Major, that, if I have to turn them loose, will make it impossible to guarantee the safety of your friends," he said, then turned and left the room.

* * *

Several helicopters swept above the mesa, guarding all roads leading from the scattered community that lay west of Santa Fe. A military troop transport vehicle raced toward the earth-colored building that hid just below the promontory against which it nestled.

Robert Cooper had hedged his bets. He enlisted the help—extortion though it was—of Mark Lansing, in pursuing the four who represented a threat to the secrets he harbored. But, at the same time, he ordered an all-out assault on the desert community, where, his sources had informed, Gessel Kirban had been secretly conducting experiments independently. Or, more likely, on behalf of some Israeli clandestine service.

A dozen soldiers wearing desert camouflage jumped from the back of the transport, rifles at the ready. Two kicked down the front door of the small, flat-roofed building, while other soldiers crashed through side and rear doors. Still others bashed in the building's several windows with rifle butts.

Five minutes later, the first lieutenant approached the major in charge.

"Sir, the building is empty. The targets aren't there."

The major then spoke into the field phone he held. "Sir. We have landed, and the desert rats have deserted."

The Director of Covert Operations slammed the receiver, a profanity hissing from between his clenched teeth. He studied the dilemma for several seconds, then pushed the intercom button on the desk phone.

"Miss Catlitt, call Andrews, and have them get a plane ready. Tell them to file a flight plan for New Mexico...Santa Fe."

Several miles away, Mark Lansing brooded while he dialed the pay phone in the lobby of Andrews Air Force Base Bachelor Officers' Quarters. He wanted to take no chances that the small suite Cooper had secured for him had been bugged, or the phone had been tapped. Lori had been right about the man. She had not trusted him from the start.

Lori... she was his life, his future. Without her, nothing else would matter. And, she was missing. He had to find her. Not for Robert Cooper, and whatever phony cause he claimed to want to protect. He had to find Lori because he loved her more than his own life.

"St. Paul Presbyterian Church," the woman's voice answered in a Texas accent.

"Ma'am, my name is Mark Lansing. I'm a captain, I mean, a major, in the Marine Corps. I just returned from overseas, and I'm looking for some people it's vital I reach. They've moved, and I'm looking for a mutual acquaintance, hoping he has had contact with them."

"Yes? How may I help you?"

"Rev. Christopher Banyon is the mutual friend. I know he's no longer the pastor there, but I was hoping you might tell me how to get in contact with him."

"All I know is that he's in Israel, Major," The woman said. "I have no idea where he can be reached, but if you like, I'll be sure to get in touch with you if and when I find out anything more."

"Yes. That will be great. Please do. I'll give you a couple of numbers," Mark said, probing his pockets for the slip of paper with the phone numbers.

"Wait!" the church secretary interrupted. "Pastor Banyon has a good friend in San Marcos. His name is Randall Prouse; he's a professor at the college there."

Mark heard the woman rummaging through her files.

"Yes! Here's the number," she said. "Now, I know that Pastor Banyon and his wife, Susie, went to Israel with Dr. Prouse on an archaeological thing of some sort. But, I'll bet Dr. Prouse's wife didn't go. They have a whole passel of teen-age and college-age children, so she stays home to deal with them. Her name's Ruth. Yes, Ruth Prouse. Would you like her number? I'll bet she could find where they're staying."

Mark stood 15 minutes later, trying to find the key to the suite. He thought through the rest of his schedule for the day. Somewhere, he had to find time to call Ruth Prouse again. Her teen-age son hadn't been any help when he called after hanging up from his conversation with the church secretary. About all he got were grunts, and "yes," "no," and "I don't know." The kid mumbled that he guessed his mother would be back about 5 p.m. That would be Central Time, Mark considered. He would try again.

Meanwhile, he had a meeting scheduled with someone in the Undersecretary of Defense's office, a debriefing of his time fighting with the Israeli Air force. About the technology, what it accomplished, from his viewpoint. At least, that's what the meeting would be about, a colonel at the Pentagon had told him that morning.

He just wanted to leave, to pull up stakes. Get his stuff and go somewhere they couldn't find him. He wanted more than anything to find Lori.

"Major."

Mark knew, in his gut, who they were before he turned to see the men approaching from down the hallway. The same two that had picked him up when he got off the plane from Paris.

"We'll need you to get your things and come with us, Maj.

Lansing," the taller man said.

"Where this time?" Mark asked, standing in the doorway, having just managed to get the door unlocked.

"Director Cooper wants you on the ramp. He's got orders for you to accompany him to New Mexico," the shorter, older agent said.

* * *

Early morning, Qumran— June 18, 1967

"The man was dying, Chris, but he knew what he was saying," Randall Prouse said, scanning the barren hills so familiar to him.

He sat behind the driver of the 1950 Ford sedan. Christopher Banyon rode on the right side of the back seat, with Susie in the middle.

"It was so strange, Randy," Christopher said. "He knew, in that time of his dying, that all these weird things have been happening to us. It was as if the Lord was talking to me through that poor man's last breath."

The experience had shaken the minister, and he had hurried to read the Scriptures when they left the death scene near the western wall. He felt now, while the old Ford rattled down the rutted road near the Dead Sea, that the weight of history itself was strapped to his back.

"If so, it's an honor…Right? Don't sweat it. The Lord, who has started a good work in you, will finish it. That's what the Word says, my friend."

The minister smiled inwardly at his archaeologist friend's philosophical-theologizing. This part of the world turned Randall Prouse on, held no fears over his head. The man was more at home here, than at San Marcos, Texas.

For Christopher Banyon, the rugged life of adventure in a land as foreboding as it had been two millennia earlier—with a young wife, who trusted him completely for her safety—the journey to the caves of Qumran was a bit more intimidating.

"Yes," Christopher said. "That's what the Word says."

Randall Prouse's mind was on his Russian-born archaeologist friend who hadn't made it to their Wailing Wall meeting. "We'll be okay, but, I wish Ilusia Karpin could've made it. Hope and pray he's not been ambushed. We'll be fine, though. I know this territory about as well as he does," he said as he looked to the driver.

"I take you to this point," the Arab driver said, after stopping the car. "They allow no farther with vehicle."

"Thanks, Kahleed, "Randall Prouse said, handing the man who operated his own one-car taxi service the equivalent of $20. "You meet us back here at 6 this evening. There'll be that much for you, again, okay?"

The Arab driver bowed and grinned happily. "Yes, yes, Dr. Randall. I shall be here promptly at 6 p.m."

"The cave where the Bedouin boy found the first scrolls is about a two mile hike," Prouse said, jumping the heavy canvas backpack onto his shoulders, after plunging his arms through its straps. "You should be well enough acclimated by now to make that distance without too much trouble," he said, a bit of humor in his voice.

"Susie will be okay. She walks three miles a day when she's back home. But, I don't know about yours truly," Christopher said, securing his own backpack in place.

"Yeah, well, we'll find out about your conditioning," the archaeologist said, striding in the direction of the cave, famous for one of the greatest finds of history. They hiked at a quick pace.

The uneven terrain, dotted with salt-based boulders that jutted from the ground, made a smooth stride impossible, and the quickly rising temperature slowed them more, the farther they walked along the southwest edge of the Dead Sea.

The archaeologist talked while they moved over the hard, salt-compacted ground. "The people who lived in the area, about 130 B.C to about 70 A.D. or so, were the people we've given the name, the Dead Sea Sect, for obvious reasons. They lived in caves, tents, and even some crudely constructed stone buildings along these hills and ridges." Prouse swept his hand in the air, indicating the area where archaeologists had, through the ages, found key evidence of the sect.

"Manuscripts in Hebrew and Aramaic have been found, that describe the life of Qumran community in those days. They are known as the Manual of Discipline, the Damascus Document, the Thanksgiving Psalms, and the War scroll."

Christopher, helping his wife step over the weather-rutted areas and large rocks, smiled to himself while they trailed their big friend. Randall Prouse no doubt missed being behind his lectern before his classes at San Marcos College. He lectured as if tutoring a freshman class on a field trip.

"The documents tell about the society's origin and history. They lay out the community's rules of life. They expound on the sect's expectations for the dawn of a new age. They are prophetic in flavor. I've seen 'em. Exciting stuff!" Prouse stopped, turning to let the students of his impromptu lecture catch up.

"The sect was an extremist spin-off of the Jewish apocalyptic movement. That group's basic doctrine was that the end of time would come soon."

Seeing his fellow hikers were again on his pace, he began walking while continuing the lesson.

"They believed, apparently, that when the end would come, Israel would be freed from its oppressors. The wicked would be destroyed, and God would raise for himself a community of elect who would escape divine judgment. They believed they would be the nucleus of God's future people."

The archaeologist again stopped, and turned to Christopher and Susie.

"You want to rest?"

Both, though breathing heavily, shook their heads, "No."

He resumed walking and talking. "The sect believed that God had decreed the division of mankind into two antagonistic camps. One, He called the sons of light. The other, He called sons of darkness. The one would be led by a superhuman prince of light. The bad guys would be led by an angel of darkness. The Dead Sea sect believed one people would reap divine bliss, the other divine damnation. They determined to shape their community in a way that would assure they achieved the former, rather than the latter. They would be princes and leaders under God's future economy of things."

"Sounds familiar," Christopher said, breathing hard, wondering how the heavier, older man could walk and talk without losing his breath.

"It does, doesn't it? You would think they had divine revelation, or something," Prouse joked.

"That part about the angel, and sons of darkness is interesting, for sure," Christopher said.

"The Romans finally dealt with the group, some time after the 70 A.D. destruction of the Temple, and Jerusalem."

Christopher blocked the rest of his friend's lecture from his mind while he stumbled forward, helping his wife negotiate the terrible terrain. His mind focused, instead, on what lay behind, and, what lay ahead.

His life was marked early on to do something beyond merely preaching the Gospel. Of that he had been certain. The night as a youngster splitting wood for the fireplace of his boyhood home, the voice that was like wind had called to him.

"*Feed my sheep*," he had heard that frigid February night, while the big snowflakes began falling.

It was the message heard by Christ's disciple, Peter. It was an audible voice, and he heard it plainly, though cerebrally, now. "*Feed my sheep.*"

But the voice the night of the storm, of the dark, electrically charged creature that was intercepted by a supernaturally empowered something or the other, the voice coming over the dead phone line that night, it had commanded him to "*Watch for the bene elohim.*" The *bene elohim* was, they were, fallen angels. Thrown out of heaven in the satanic rebellion.

The strange impressions when he had studied and prayed while pastor of the St. Paul Presbyterian Church. He was to feed Christ's sheep. He was plainly impressed, though not told audibly, to feed Christ's sheep the prophetic Word of God. The weird nightmares experienced by Mark Lansing and James Morgan—men who were not of the flock, who weren't believers in the message that Jesus Christ died for the sins of mankind. Their encounters with creatures like the one who was intercepted that stormy night in his own night-vision.

Laura Morgan's coma and miraculous recovery. The desperate calls from Taos. The strange storm on Mount Olivet. The answer, almost immediately, when Israel overwhelmed Arab forces that outnumbered them by millions.

The scroll fragment, bearing a message about the *bene elohim*. The words of the orthodox blackhat before his trip into eternity, telling him to come to this God-forsaken place, to go to the cave and take with him the scroll fragments.

The final words, *"Old men shall dream dreams, young men shall see visions."*

Randall dropped the heavy backpack to the ground. He looked around the region, seeing no competition for exploration of the caves. He had figured correctly. June near the Dead Sea was not prime time for archaeological ventures.

"Sit on my backpack," he said, leading Susie by the hand and elbow, and seating her on the bulky package of canvas.

"There's the cave," he said, pointing at a dark shadow near the top of a slanted mound of earth. The cavern resided within a cliff-like promontory of orange-red hue.

"We've got it all to ourselves today," the archaeologist said.

"I wonder why?" Christopher asked, wiping the heavy beads of sweat from his forehead and face with a hotel hand towel from his backpack.

He poured water from the canteen he took from around his shoulder, into a cup. He handed the cup to Susie, who looked around the area while she drank the water.

"This is a strangely beautiful place," she said quietly, between sips.

"A girl after my own heart," Prouse said with a smile. "Not many people appreciate this terrain."

"Like west Texas, only worse," Christopher said before taking a drink from the canteen's opening.

"Like west Texas, only better!" Prouse corrected, drinking from his own canteen.

The minister looked at the barren landscape, and vocalized his thought. "What in the world are we doing here? Can there be anything to the old man's words?"

"Come on, Chris! Where's your spirit of adventure?!"

"It's melted away, I think," he retorted.

"God has us here for a reason, Chris. You know that. It's a wonderful place," she said, looking at the distant desert-like landscape, broken by jagged cliffs made of earth, rock and salt.

"Only you could see good in such a place," her husband said with a smile, taking the cup from her and refilling it with water.

"I'm with her. It's a great place," Prouse said, screwing the cap onto his own canteen, then putting his binoculars to his eyes to get a better look at the cave's opening 300 yards in the distance.

"The Bedouins found the cave in February of '47. The region has been a veritable feast ever since."

Prouse was again in lecture mode, while he and Christopher dropped their backpacks. They stood at the base of the earth mound that led upward to the cave high above.

"Anything live in there? Like animals, bats?" the minister asked, straining to look at the opening.

"Maybe a few insects," Prouse answered. "But, there's too many visitors to these caves for wild animals to take up residence. Besides, you won't find many mammals in these parts."

The seriousness of their reason for coming to this place pervaded the thoughts of the three, while they gazed upward.

The archaeologist carefully took the ancient fragment from its felt wrappings, and read the Hebrew words: "'*War in heavens and on earth shall begin the consummation when first scroll words shall be found.'"*

Prouse read the last of the words, after hesitating to grasp the significance of his first reading.

" *'Watch for the bene elohim...The bene elohim deludes when approaches the great taking away.'"*

All were silent for several seconds, deeply within their own thoughts. The men, in particular, had been over the writings a hundred times before. Finally, Susie spoke.

"The scrolls were found in 1947. The war for Israel's nationhood took place in 1948. Do you think that's the meaning?" she asked. "And the next fragment says to watch for the *bene elohim,* the sons of god, angels, fallen angels. It says they will appear in the time of 'the great taking away'."

"It says they will delude when the great taking away approaches," Randall Prouse said.

"As it was in the days of Noah," Christopher said beneath his breath.

"What?" Prouse said.

"Oh, I was just remembering. Remember? I told you about the strange impressions I've been getting for so long. To preach about the Scriptures in Luke 17:26 and 27. 'As it was in the days of Noah, so shall it be in the days of the coming of the Son of man.'"

"Yeah, I remember you telling me," Prouse said. "The people of the Flood were definitely taken away," he concluded.

"Yes, but I believe, more to the point, that the people in the ark were taken away, out of danger, out of the destruction that was the result of God's judgment."

"The rapture?" Susie Banyon said. "Do you think this has something to do with prophecy about the rapture?"

The minister's eyes narrowed in concentration. "The taking away...like in Noah's day..."

"It fits," the archaeologist said. "These *bene elohim* –the sons of god, or fallen angels—will again assault the earth like in the days of Noah, before the Flood that took Noah and his seven family members safely away. God's wrath then fell, and destroyed the world in judgment."

"I must admit, I've never known much about the so-called rapture theory. We weren't taught that. We were told, as a matter of fact, that it was something cooked up by a teen-age girl in her dementia, later viewed as a vision and put forward by John Darby," the minister said, remembering his days at seminary.

"Then the Apostle Paul must've been demented, too," Prouse said. "He was the first to write about the rapture."

"What delusion?" Susie said. "What kind of delusion? And, what does it have to do with 'the great taking away'?"

"Delusion about the rapture?" Prouse said, as if to himself.

"Well, this is why we came. Let's see what's in that cave. My need to know has overcome my fright…I think."

With his not entirely self-convincing bravado, Christopher dropped his backpack to the ground, and said, "I guess it's up to me. The old gentleman in the black hat said nothing about others helping with this."

"Are you sure, Chris?" Prouse said. "I can stand just outside."

"No, I think I'd best do this the way it was told to me."

"It's okay," Susie said, looking into her husband's eyes, seeing not the courage he was trying to muster, but the Lord's servant she loved and admired.

He took the velvet-covered scroll fragments from Prouse.

"Better take this," Randall said, handing Christopher the flashlight he had just retrieved from the backpack.

The minister started to wedge the folded velvet cloth containing the scroll fragments between his pants at the belt buckle and his stomach, but thought better of it. It might damage the precious artifacts.

He unbuttoned the chamois-like khaki shirt, stuffed the cloth carefully within, then rebuttoned the garment.

He started up the steep bank toward the cave opening, using

his fingertips and toes of his boots to crawl upward. Forty feet later, he peered into the dark opening, then flipped the switch on the flashlight, and swept the interior with the bright beam.

He turned to look at his companions, who stood far below looking upward at him. He smiled a grim smile, gave a brief wave, and disappeared into the cave's black mouth.

* * *

Taos – 2 a.m.

Mark rode in the back of the government jet the entire trip from Andrews to the private strip near Taos. The compartment door had remained closed between where he sat, and the group of five officials, including Robert Cooper. No one had checked on him; it was if he was deliberately quarantined as punishment for some unspecified transgression.

The door opened only after the jet landed and had rolled to a stop in its parking spot.

The six men had stepped from the plane at 1:45 in the morning, and soon rode toward the underground complex. The men conversed between themselves, now, but said nothing to Mark, who thought of Cooper's words earlier.

"I'm depending on you to find them and bring them to me, to the complex. For their own good, as well as for national security. Once that's done, we can reunite you with your father."

The new Director of Covert Operations for the DOD had, in the same breath, sounded consoling and sinister. He offered hope mixed with threat.

Cooper's parting words, before leaving the conference room, played again in Mark's mind.

"There are others, Major, who, if I have to turn them loose, will make it impossible to guarantee the safety of your friends."

He stared out the window of the limousine, seeing in the early morning darkness the distant buttes, lit by the moon's eerie glow. He thought of his dad, and of Lori. What had happened that would make them run? Cooper had at first implied that Dr. Gessel Kirban had forced Lori and her mother and father to flee. Then, Cooper changed the story to indicate the four escapees must be brought in for unspecified national security reasons.

Mark hadn't had time to call, to ask Ruth Prouse where he might reach her husband and Christopher Banyon, so he could find out how to get in touch with Lori. The church secretary had said the minister and the archaeologist—along with Banyon's new wife—had gone to Israel on an archaeological quest of some sort. The secretary had said Prouse's wife would have stayed home to deal with their children's goings and comings. He would contact Ruth Prouse at first opportunity, Mark promised himself. Maybe she could put him in touch with the preacher, who would know about Lori's mother. Maybe they had been in contact; maybe she had given the preacher her phone number.

Thoughts of his father moved through his mind. His dad, the way he had been when Mark was 7 years old. He was a tall man, Mark remembered. But, maybe he just seemed tall because Mark had been only 7. His Dad was always preoccupied with one thing or another, he remembered. Probably with the physics of the government projects on which he worked.

But, his Dad always took time to help him build model planes, he remembered with an inward smile. His Dad helped him make balsa models that would actually fly, as well as models of hard wood, which were only to be looked at on the top of his chest-of-drawers.

Was his father alive? Was Cooper playing some cruel hoax, just to get him to bring Lori and the others back under Cooper's control?

Lori…she was right all along in her apprehensions concerning the man. Robert Cooper was untrustworthy, at the very least.

He would find a phone he could trust at first opportunity.

* * *

Prouse looked to the eastern sky, above the rocky ridge a quarter mile beyond the cave Christopher Banyon had entered just minutes earlier.

"I've never seen this," he said in a tone of astonishment.

"What?" Susie said, trying to follow the archaeologist's line of sight while he stared at the phenomenon.

She saw the reason for his amazement at the moment he spoke.

"I've never seen a storm front that looked like that, coming from the east. Not in this region."

The clouds on the ridge-broken eastern horizon were black, as black as any he had seen, even more ominous than the dark clouds of the tornadic storms that often raked his native west Texas, and Oklahoma to the north.

"This never happens at this time of year, for sure," Prouse said, starting to gather his big, canvas pack, and the one that Christopher had worn.

"We've got to find some place, Susie. We've got to get out of that storm." Lightning fired in a thousand streaks while the clouds rolled toward them. "We're sitting ducks on this flat land. We're the only lightning rods around for miles," he quipped, holding Banyon's backpack while grasping Susie's arm with his free hand. "We've got to go in the cave. We have no other choice."

Thunder growled, then became crashes, while the jagged bolts of lightning did their work. Prouse pulled the woman up the steep grade toward the cave's gaping mouth, while the first large drops of rain began pelting them.

A deafening clap of thunder blasted overhead and they hurried into the opening. Prouse and Susie Banyon turned to see that the early afternoon now looked to be night.

The wind drove rain so hard that all beyond their immediate view was obscured. The sloping area leading to the cave that they had just scrambled up was now a mound of mud.

"Where's Christopher?" Susie said, her eyes searching the almost impenetrable darkness of the cave's interior.

"There must be an opening," Prouse said, taking a flashlight from the backpack, after dropping the canvas bag to the cave floor.

He searched the cavern with the beam, finding, finally, a small opening along one side of the cave's back wall. He examined it carefully, realizing immediately the fact he didn't like. He wouldn't be able to fit through the opening.

"Chris!" Prouse shouted into the opening just large enough for the minister, more slightly built than himself, to have slithered through.

"There's no way I can fit through that opening," the archaeologist said with disgust, after listening, but not hearing a response to his shout.

"I can," Susie said, bending to look through the opening, seeing only blackness.

"Are you sure you want to?" Prouse said, shining the flashlight's beam through the opening.

"Yes. If you think I should," she answered.

"Don't see why not," he said. "I don't think there's much danger of there being any deep drop-offs here. But, you'll have to watch your step."

She said nothing, but Prouse saw fright in the brown eyes.

"You know you don't have to do this, Susie," he said.

"Oh, I need to, Randy. I really feel that I do."

"The way it's worked out, I think you're right. Seems the Lord has made it so that only you and Chris can fit through that opening. Who am I to argue with Him?"

He didn't think the logic was all that sound, but his words were meant to lighten the mood, which they did.

"Watch very carefully for pits. Like I said, I don't think there will be any, but watch your step. Okay?"

"Okay," Susie said, taking the flashlight from the archaeologist, who tried to keep her from hitting her head on the lip of the opening when she knelt, then lay on her stomach and began slithering through.

"Let me know what's going on," he said, bending to watch her stand and shine the light to illuminate her new surroundings.

Prouse tried to soothe his worry about the two by arguing silently with his fears that there had been hundreds—maybe thousands—of people slip into that small opening since the cave was discovered. There had been no reports of any who never came out—so far as he knew.

One thing sure, he thought while going back to the mouth of the cave to watch the horrific storm raging just outside, he would never be one of the thousands who would go through the hole ...

* * *

"Stay with him," Robert Cooper said to his agents in a lowered volume, so as not to be heard beyond their meeting in the hallway. "I want at least two of you with him at all times, understood?"

The three mumbled their understanding and agreement.

Mark Lansing sat in an adjoining room, alone with his Marine Corps duffel bag full of his things. He stared at the wall in front of him, his thoughts racing through his fatigue.

He was a prisoner, although not a prisoner that had been told he was one. But, he felt the bars, as surely as if they had locked him in a cell. He was tired, frustrated...and, angry.

The strange hum vibrated the air around him, assaulted his senses, and added to his agitation. The Taos complex, he now viscerally knew, was a place of embedded evil. It—they—had done whatever they had done to Lori. She was able to get away from them, and now they treated him like a prisoner. Cooper intended to use him as a bloodhound to track down and turn over the girl he loved to the people responsible for this hellish place.

Nausea crawled in his stomach. No doubt it was partly because he hadn't eaten since noon the day before. But, the convoluting sickness he felt was fueled by nerve-jangling realization that Lori, her mother, and her father, needed his help, and, here he sat, not yet knowing how to get to them…and at the same time lose his watch dogs.

The door opened and Robert Cooper strode in, Mark thought, looking as fresh as he had during their conversations 12 hours earlier. The man had had no sleep; he was sure of that.

"Now, Mark, I want you to know we're not lying to you about things," he said with a forced smile that looked more like a grimace.

"I realize what I'm about to show you will somewhat disturb you. But, your father is making big strides," Cooper said, walking to a television monitor recessed in one wall.

Mark turned to follow with his eyes, the Director's walk to the monitor. Cooper manipulated several of the buttons on the monitor, and an image appeared on the screen in color. It was the image of a man, sitting, looking out a window, sunlight framing his profile.

The man looked old, with graying hair that receded high on his forehead. His face was pale, and wrinkled, but the gray-blue eyes seemed to spark with a degree of youthfulness while the camera zoomed slowly in, and then out again.

"It's your father. He's now 47. He is coming along quite well, the doctors tell me."

Mark's sensation was one of being disembodied. As if he watched the monitor through another person's eyes, experienced everything through someone else's senses. He felt no emotions, watching the monitor showing the man Cooper claimed was his father. But, for reasons he couldn't fathom, a single tear streamed from the corner of his right eye and rolled over his cheek.

"You can be together with your dad again, Mark. Wouldn't you like that? All you have to do is help us bring Gessel Kirban and the others back into the Taos fold," Cooper said in a business-like fashion, as if offering Mark a deal he would be a fool to refuse.

* * *

Susie Banyon made her way along one side of the low-ceilinged cave. The violent sounds of the storm faded the deeper she went into the cavern. Rifts in the cave floor gaped at various points, and she shined the beam into them. Although they appeared bottomless, they were narrow, and presented little threat while she moved farther along, hugging the wall.

A hundred feet into the cave brought her to a dead-end, but, looking carefully while she approached the blockage, she saw an opening along the wall. It was narrow, but she easily slid through, the flashlight's beam illuminating a larger cavern.

Her husband sat on a small boulder in the distance. She snapped the flashlight off when she saw that he looked to be engulfed by a yellow field of light. She surmised that he must have his flashlight resting on something, shining upward, onto himself.

Christopher sat staring straight ahead—at what, she couldn't tell.

Susie stood motionless, and silent, 20 feet to the right and rear of where Christopher sat.

"Come, Susie," he said. "I've been expecting you."

She blinked in amazement. He had been expecting her? She walked, without saying anything, toward him.

Her husband reached with his right hand to take hers.

"Where two or three are gathered together, there I am also," Christopher said, without looking at her.

Susie felt inexplicable warmth bathe her senses. Her sensation was one of peace, comforted by the words she recognized as from Scripture. She remembered that they were the words of Jesus. "For where two or three are gathered together in my name, there am I in the midst of them."

Susie sat beside Christopher, noticing that she, too, now seemed at the center of the yellow glow of light. She saw that his flashlight was lying at his feet. Its glass was dark.

The minister put his arm around his wife and pulled her close.

"I was told to await your coming to me," he said, gently

holding her against his body.

"How were you told?" she asked.

"I was told in my spirit," he said.

The explanation wouldn't have satisfied most, Christopher considered. But, he knew it would satisfy this woman of faith. Neither did she question the light that surrounded the—somehow comforted them. The light grew brighter, until it almost blinded them. Their minds seemed in synchronization with each other's thoughts—with the source of the light that embraced them.

"*Place the parchments before you,*" they heard the inner-voice say in a wind-like whisper.

Christopher removed the felt covered pieces from his shirt, removed the cloth, then leaned forward to put the pieces on the cave floor just in front of his and his wife's feet.

The voice spoke to their innermost thoughts. "*War in heavens and on earth shall begin the consummation when first scroll words shall be found.*" The words sounded again, the thought echoing within their heightened senses. "*Watch for the bene elohim...The bene elohim deludes when approaches the great taking away.*"

Silence spoke as mightily for the next seconds as had the voice. The thoughts then came to them—words that supernaturally imprinted their brains with all that must be accomplished. The fragments began to glow while they lay in front of Christopher and Susie on the cave's floor. The pieces of ancient material burst into flames, then were gone, without a trace of ever having existed.

Randall Prouse stood by the narrow opening in the wall while Susie, and then Christopher emerged into the first cavern. He took Susie's hand to steady her when she straightened.

"The fragments are gone," Christopher said when he stood and brushed dirt from his khaki pants.

"Gone?" the archaeologist said.

"Randy, they literally went up in flames. Not even a trace. The Lord was finished with them. They had served their purpose."

"Well, we understand...I guess," Prouse said. "I don't know if Yadin will, though."

They gathered the backpacks and walked toward the mouth of the cave. Prouse wanted to ask a thousand questions about their experiences within the other cavern, but didn't. There would be time...

"That storm...I've never seen anything like it. But, it's been over for about 30 minutes," Prouse said, leading the way.

"We're going to be muddy messes by the time we get to the bottom of the dirt mound," the archaeologist said. "We'll have to slide down in all that muck."

He stopped at the mouth of the cave, and stared in disbelief.

"What's wrong?" Susie asked, not able to see around their big friend.

"Strange, indeed," Prouse said, looking out over the surrounding terrain. "Everything's perfectly dry...like there was never a drop of rain."

Chapter 16

The vibrating hum had stopped, and Mark's thoughts became better defined while he sat, his legs stretched, his feet crossed in the big chair. The quarters were luxurious, he thought, looking around at the elegant interior of the three-room suite.

The one thing that stood out, though, he considered while scanning the walls, there were no windows. Of course, the suite was at least one floor beneath the entry level of the complex. No need for windows.

But, he sensed that the lack of windows, and the fact that there was only one door at the center of the small kitchen/lounge room, had an additional purpose—to imprison him, albeit in a sumptuous manner.

Mark stood from the leather recliner and walked to the door. He tapped on it, and tried the knob. The door, made of what felt to be almost solid steel, swung open. Mark stepped into the hallway, and looked in both directions. Nothing but cream-colored walls, its surfaces broken along their length by other doors like the one he had stepped from moments before.

Maybe he was imagining the prisoner bit, he thought, opening his door and walking back into the suite. Robert Cooper's words, before Mark was issued into the suite, were meant to reassure, he imagined. They didn't.

"Please feel at home, Mark. Anything you need is at your fingertips, including room service. Just use the phone, like you would in a hotel room. Dial 9 to get out."

The Director, after playing the part of concierge, appointed two of his young goons to accompany their "guest" to the suite. "We'll talk later today. Meanwhile, get some rest," Cooper had said, while Mark and his agent-companions walked away.

Mark tried the phone again, picking up the green receiver and dialing 9. He heard the dial tone change from the complex tone to that of the public line. He dialed the 0 and a woman's voice asked, "May I help you, please?"

He read the number from the piece of paper he had taken from his wallet, then listened while the connections were in process along the lines leading from the complex, and New Mexico, toward Texas.

"Hello," the sleepy-sounding woman said in a soft, Texas drawl.

"Ma'am, I'm sorry to call so early," Mark said, looking at his watch and seeing that it was 5:35 a.m., then calculating that it would be 6:35 in San Marcos, Texas.

"Are you Ruth Prouse?"

"Yes," the woman answered, sounding more alert.

"I'm Maj. Mark Lansing. I'm a friend to your husband's friend, Rev. Christopher Banyon."

"Yes, I know Chris," she interrupted. "He and his wife, Susie, are in Israel with my husband."

"Yes ma'am, I know. And, that's why I'm calling. I need to get in touch with Chris…Do you have a number where he can be reached?"

"How did you get this number?" Ruth Prouse asked with caution in her voice.

"I got it from the church secretary of St. Paul Presbyterian Church. I'm sorry, but I failed to write the lady's name down."

"I will have to go to the other phone, Major…" she hesitated to get the name again.

"Mark Lansing," he said.

"Hold a moment, while I go to the other phone."

In a few seconds, Ruth picked up the kitchen phone and Mark

heard paper rustling.

"Major, here's the number of the hotel where they are staying. My husband is in 833. He can get Christopher for you."

"Thanks, Mrs. Prouse. I really appreciate the help," Mark said, after she had read him the number.

When they said goodbye, he held the receiver to his ear a few seconds after she hung up.

Yes. He heard the extra clicks. Just as he suspected, their conversation had been monitored.

* * *

Sharkton Cove, Maine, June 20

The trip had been grueling. Lori had driven the mid-size truck-van most of the miles across country, and her arms, shoulders, neck and hands ached from the struggle. She pulled into the Texaco service station, looking in the truck's long side mirrors to see Gessel Kirban's Jeep wagon follow her vehicle to the side of the station's main building. She stepped from the GMC's high running board, feeling the blood flow more normally again into the muscles of her cramping legs. She stretched, feeling the stiffness of her body begin to dissipate.

They had come a long way from Santa Fe, New Mexico. The sign they had passed only moments before was a welcome sight. "Welcome to Sharkton Cove, Population 4,700."

The three of them had spent the night before in Boothbay, at the home of Grace Banyon, whose hospitality had meant much to the travelers. Their trip had been grueling, made worse by constantly checking rearview mirrors all the way from New Mexico.

"If they really want us," Gessel Kirban had said more than once, "they will get us."

"Not as long as the Lord is in control," her mother had said, in answer to the scientist's pessimism.

Lori didn't know anything about whether the Lord had assisted them. Didn't know why the government goons from the complex hadn't thrown a roadblock up somewhere along their way. But, she did know the trip had been uneventful, with the exception of when her father had gotten carsick somewhere in New York State. He was improving every hour, and she believed things were going to improve even more, once they settled into the home to which Grace Banyon had directed them.

Mark...things wouldn't be better, until she was with Mark.

Her self-reminder brought a pang of sadness that caused tears to stream in a thin line down her cheeks. Mark would soon join them, she assured herself, straightening her shoulders and wiping the tears with her fingertips while she walked beside the truck's enclosed bed toward Kirban's Jeep wagon.

She opened the left rear door of the Jeep, and slid into the seat beside her father. He looked into her eyes, stared for several seconds, his expression one of confusion. He recognized his daughter, then, a fleeting, but definite smile, came, Lori saw with delight. She kissed him on his cheek.

"Hi, Daddy. Are you feeling better?" Lori said, reaching to straighten the curl of hair from his forehead.

"He's doing just fine, baby," Laura said from the other side of her husband. "He's been pointing to things he recognizes more and more."

James Morgan turned to look at Laura while she spoke. She, like their daughter, kissed him, and squeezed his arm with her right hand. She had lost him in the crashed T-38, and, thanks to her Lord, he was again with her. It was like the resurrection, she thought, silently thanking God for the one-hundredth time since they left New Mexico.

Morgan tried to speak, but managed only, "soon..."

"Soon? What's soon, Daddy?" Lori asked, trying more to get him to talk, then to get his thought. "We will be there soon? Is that what you mean?"

Her father's eyelids narrowed in concentration, his forehead wrinkling above his graying eyebrows. He shook his head to indicate no.

"Soon…" he said again, tried to say more, then gave up, a look of frustration on his face.

"The effects seem to be not unlike an aphasic stroke," Gessel Kirban said from behind the wheel in the front seat. "Your husband is having trouble collecting his thoughts, then verbalizing them. But, I think that, unlike an aphasic stroke, where there is major damage on the left side of the brain, the colonel will snap out of this inability to reason. I am convinced that the precognition neuro-diviner does no permanent damage."

Lori looked deeply into her father's eyes. "Do you hear the doctor, Dad? You're going to get well—soon." She emphasized the word "soon," and James Morgan's tenseness seemed to diminish.

Fewer than 30 minutes later Kirban's Jeep Wagon, followed by Lori and the GMC van, turned onto the narrow gravel road. Lori remembered the words of Grace Banyon.

"It's an old house, that we've always joked about being haunted. But, don't let it frighten you. It belonged to my aunt— Christopher's great aunt—Annabel. Annabel Lee, as a matter-of-fact. But I don't think she was the inspiration for Poe's poem," Grace had said with a laugh. "But, the old place can be pretty spooky on the proverbial 'dark and stormy night'."

This day was bright, but when the old dwelling came fully into view around a copse of trees, Lori could imagine, from her elevated position in the high cab of the van, that on a dark day, or stormy night, the old house could have been the inspiration for an Edgar Allen Poe poem, or story, had he seen it.

The road leading up to it had a name that could evoke thoughts of sea storms, and women with telescopes scanning the ocean's horizon for their returning seafaring men.

"Crab Cove Road," she thought, definitely fit the scene, with the ancient three-story gothic-style home, standing out starkly in the blue-green grass on a bluff that overlooked the colorless Atlantic. Poe would've loved it, she thought, while she herded the big truck to an open space just off the rutted drive near the front of the storm-weathered house.

Lori got out of the cab, and turned her eyes upward toward the home's front turret, with its several dark windows bordered by shutters.

The house's slat-planked, dark gray surface, with a bluish tint, needed repainting. Its once-white trim now was faded to a blotched tan. The shutters on either side of the long windows had broken slats, and, like the rest of the home, begged for fresh paint.

Grace Banyon had told them that the interior was in better shape than the exterior. Christopher, to whom her aunt, his great aunt, Annabel Lee Mitford, had deeded the house, planned to refurbish it when he could afford to. He would spend his summers doing as much to bring it back to its former glory, as his time permitted.

It was a gracious gesture—the minister offering them use of the house—Lori thought, rounding the back of the big van. Dr. Kirban was intrigued with the fact that Mrs. Mitford's husband had been a physician. He had, Grace had told them, a full laboratory in the basement. A lab few had set foot in since the 1940s.

Just great, Lori thought, seeing Gessel Kirban help her father out of the back seat of the Jeep wagon. *Just great, if one were a horror movie freak...*

But, the house was remote. And, it did have a place where Dr. Kirban could work on learning more about the projects and how to help her father recover.

Kirban and Lori's mother worked at the back of the Jeep, removing things to transfer to the home. Lori helped, but then became concerned for her father.

"Where's Dad?" she asked.

All three looked around the new area. James Morgan was not in view.

"Dad!"

Lori trotted toward the side of the house, continuing to call.

She saw him when she rounded the corner of the rear of the home.

"Dad!" she shouted, seeing him standing on a large rocky area, looking toward the Atlantic Ocean far below. "Daddy! Don't move!"

She ran to his side, and clutched his arms. "Be careful, Daddy," she said, her heart racing.

"It's okay, Sunshine," her father said, patting her arms while they wrapped around him. He freed himself from her embrace, and put his arm around her.

Laura, out of breath after running toward her husband and daughter, joined them on the rocky point.

"Everything's going to be okay now, SuperL," he said, putting his free arm around his wife, then kissing her.

* * *

Jerusalem, near daybreak, June 21, 1967

A swirling cloud surrounded him. Mini-bolts of lightning struck at him, but didn't hit him. He nonetheless sought cover. Cover that was nowhere to be found, while he seemed to glide on some unseen conveyance along the back alleys and narrow passageways between dilapidating streets.

The darkness surrounded only him, and he couldn't understand why no one noticed. The Jerusalem natives were oblivious while he glided on a cushion of air toward the easternmost edge of the city.

He was on a mission. A mission to do what, he didn't know. But, he did know that it was a most important mission.

The cloud, with its lightning, was gone. He stood in bright sunlight, about to step off a curb and onto a street, across from which he saw the black-hatted Jews bowing while reading from the Torah.

He looked down. He wore a black garment that covered him even to the toes of his sandals. He reached to feel the hat he wore. A large-brimmed hat. He pulled it from his head and looked at it.

A black hat, like the one's worn by the men at the Western Wall across the street.

Somehow it seemed right. But, at the same time, it bothered him. He wasn't Jewish. He was a Christian—a Presbyterian. His robes were gray and maroon…He wore no black hat. They would know. Know that he was Presbyterian.

Something moved him, an unseen, powerful presence that forced him forward. Christopher next found himself standing beside a bowing, chanting, bearded black hat worshipper. The man paid him no attention, keeping, instead, his eyes upon the Torah he held with both hands in front of his eyes while he bowed toward the wall and the Temple Mount.

He had no Torah, himself. But, there was something in the large pocket of the black robe. The robe which was now the robe of his own faith, gray with maroon trim. It was his Bible, the one his mother had given him as a teenager.

Scribbled in the upper left corner of the inside cover were the familiar words Grace Banyon had written there on his fourteenth birthday: *"Trust in the Lord with all thine heart; lean not unto thine own understanding; In all thy ways acknowledge him, and he shall direct thy paths. Proverbs 3: 5-6."*

He opened the Bible and something fell out of its pages. The parchment pieces! The fragments with the Hebrew words on the first: *"War in heavens and on earth shall begin the consummation when first scroll words shall be found."*

On the second fragment, the words: *"Watch for the bene elohim. The bene elohim deludes when approaches the great taking away."*

But, the fragments had burst into flames in front of Susie and him, while they were in the cave …had disintegrated to nothingness!

He looked again at the fragments. They had transformed into a single piece of parchment. The words were in English.

"Go to Sharkton, Maine. On Crab Cove Road is your Salvation." In that moment of epiphany, Christopher knew what

he must do. He moved forward, rolled the paper into a scroll, and stuffed it into a crack in the ancient wall.

In the next instant, the paper was being tugged, and Christopher gripped hard with his fingertips and thumb. He almost retrieved it from the crevice when he saw a dark hand that seemed to consist of nothing more than black smoke. It appeared to be attached to nothing, just an armless, black hand of swirling smoke, its fingers gripping the paper and trying to wrench it from him.

"Chris!"

He heard Susie's voice as if it were far away, down a deep shaft.

"Chris! Wake up!"

Christopher sat up in bed beside his wife, his eyes open wide, the room coming into better focus with each blink of his eyelids.

"You were having a nightmare," she said, reaching to steady him, then helping ease him back to a lying position.

"Yes, quite a nightmare," he said, trying to bring his thoughts again into the waking world.

* * *

Sharkton, Maine, 11:18 p.m., June 20

Unlike the huge, Victorian-gothic home's facade, the interior had been well cared for. Grace Banyon had been right. The person the family had paid to keep things dusted and in good repair was conscientious, and the old place didn't creak nearly so much as Lori had anticipated.

She lay near exhaustion from struggling with the van for the last several days. Her brief thoughts of her new surroundings turned to thoughts of Mark. How much she did miss him. Again, the tears came. She should be happy. Her family was together again. Her father had made a near-complete recovery, according to Gessel Kirban. Her mother had said that the recovery was a miracle.

If God could perform such a miracle in these modern times,

could he perform one more for her? Could he bring Mark to her again?

Lori wiped the tears with the pillowcase and said a quick prayer to a being she didn't know.

"Please bring him to me," she said in a whisper. She chastised herself for doing so. Not so much because she didn't really believe in a deity that was interested in her problems, but because she was so presumptuous as to think that after ignoring that deity, He would now snap to attention and grant her request.

"But, dear God, if you are there, please grant this prayer," she said, wiping the tears again, before drifting off into much-needed sleep.

Upstairs, in one of the six bedrooms, Laura looked at her sleeping husband. He looked so much older than before the accident in which he, along with the Wing Commander, was reported to have been killed.

She brushed back his still dark, but graying hair from his right temple, then a tear from her own eye.

"Thanks, Lord," she breathed. She was grateful—thankful beyond her ability to express. James was back. His sensibilities had returned, and she knew things would get better from here. Despite the things they had all been through, and the fact they were probably being pursued—by whom, and exactly why, she didn't know—things would be better.

Gessel Kirban was determined to find out. With God's help they would find out together.

Lori. Their sweet daughter had put up a good front. Had been strong for her mother and dad. But, she loved Mark so, missed him so much.

"Dear Lord," Laura prayed in silence while continuing to stroke her sleeping husband's face. "Please bring these kids together. And, please let Mark and his father have a reunion as wonderful as mine and Lori's has been with James."

* * *

Gessel Kirban, like his fellow travelers, was tired. But, the excitement of his new surroundings helped lift his strength to a level that would give him another hour or two of consciousness.

The basement—a full basement that served as foundation for the huge house above—was more than promised.

"My uncle, Dr. John Mitford, had a modern laboratory for its time," Grace Banyon had told him before they had left Booth Bay. "It's a real interesting place," she had told him, in describing the lab.

It was indeed a most interesting place, he thought, while he arranged the instruments of his own experimentation—things brought from his private Taos laboratory. Kirban turned the brass levers of the several Bunsen burner spigots. Hearing the hiss, and smelling the gas, he smiled. He was home again...

He opened one of three boxes of the same size, and carefully removed its contents. He held the gleaming golden precognition neuro-diviner at arm's length, and smiled again.

Here, there would be time to learn all there was to know about this marvelous instrument. He wondered how he might begin the process of convincing Laura Morgan that her husband and daughter must again wear the helmet.

* * *

Taos 12:33 a.m., June 21, 1967

Thoughts of his father pricked at Mark's troubled semi-sleep. He was dog-tired, but couldn't relax in order to drift far enough away from his worries to drop into that restful realm, toward which he struggled.

He saw his Dad's face amidst a swirling cloud of gray-blackness. It was the face as he remembered it when his father would sit across from him at the kitchen table. It was again 1947, and his Dad was helping him construct one of the model balsa wood gliders they both loved.

Mark's sleep-thoughts next centered on a beautiful, smiling face. Her eyes sparked love for him in a way he knew would come only once in a lifetime. His eyes snapped open and he sat up in bed, blinking, trying to regain his sensibility.

Lori. Every part of him ached for her, longed to hold her close, feel her warmth and vibrance, return her love for him. He sat on the edge of the bed, wondering where he was, his thoughts still a blur.

Mark couldn't see his surroundings beyond his own feet. Not even the carpet beneath them. Was he losing his sight?

The room filled with thick smoke, which had no odor. He fanned it with his hands, trying to see through the opaqueness. A brilliant stream of light pierced the cloud, and it opened up a tunnel through which he caught a glimpse of something...someone.

Lori!...It was Lori!

She stood, beckoning him. Dressed in a white gown of sheer translucence, she held out her arms to him, the gown's diaphanous sleeves undulating, a gentle wind moving them in slow motion while her long, slender fingers bid him to come to her. He tried to move from his sitting position on the edge of the bed. But, it was no longer the bed. It was a big stone of some sort, and he struggled to get up. Finally, he was free of it, and he tried to move toward Lori, who smiled, turned, and began walking away into the smoky distance. She turned back to him, then, and again beckoned him with a motion of her hand.

He followed. Tried to catch up to her. His legs moved as if they were trying to run through thick oil. He managed to draw to within several feet of her, and reached to take hold of the gown she wore, which flowed gracefully behind her while she glided forward. He grasped the gown, felt its cool, silky softness in his hand. She would be in his arms within moments...

When he reached to embrace her, he felt nothing. Lori was gone!

He stood in the smoky surroundings, holding the gown. The girl he loved was gone!

He saw in the distance, a strange, rock-covered barrier. The scene before him became clear while he walked toward the huge wall-like structure. He felt the surface with his fingertips. Had Lori gone through an opening somewhere along the wall?

He continued to feel, probing with his fingers the deep cracks along its ancient surface. His fingers touched something in one of the cracks, and he grasped it, pulling it from the opening. A thick piece of rolled up paper. He unscrolled it, and read the words: "*Watch for the bene elohim. The bene elohim deludes when approaches the great taking away*," it read.

The words then changed before his astonished eyes: "*Go to Sharkton, Maine. On Crab Cove Road is your Salvation.*"

The words became red hot in appearance, then white hot, and he felt their heat. The instructions burned themselves into his brain, just before the paper burst into flame, causing him to drop it.

Mark blinked, finding himself standing in the suite's small kitchen. Another sleepwalking episode! Had it been another of the night terrors, with the dark beings directing his movements? Or something other?

He looked in the refrigerator, withdrew a can of beer, and searched the cabinet drawers for a church key. He opened the can, took a sip, and sat at the small table. It seemed so real, yet so surreal. What did it mean?

Mark rolled the cold can over his forehead, while he tried to remember details. Tried to remember Lori, and her part in the… dream…or whatever it had been.

His thoughts could center on only one part of the nightmare, the words on the paper that had burst into flames.

* * *

Over the Atlantic, June 23, 1967

The 707 co-pilot looked to the western sky through the windshield. He shifted to get a better look at the looming blackness he hadn't noticed just minutes earlier.

"Johnny, you get any word on that weather?" the co-pilot pointed out the storm they were approaching at more than 500 knots.

"Where'd that come from?" Johnny Bristow asked, rising partially from his seat to see the building thunderstorm. "There's been nothing about a system of that size," he said.

"Better get us some new numbers," Jeff Blackston said from the left seat. "Better do it quick, because I don't think we've got much time to adjust," the pilot concluded.

The ride had been smooth, uneventful. Just the way Christopher Banyon liked it. He had dozed off and on for the past several hours since leaving Paris.

He looked to see the angelic face of his wife, who slept soundly beside him.

"Looks like something's brewing," Randall Prouse said, leaning over Susie while standing in the aisle.

Susie stirred and struggled to find consciousness, awakened by their big friend, who stood above her talking to her husband.

"What's wrong?" she asked, able, finally, to understand there was a problem.

"It's nothing much, I don't think. Just a thunderstorm up in front of us," the archaeologist said, trying not to sound alarmed.

"The captain will probably be telling us to buckle up, just for precaution," he said. "I better get in my seat."

With that, Prouse moved to his seat several rows back, and clicked the buckle of his seatbelt.

Christopher looked through the window just above the left wing. He saw in the distance a tapering cloud of dark gray.

"The main part of the storm must be to our right," he said to his wife, who strained to look past him, then looked across the aisle to the window opposite theirs.

"It looks darker over there, but I can see only a tiny bit of sky," she said.

"It's been so smooth, not a cloud. It sure came up fast,"

Christopher fretted. "The pilot said it looked like clear flying all the way to New York, according to the weather people."

"Guess you can't depend on the weather people," Susie said. She added, "Except for the main Weather Person."

Christopher smiled, knowing whom she meant. If only he had her faith...

The intercom chimed, and the expected "Fasten Seatbelt" light came on.

The TWA captain said, "Ladies and gentlemen, as you can see, the fasten seatbelt sign is on. Looks like we'll have a bit of a bumpy ride for the next 20 or so minutes. We will try to make it through this turbulence with as little inconvenience to you as possible."

They felt the first bounces of rough air, the belly of the 707 bumping hard against the pockets of turbulence, as if it were a small speedboat slapping against choppy water while at full throttle. The violence increased, the whole aircraft seeming to move at unnatural angles. The huge wings rose and fell as if fluttering like an actual bird struggling against a Texas thunderstorm, the minister thought, while watching out his window.

He guessed he should say a prayer. Better yet, he should ask Susie to pray. She was the one with the greater faith, he thought, only half-joking to himself. In the cockpit, Jeff Blackston wrestled with the plane's controls, while his co-pilot assisted him.

"We've got to get above this, guys. Are we clear to get altitude?"

"Yes, Captain," the navigator said. "We're cleared to do whatever is necessary."

"That's a little bit late, looks like. We're in the middle of it now. Don't think I've seen one I couldn't get over...or around."

"If we could've started a little earlier," the co-pilot said, letting the thought die.

"Yeah, it was on us too quickly," the pilot said. "But, we'll be okay."

Randall Prouse did what he always did in these situations. He watched the flight attendants' eyes. He looked for unease, and did see concern that bordered on panic in the eyes of the stewardess who lurched from seat to seat while going to strap herself in.

He offered his own prayer, and knew he was joined by at least two others in the plane.

The archaeologist flew the Atlantic often, at every time of day and night, at every time of every month. He had never been in such a storm, he thought, gripping the armrests hard, and praying harder.

It was as if they had caught up with the same weird storm that had sent them into the cave near Qumran. The storm that, despite producing horrendous rain, inexplicably left the land completely dry—as if there had never been a storm.

The ink-black sky seemed to ignite with irresistible violence while the 707 rose and fell hundreds of feet in a matter of seconds, no matter what Blackston and his co-pilot did to try to control the aircraft.

Passengers remained abnormally quiet, except in the moments when the bird fell hard into storm-created troughs, its fall interrupted by sudden updrafts of great power. Shrill screams, even from the stewardesses, split the air, drowned out sometimes by tremendous thunderclaps.

The engines roared loudly with each forced inflow, each massive super-burst of storm driven -wind.

Christopher prayed silently while he saw the pyrotechnics beyond the shuddering wing. He held Susie's left hand tightly, watching the brilliant discharges fragment the whirling clouds of night-like darkness.

His eyes seemed to pierce the maelstrom, his vision invading the angry vortexes just beyond the 707's wingtip. There! In the center of the wind-generated violence! Susie felt his grip tighten, and she had to remove her small hand from his, or it would be crushed.

"What's wrong, Chris?" she asked.

His eyes were wide, and he paid no attention to her question.

"Chris?" she said, louder, gripping his arm to get his attention.

But, his mesmerized mind would not be reeled back into the plane. Not even by the woman he loved. The scene before him was apocalyptic. His brain and spirit were held fast in the supernatural conflict he witnessed.

Gigantic, human-shaped beings clashed within the whirling storm clouds. One was black, flashing sparks of lightning-like flickers while it swung a red-hot, glowing sword. The other was a creature of spectacular light, emitting every imaginable color in electric-like discharges, wielding a sword as bright as when looking directly into the sun. When the swords met in combat, the violent atmosphere surrounding the 707 burst apart in one massive explosion, and then quickly closed again in preparation for the next clash.

"Lord God!" Christopher said, his mouth open, his eyes wide, unblinking.

"Chris!"

Susie tugged at his arm, then tried to turn his face to her with her hand. His head turned again to the terrifying spectacle.

"Chris?! What's wrong?!"

"Can't you see them?" the minister asked, calmly, without emotion.

"See what? The lightning?"

Susie looked past him, through the window, seeing only the lightning and the blackness that rolled over the wings while it cut through the storm at 500 knots.

"They're trying to kill us. They want to stop us, Susie," he said in the same unemotional tone.

"Who?" Susie said, again looking past her husband, and seeing only the spectacular flashes of lightning.

"But they can't. The Lord God is our strength and fortress," he said, seeing through supernaturally opened eyes, the gargantuans engaged in titanic battle just beyond the shuddering wing of the 707.

* * *

Sharkton, Maine – June 23

It was cool, almost fall-like. Lori had left her clothes in storage somewhere in San Antonio. She had nothing for such chilling weather.

But, her mother had found a navy watchcap and a navy, heavy cotton turtleneck pullover in a box in the basement. The oversized sweater felt good, and it, with her well-worn denims, kept her warm while she walked along the steep ridge behind the old house. She stopped and looked over the Atlantic, her hands deep in the hand warmer pocket of the turtleneck.

Laura watched her daughter from the rear-most turret window on the third floor. She smiled, seeing loose strands of Lori's golden hair stream straight back beneath the watchcap, the stiff sea breeze bringing to land a slight sample of what autumn and winter would be like, living in Annabel Lee Mitford's seaside home.

She watched Lori kneel to pick a stone from the ground, then fling it as far as she could. Her daddy always told her she shouldn't throw like a girl, Laura thought, another smile of nostalgia crossing her lips.

Lori's father had wanted a boy, of course, she thought. They all do. Girls can always come later. The first should be a boy…

But, James would not have a baseball team full of boys in trade for his "Sunshine."

His first look at the baby with the straw-colored hair made him think of bright, cloudless days…of springtime, and lemon-colored butterflies on vivid-hued flowers that blanketed rich, green meadows.

Well, she thought, maybe that was hers, not James' vision of their baby girl. He did call her "Sunshine."

The name still fit, Lori's mother thought, watching her daughter pick up another rock, and throw it like a girl toward the whitecapped Atlantic.

Lori stood again with her hands thrust deep into the sweater's tunnel-pocket. The cold wind stung her face, and tried to but couldn't dry the tears that kept filling her eyes and trickling over her cheeks.

She mopped the tears with the sleeve of the sweater, and wished for Mark. *Dear Lord,* she thought, *please bring him back to me.*

Always the guilt came. What right did she, a sinner, have to ask God to do anything for her?

"But, Lord, if you will bring him to me, I'll..." She let the promise die, imagining the Almighty's words.

"You'll...what?"

Lori watched the gulls, white against the overcast skies, dive and swoop beyond the ridge, hundreds of them, sweeping toward the water in constant search of food.

"You are there. I know you are there," she said in words that were erased by the harsh wind.

* * *

Robert Cooper grew more frustrated by the second. He shouted into the phone, his face reddened with his rising anger.

"You mean we can find a single Russian spy, hiding out in a city of eight million people, but we can't find a bunch of civilians traveling with a U-Haul nearly the size of a semi-tractor-trailer rig?!"

He listened to the response on the other end of the line, and then interrupted the agent. "I'll tell you something. If you don't have a lead on these people by this afternoon, I'll find someone who can do your job. You obviously can't do it! Find them! Do you understand me?!"

He slammed the receiver onto its cradle, not waiting for a response from his underling.

The door to Gerhardt Frobe's office opened, and a female lab technician walked in.

"You just walk in?!" Cooper shouted, his complexion again reddening. He noticed, then, the sallow skin, the glassy eyes beneath the lab tech's glasses. He saw the wicked grin that crossed the young woman's face, and his blood ran cold.

"Maybe you are the someone who will be replaced," the woman said, starting the words with her own voice, but finishing with an echoing voice from another world.

Cooper's face went from hypertensive to ashen. His senses darkened, realizing the threat he faced.

"What is the problem, Mr. Director?" the voice asked with a snicker, the words moving in and out of human and non-human intonation.

The woman walked in front of the desk, behind which the Director of Covert Operations sat, his eyes betraying his fear.

"Cat got your tongue, Mr. Director?" the thing possessing the woman said. The mouth of the Dimensional's host gaped, the creature's laughter sounding as if it issued from a cavernous abyss.

"I'm...we're trying to get a line on them," Cooper said, his forehead beginning to bead sweat.

"It's not working," the thing growled from deeply inside its host.

"We will use drugs on Lansing—make him work for us in finding them. I'll take off the velvet gloves," Cooper said through clenched teeth, his rage again beginning to rise.

"And, he will react like a drugged robot, you fool," the voice of the thing possessing the young woman said. "Subtlety has always worked better for us," it said. "Iron always goes to a magnet, bees to honey. Let us turn our bee loose, Mr. Director...see where he flies."

Robert Cooper, who had stood in the presence of the evilness that pervaded Gerhardt Frobe's office, sat again in the swivel chair, removed the silk handkerchief from the pocket of his navy pinstriped suit, and mopped the perspiration from his forehead.

The thing spoke again from within its host. "Our young

friend will never expose his…true love…to us. He knows we are extorting him, to get to her, and the others. Set our bird free. He cannot resist homing in on his…true love."

The voice seethed with contempt and sarcasm while it instructed Cooper.

"Subtlety, Mr. Director. Set our bird free…"

* * *

TWA Captain Jeff Blackston looked over the cockpit gauges. Everything had settled to normal range.

"Take it, Brian," he said, releasing the flight control when his co-pilot had the bird firmly in hand.

The pilot flexed his fingers and rubbed his forearms while gyrating his neck and shoulders to loosen the tensions. His body ached from more than 20 solid minutes of wrestling with the 707.

"I've never seen one like that," Blackston said, fingering the intercom switch. "Stewardess Jurgens," he said into the mouthpiece of his headphone. "Will you come forward, please?"

Moments later she opened the cockpit door and stuck her head inside.

"Yes, sir?"

"How are the passengers?" Blackston questioned, still stretching his tense muscles.

"Some are pretty shook up. But, Everyone seems okay," she said.

"Think we could get some coffee up here, sweetheart? Looks like clear sailing to the Apple," the captain said.

"Sure," the girl said, and started to close the cabin door. She opened it again.

"Thanks, guys…Good job," she said, before going to get the hard-earned coffee.

Christopher Banyon pulled his wife's left hand to his lips and kissed it.

"Looks like your prayers brought the sunshine again," he said, feeling wrung out by the spectacle he had witnessed during the storm's most furious moments.

Susie said nothing, but leaned to her left to peck him on his cheek with her lips. "The Lord is with us, Susie. If ever I doubted, I know now. I've seen His forces in action."

His wife snuggled close to his arm. "Was there ever any real doubt?" she said, at the same moment starting a silent prayer of thanks for coming through the storm safely. Susie felt a presence while her eyes were closed. She opened them wide, in surprise.

Randall Prouse leaned forward to be heard above the engine's whine.

"Chris, I didn't know what I was signing up for when I got hooked up with you," the archaeologist joked. "Is there anyway to resign from this outfit?"

"Only if you want to be on the losing side," the minister said, solemnly, but with facetiousness equal to that of his big friend's.

* * *

New York City looked good to Randall Prouse several hours later, while the 707 circled over the Atlantic in its approach to JFK. He saw the familiar part of the skyline, and the new excavation that would grow to become the World Trade Center on the lower east side of Manhattan. The construction presented a massive gouge in the earth. The planned 90-story skyscrapers would, by 1970, change the world's greatest city for the better, he determined. But, as always, New York paled in comparison to seeing San Marcos after one of his long trips away from the Texas city ... and from Ruth.

* * *

Taos – June 24

"You are free to take your father and go," Cooper said, handing several pieces of paper to Mark. "Your orders have been cleared to return to Egland," he said, turning, then, to take his seat behind the late Gerhardt Frobe's big desk.

Mark was stunned, and could only think to ask, "Dad…When can I see him?"

"He's not exactly at full health. But, they tell me he's about as well as can be expected. He can travel, without major medical attention," Robert Cooper said clinically. "Agent Browne will take you to him."

Cooper spoke into the intercom on the desk. "Agent Browne… Will you step in here, please?"

The office door opened, and a tall agent from Covert Operations stepped into the office.

"Will you show the major to Suite 310?"

Mark's reasoning returned to full functioning, while he watched the stocky Director go through the long drawer of the oak desk. Cooper withdrew a thick envelope from the drawer, then stood and walked to Mark.

"Major, these are your father's medical records—in brief, of course. After this many years he has a warehouse full, as you can imagine. These are all you will need. Most are classified, and must remain with the Defense Department."

Mark took the envelope, his hatred simmering just below the surface of his emotions. He must remain calm, take full advantage of this—this what? They were just going to let them go? The thought flew in the face of everything he had learned about this man, about the clandestine service he ran. They would never just let him and his Dad go, not without arranging to track them wherever they went.

"You served your nation well, Maj. Lansing. The President— we all are very proud of you and grateful to you for what you've done," Cooper said, reaching his hand to Mark, who, not knowing quite what to make of it, took the hand to complete the congratulations.

"You will see that your orders contain a 30-day leave. We insist you take it, before returning to Egland."

Mark started to ask why they wanted him to take the leave, to ask what they had planned for tracking him, while he blindly, foolishly led them to Lori, and the others.

"You'll see, too, that your government will pick up the tab for your father, any time he needs medical attention. So long as it's at a military hospital. Except in cases of medical emergencies, when he's not near a military facility. In that case, we'll take care of expenses until such time as he can be placed in a military hospital."

Cooper was a cool, calculating deceiver. Perfect for his brand of clandestine evil, Mark thought. While Cooper plotted to destroy his victim-to-be, he calmly pulled off the role of the typical government bureaucrat, giving a standard release-from-duty lecture.

"You're free to leave when you get your father. Agent Browne will brief you on military transportation, if you choose to leave the Taos area," Cooper added.

Mark stood silently, fingering the papers. He turned, then, to follow the agent from the room.

He stopped and turned to look at Robert Cooper, who said with a tight-lipped smile, "Good luck, Major."

Chapter 17

H e sat there, stooped, wrinkled, and gray-haired, in a brown leather flight jacket. He didn't look up when Mark approached, strange emotions running through the younger man's mind.

"Dad?"

Clark Lansing looked upward, then straight ahead again. There was no hint of recognition in the older man's age-yellowed eyes.

Mark knelt on one knee in front of his father. He reached out to grasp him on both arms, looking into the eyes of the Dad he hadn't seen since that day in July of 1947.

"Dad…"

Mark's words choked in his emotion- constricting throat, but he managed, with eyes glistening, to say, "It's me, Mark. Dad, it's your son."

Clark Lansing looked at the younger man's face, but still there was no recognition.

Mark leaned forward in front of his father on both knees, and hugged his Dad. Clark Lansing made no attempt to return the embrace, his arms hanging limp at his sides.

Mark loosened his grip, and held his father at arms length.

"We're going to get you well, Dad. That's a promise. You're going to get well real soon."

The prematurely old man's eyes seemed to focus, understanding crossing his age-creased face.

"Soon," Clark Lansing said, parroting his son's words.

"We're ready, if you are, Major."

The tall agent named Browne stood in the doorway of Suite 310, watching Mark help his father to his feet from the small sofa.

"The flight will leave as soon as we get there," Browne said, picking up one of Clark's suitcases.

"Thanks," Mark said, lifting another bag from the floor, then assisting his father from the suite. The older man looked into the eyes of the son he didn't recognize. His own eyes narrowed in concentration.

"Soon," he said, with authority in his voice.

"Soon," he repeated, before his eyes again took on a stuperous glaze.

Mark watched out the porthole of the little T-39 Saberliner, seeing the earth tones of brown, gold and red make the transition to varying tones of green. His father sat beside him, his seat partially reclining. He was asleep, having said nothing since they left the complex at Taos.

They would touch down at Egland Air Force Base in just over 2 hours, the pilot told him. There, he would be reprocessed into duty as a fighter pilot... He presumed, as a member of his former flight, assigned to the F-4s.

The forced leave time, he knew, was so that he would use it to find Lori. So they could follow him to Lori and the others. They particularly wanted Gessel Kirban. How could he elude them? He had to find a way.

But, how could he find the fugitives, when Cooper, with all the United States investigative services at his command, couldn't find them? He looked at his sleeping father. The technology had done this to him. What was it all about? How had the brief time he had been involved with the PND helmet affected his own brain?

His mother. He hadn't thought of it. What would she do when she learned his father—her husband—was alive? Her first husband...

His mother was strong. He would do all he could to make it easy on her. Remind her that Clark Lansing had been legally dead for more than 13 years. He would smooth the way, before explaining everything.

They…Cooper…whoever was responsible had destroyed his family, when his Dad was…caught up in whatever happened.

What had happened? How does a man just vanish from an airplane?

So many troubling questions, things that he must find answers to, so he could put his life in order.

Lori. The essence of everything he loved.

He struggled to stay awake, but Lori's loveliness was the last disintegrating image in his mind's eye, while thoughts of her faded into restful sleep.

* * *

Sharkton, Maine—June 25

"These things, I do not know how else to say it. They mentally, physically, spiritually possess their host—their 'victim' is perhaps a more appropriate way to say it. For the ones possessed do not, I presume, invite these Dimensionals into their bodies, their souls."

Dr. Gessel Kirban spoke into the microphone of the large reel-to-reel recorder. He stopped and punched "replay," making sure his notes were stated correctly.

"Those things, what are they, Doctor?" The unfamiliar voice startled Kirban, who turned to see James Morgan, accompanied by his wife and daughter, standing at the entrance to the basement laboratory.

Kirban placed the microphone on the table beside which he sat, got up and hurried to Morgan.

"Your recovery is remarkable. No, it is phenomenal!" Kirban said, taking a penlight from a pocket of the smock he wore. He lifted James' right eyelid, and shined the light into the retina. He did the same to the other eye.

"I hope you don't mind," the scientist said, after the fact. "Truly, truly remarkable!" he said, shaking his head.

"There's nothing magic about it, doctor," Laura Morgan said, hugging her husband, and admiring him.

"It's an answer to my prayers," she said with a bright smile, hugging him again.

"I'm sure the good doctor has other thoughts, SuperL," James said.

"Don't be too sure, Colonel. These things are not of this world. And, I find it impossible to believe they, if physical, extraterrestrial creatures, could travel from such far distant worlds at sufficient speed to make this lonely planet feasibly accessible to them."

"What, then? What are they?" James asked.

"Dimensionals. That's how Gerhardt Frobe termed them. I believe these dark beings are interdimensional. They can pass from their plane of existence, to ours, apparently as they will."

"They are *bene elohim*—fallen angels," Laura said, interrupting the scientist. "He—Dr. Frobe, or that thing possessing him, told us so."

"I just don't know," Kirban said, shrugging. "Whatever they are, they exist. Their form and materiality are foreign to anything we know. But they are real."

"I can't remember anything," James Morgan said, his tone laced with frustration. "Last thing I remember is doing a nosedive in the T-38. Next thing I knew, I was standing out there looking at the ocean."

"That thing inside Dr. Frobe said they wouldn't fail this time. I believe they are the same as those beings that tried to invade the human race in antediluvian times—the time before Noah's Flood. They're the things Pastor Banyon has been preaching about," Laura said.

"Why? What would be their purpose?" Laura's husband asked in a tone mixed with equal parts curiosity and skepticism.

"Perhaps that's a theological question that another must address," the scientist said.

"Rev. Banyon can tell us," Laura said. "The Lord has been dealing with him on that very thing."

* * *

Christopher studied the page. He then thumbed through the following pages in rapid succession to find a Scripture for which he had been searching. But, his tired mind wasn't really into his study this morning. Their final leg of the trip the day before from New York to San Marcos had seemed to last forever, and his fatigue made him irritable.

Why hadn't they got the telephone on line yet? He had tried to call from New York, from their stopover in St. Louis, and several times since, from the home of Randall and Ruth Prouse. The telephone at the Sharkton house was still not in service. He picked up the receiver from the phone on Prouse's cluttered desk and dialed yet another time. He heard, like all the other times, the rapidly buzzing busy signal he recognized as different from the regular busy signal. The line was still not connected to his Aunt Annabel Lee Mitford's old home.

They should have gone directly from New York to Sharkton, he thought. But, their things were here, in storage at San Marcos. Susie must have her own things…

"Any luck yet?" Randall Prouse asked, after opening his study door and poking his head through the opening.

"Only bad luck, I'm afraid," Christopher said, frustration in his voice. "I double checked to see that the new phone number that's to be installed is right. The phone company assures me it is. But, it's still not up and running."

"They'll get it installed soon," Prouse said. "Keep trying. It will be up and running at any second," he encouraged.

"I'm off to school for a couple of hours," the archaeologist said. "Got to justify my expenses to the department head, you know?"

When he closed the door to the study, Christopher bowed his

head. Before he could begin his prayer, the phone rang.

He started to answer, but realized he wasn't in his own home. There was a knock on the door, and Susie said, after opening it, "Ruth says there's a call for you, Chris." He lifted the receiver.

"Hello?"

"Rev. Banyon?"

Laura Morgan! After several minutes of going over all that had happened during the past days, Laura said, "Dr. Kirban wants to speak with you. Do you know him?"

"No...Only that he is Randy's friend and colleague," Christopher said.

She introduced Kirban, then he was on the phone.

"Reverend..."

"Please, call me Chris," the minister said.

"Very well. Is Randall there?"

"No. He had some business at the college where he teaches," Banyon said.

"Then I tell you...Chris..."

The Israeli scientist paused, as if calculating the precise wording needed.

"I am but a scientist, so do not understand things of theological import. I am convinced, Chris, that we are dealing, here, with something beyond my job qualifications."

"The dark beings?" Christopher asked, a chill running down his spine. "The things a former colleague of mine calls Dimensionals," the Israeli said.

"I agree, Dr. Kirban. These Dimensionals are beyond both of our job qualifications, as you say. But I know someone whose job description covers even these strange matters."

"I believe we are thinking in terms of the same authority," the Israeli scientist said.

"My wife and I will head up that way tomorrow morning. We can explore these things, together," the minister said, his mind racing with questions.

"There are certain procedures I would very much like to try

in pursuing these matters," Kirban said, his thoughts also running ahead to consider the possibilities.

* * *

He had lied to the Marine Corps, something akin to sacrilege even within his own, personal economy of ethical behavior. To the Marine Corps, the lie was a court martial offense. But, he didn't care. His government had used his father, had used him. Turnabout was fair play, and he would put them off the scent by any means possible, while he looked for Lori.

They had used them both, and for that he couldn't find within himself to trust any part of the government watchdogs, not even his much-beloved Marine Corps.

What had they done with Lori? To her? What would they do with her? They had kept him from his father for 20 years; had allowed his mother to remarry, rather than divulge the truth that her husband was kept alive as part of some…what? What was it all about? They would be just as ruthless in dealing with Lori and the others who were with her. They were capable of anything…

He must get answers. His gut told him the dream, or vision, or whatever it had been, pointed him in the direction he could go to find those answers.

"*Sharkton, Maine, Crab Cove Road is your salvation.*" The remembered words were as clear now as when they first burned into his brain during the nightmare.

He reported, as all Vietnam-eligible F-4 stateside pilots must, where he could be found during his leave time. He lied that he would be staying in the area of Florida that surrounded Egland, mostly Destin and Pensacola, because his father couldn't travel far from a military hospital in his condition.

Mark looked at his Dad, who sat next to the big window of the aircraft equipped with pontoons for water landings. They had been given the ride with a friend, who asked no questions, and who, Mark knew, would say nothing of them hitching their way to

Maine on his "air-boat," as Greer Swenson called it.

They had made the trip from Florida's upper Gulf coast in a series of hops. Swenson delivered boat and ship parts to a number of locations along the East coast, and Boothbay, Maine, was the last port of call before he flew back to Florida.

Mark had checked everything he could check, looking for any sort of tracking device. There were none. They were in the clear, and he looked forward to searching to see if there was, indeed, a Crab Cove Road in the tiny town called Sharkton.

"I'll be back in Boothbay in about a week," the short man with a small frame said, offering Mark his right hand. "Check with the port master. I'll have to file my flight plan to include putting in here. I should be back here in six or seven days…"

"Can't thank you enough, Swen," Mark said, pumping his friend's right hand in gratitude.

"You just take care of your old man," Swenson said, before thinking better of what he had said. "I'm sorry, Mr. Lansing. I mean take care of your Dad, Mark."

"You know I will," Mark said, putting his arm around his father's shoulder and giving him a hug. "We've got a lot of catching up to do, right, Dad?"

Clark Lansing glanced nervously at his son, then at Swenson.

"Soon," he said, with a serious look of concentration that turned to one of frustration.

"Soon," Mark said, hugging his father again.

"You take care, Mr. Lansing," Swenson said. "Maybe I'll see you this time next week."

They said their goodbyes, and parted ways, Mark gently leading his father by the arm toward the only place that looked like he might find answers to his questions about Sharkton.

"Sir," he said, finally getting the attention of the bait storeowner who had been talking and laughing with a number of what looked to be commercial fishermen.

"Yep? What can I do for ya?" the man asked, the broad smile he had for the fishermen's stories melting into a more businesslike demeanor.

"Can you tell me how to go about getting to Sharkton?" Mark asked.

"Yep. About seven miles or so up that a way," the man said in a thick Maine accent.

"Is there a bus or something? Someone who might could take us there?"

"Nope. Not that I'm aware. Nothin' by land. You might make a deal with old Maddow, over there."

He pointed to a small, run down building across the dock. "He'll do most anything for a dollar," the man said.

"What's the name?" Mark said.

"Maddow. Shad Maddow. Can't miss him. He's the one that looks like he's been out to sea without a break for a month a Sundays."

"Thanks."

Mark gathered their bags, and managed to hold his father's arms with a part of his fingers not clutching a bag.

They walked to the end of the pier, turned right, then right again on the other side of the water that divided "Shad's Place" from the bait shop.

Mark noticed a number of motor-boats, none in good condition, tethered to the wooden walkway that fronted the old, deteriorating building. Fish smells and other odors of the sea assaulted his nostrils when he entered. Several large barrels, rough-hewn wooden and wicker chairs and tables sat around the room on a plank floor covered partially with sawdust. Marlin and other big-game fish hung on the wall behind the counter, which was full of miscellaneous artificial baits and seafaring paraphernalia.

An old man sat in an equally ancient chair made mostly of weathered wicker. He carved on a foot-long piece of wood, and didn't look up, either when Mark and his father entered, or now, when Mark spoke.

"Are you Shad Maddow?"

"Who's askin'?" the old man said, concentrating on the piece of wood.

"My name's Mark Lansing. This is my Dad. Clark Lansing."

"What you want?" the old man said from beneath the worn-out sea captain's cap. His whiskers were white, and looked to be at least two weeks worth.

"We're just in from Florida." Mark said.

"Whatcha want?" Maddow said gruffly, without looking up from his task.

"We need a way to Sharkton. The guy over there in the bait shop said you might take us."

"How much?" the old man asked.

"How much, what?" Mark said.

"Money, son. Money."

"I thought you'd tell me."

"Take you there for twenty-five," Maddow said, then spit into the brass spittoon near his right foot.

"Twenty-five dollars? Sounds fair," Mark said.

"Plus gas. That's another dollar seventy-five."

"It's a deal. Can we go now?"

The old man said nothing, but finally cut his ocean blue eyes at Mark. They projected something far more than an over-the-hill sailor running a dying business. This was a man who lived the way he pleased, and was happy, despite his surface anger.

Maddow flung the knife 10 feet across the room. It stuck dead center in a 2-foot square surface of cork framed by gray 1-by-4-inch boards.

Minutes later, the 1930s inboard runabout moved just off the coast, northward toward Sharkton. Mark wrapped a jacket he took from his duffel bag around his father's shoulders. The wind was cool, almost biting, but the old seaman, in just a blue and white striped T-shirt and dungarees didn't seem to notice, while his passengers shivered.

"You know anything about Sharkton?" Mark said from the seat behind the empty seat beside Maddow.

"What's to know?" he said, a crusty edge to his question.

"I'm looking for a place on Crab Cove Road. You know where that might be?"

"Yep."

"Can you get us near there?"

"I'll take you into Crab Cove, herself, if that's your druther," the old man said, then spit his cud of chewing tobacco over the side.

"Yep," Mark said, a grin crossing his face.

Thirty-three minutes later, the runabout chugged into the inlet, above which jutted rugged cliffs.

The day was fading, and as the fleeting sun made its way eastward, long shadows engulfed Crab Cove and spread into the Atlantic.

Shad Maddow pulled the boat beside a wooden dock that sat on large posts. The dock rested against the cliff's sloping ridge that was cut with a pathway of man-made stone steps to the top.

"Ain't but one old place atop the bluff," the old man shouted after mooring the boat to the dock with a rope. "Don't think anybody lives there no more, not since the widow Mitford. Spooky old place."

The incoming tide was somewhat buffered by the inlet's configuration, but the little craft rose and fell while Mark climbed onto the steps of the dock. He used all of his strength to grab his father's arms and hoist him onto the dock, timing the lift just right with the boat's ascension upon the tide swell.

"How far is it to Sharkton?" Mark asked, when he had stacked the bags and grabbed his father's arm to steady him.

"Soueast, 'bout a mile and a half," Maddow said.

"You got a light?" he asked.

"No," Mark said.

"Gonna need one afore long."

The old man jumped from the dock into the back seat of the boat. He lifted a panel from the floor, pulled out a long flashlight, and tossed it to Mark.

"What do I owe you, Mr. Maddow?" Mark said.

"Just bring it back sometime. I'll be at the shop. I probably shouldn't," he groused, "but I trust you. Any boy that takes as good care of his old daddy as you gotta be trustworthy."

"Thanks," Mark said, thinking, while smiling to himself, that Shad Maddow's hard-crusted facade was not as thick as it at first seemed.

"Unhitch me, boy," Maddow said, restarting the old boat's inboard engine.

Mark pulled the rope loop from the big mooring post, and threw the line to the old man, who reeled it in.

"I'll get the light back to you!" Mark shouted to be heard above the inboard's roaring.

"See that ya do!" Shad Maddow yelled back, and turned his eyes out to sea.

* * *

Laura Morgan walked into the huge, high-ceilinged parlor, sipping on a mug filled with coffee.

"The phone is working," she said, standing in the middle of the room looking at her husband, who had been dozing.

James sat up from the burgundy, velour-covered Queen Anne-style sofa and rubbed his eyes. "Can't get enough sleep," he said, yawning.

"Dr. Kirban says you will feel groggy off and on for a long time," Laura said.

She walked to the sofa and sat beside him. "Want a sip?" she said, offering the mug to him.

"No, thanks, SuperL," he said, standing, and stretching. "I'll have a cup later."

He looked at Lori, who was curled up on a smaller sofa against one wall.

"Still our little girl," James said, admiring her from the center of the room.

"She's worn herself out wishing for Mark," Laura said. "Maybe we can find out something."

Laura was startled when the phone rang loudly on the table several feet away. Finally, after hours of being out of service for the fourth time since it was hooked up, the phone was working again.

Lori sat up, rubbing her emotion-swollen eyes, and blinking through slitted lids to see her mother pick up the receiver of the ancient, black phone.

"Hello?"

A smile came on her mother's face, and Lori sat forward to hear the one-sided conversation.

"Thank the Lord! Christopher—you just don't know what it means hearing your voice…Where are you?"

Laura's eyes widened. "Boston? When will you arrive at Portland?"

She listened to Christopher, while James sat beside Lori.

"It will be Mark on that phone, next," he said, patting his daughter's arm.

"I hope so, Dad," she said, clinging to his arm and resting her head against his shoulder.

"He wants to be with you as badly as you want to see him, Sunshine. He'll do whatever necessary to find you."

He was pleased that his words brought a quick, but genuine grin to her face.

When she finished the phone conversation, Laura said, "Chris and Susie are at Logan in Boston. They kept trying to get us until the phone was working again. They will land in Portland about 11:40 tonight. Should be able to get a ride here by early morning."

"He hasn't tried to contact you through the Air Force, has he?" James asked, standing and trying to clear the cobwebs from his thinking.

"No. They know better than that," Laura said, walking to her husband and embracing him.

"They won't stop until they get at us," James said. "Cooper

will protect his operation at all cost. I can't figure how we've gotten this far."

"The Lord, that's how," Laura said.

Gessel Kirban walked into the parlor, beaming. "I have done it," he said with excitement. "I have adapted the house's electricity to serve my experiments!"

"What does that mean?" Lori asked, amused at the usually serious Israeli scientist's burst of exhilaration.

"What it means, my dear young woman, is that the precognition device is again functional. I can, perhaps, begin to learn its secrets, which they have kept hidden."

"They? You mean the government?"

James Morgan's question sobered the expression on the scientist's face. Kirban considered a second, then said, "No, no. It is, I believe, a very, small group of self-interested people who actually know the precognition neuro-diviner's special attributes."

"You talking about Cooper?" James asked with surprise in his voice. He had considered the whole United States clandestine planning to be at the heart of the problem.

"I am convinced that these matters, these technologies, have evolved from as far back as Roswell in 1947, maybe even earlier," Kirban said. "But, these things involve interdimensional traffic. Not extraterrestrial interlopers. Mr. Cooper is probably but one of several, in a very hush-hush group that knows the truth."

"*Bene elohim*," Laura said. "They're the angels that fell, with Lucifer."

Gessel Kirban smiled, slightly, and with a mild air of condescension in his voice said, "Well, my dear Laura, we shall have to study about that a bit more."

* * *

The climb up the sloping cliff wall on the stone steps that spiraled their way to the top was arduous.

His father was exhausted. Mark, who had to carry him most of the way, then return to the bottom for the rest of their bags, sat on his duffel bag catching his breath and letting his thumping heart find its normal beat.

Mark struggled to his feet after a minute's rest. "Come on, Dad. Let's see if I'm nuts, doing what some dream tells me to do."

He did feel nuts. But, nothing else made sense, either. He had never heard of Sharkton, Maine or Crab Cove Road. Yet here they were, standing, bags in one hand, and over shoulder, with Dad in the other, looking both ways down Crab Cove Road. South led to Sharkton, north led to the bluff, where Shad Maddow said there would be a dilapidated house...

"Spooky," Maddow had called it.

His Dad needed rest. Even if the house was dilapidated, they could, maybe, rest on the porch, or in a room for the night. Tomorrow, they could walk the mile and a half into Sharkton down this same road.

Shadows had all but quenched the sun's lingering rays, the Atlantic growing darker by the second. Yet the scant light continued to provide a gorgeous vista, Lori thought, seeing the ocean go from dark purple close to the shoreline far below, to an orange-red on its farthest horizon.

She stood before the ceiling to knee-level window in the old home's northeastern turret, imagining how she would begin the painting she planned. This time of evening would be impossible. The project would take too long. She would have but a half-hour or so to catch the magnificent gradations of hues. Taking into account the weather—whether clouds, or clear skies—the wait for just the right minutes to complete such an oil painting made a project at this time of evening impossible. She would have a look in the morning. The dawning sun on the horizon should be as beautiful, and would provide more time to paint each day.

Lori's eyes saw the golden-red turn lavender, but her mind saw only Mark's face on her imaginary canvas.

She turned, and for the hundredth time today, wiped a tear from her face. She walked down the few stairs and traversed the hallway that circled the home's upper floor. The light was dim from two low-wattage lamps attached to the wall by brass fixtures. Such a house should frighten her, should seem more forbidding, she thought, smiling to herself.

"But, who cared? How could anything a ghost do be worse than being here, not knowing about Mark?"

Her thoughts brought her to the southern turret, and she stepped inside the rounded room after springing up the several steps. She would check the vista this window presented. Maybe the painting could be even more appealing as a landscape from this high perspective.

The rutted, graveled road disappeared into the thick cluster of trees. The dusky hour all but obscured the little road, but its brighter appearance than the sea-grass bounding it on either side made it stand out from the surrounding terrain.

Something moved along the road. Yes. Two people, one taller, carrying something. The other, stooped and shuffling beside the taller one.

"Somebody's here. Lights on all over the place," Mark said. "Ghosts don't need lights, do they, Dad?"

Clark Lansing said nothing, his expression unchanging.

Mark looked upward to the turret. Someone looked down at them. Someone with a sleek, feminine form, framed nicely by the turret's light.

"Let's see what we've got here, Dad," he said, nudging his father's arm while they moved again toward the old house.

Several lights came on, displaying a rounded wall, along which the row of lights illuminated the porch that curved around the house. The porch had a number of spindle-hewn columns that supported the spined and spiked porch roof at points 8 feet apart.

"Spooky would be the right word, if not for all the lights, huh?" Mark said to his father, whose only acknowledgement was to cut his eyes upward toward the home's many gables and spires.

The front door opened, and James Morgan stepped onto the porch. He squinted to better see the visitors.

"Who are you?" he questioned, worrying that it might be a surreptitious way to win their confidence with two apparent strangers, rather than a force of many.

"Mark Lansing!" Mark shouted from more than 80 feet down the road. "This is my Dad, Clark Lansing!"

Mark Lansing. The name pierced his recovering memory. Clark Lansing. Could it be?

James quickly calculated the possibilities, the probabilities. If these were Mark and Clark Lansing, how could they have found them? Were they, either accidentally, or under duress, leading Cooper and the Taos goons to the fugitives they sought?

James scanned the forested area behind the two men for any signs of anyone who might have accompanied them. He listened to try to hear movement. Only the chirp of crickets and other night creatures.

"Mark! Is it really you?!" James yelled, deciding there was no threat.

Lori burst from the doorway when she heard Mark's name. She took the porch steps in two bounds, ran by her father, and sprinted to her objective.

Mark dropped the duffel bag from his shoulder, and the two smaller bags he carried in his left hand. He released his father's arm to catch Lori, who threw her arms around his neck and kissed him.

He held her suspended from the road in their joyous embrace. "Oh Mark!" Lori could say no more, her words becoming sobs of happiness. Their reunion melted into a lingering kiss that removed from their presence, for that long moment, consciousness of everything and everyone around them.

When Mark slowly put Lori's feet on the road, Laura hugged them both and kissed Mark.

James Morgan, who had grabbed Clark Lansing by his arm when his friend started to wander off in the direction of the house, led Mark's father back toward the group, while offering his hand.

"I don't know how you knew we were here, Mark, but I've never been happier to see a fellow jet jockey," Lori's father said, shaking Mark's hand.

Lori walked with Mark toward the old house, her cheek against his chest, both arms around him, feeling the hard muscles of his body move beneath the sweat shirt he wore, feeling his strong right arm hold her to himself. She released her grip around his waist just long enough to again remove tears from her cheek with a slender index finger.

* * *

Boston's Logan Airport was closed in by a heavy fog. The voice echoed loudly from the speakers throughout the passenger lounge.

"American Airlines Flight 327 to Portland, Maine has been cancelled due to weather conditions."

"I knew they were going to cancel," Christopher Banyon said, plopping the *Boston Globe* onto the empty chair next to his in frustration.

"Passengers need to check the American Airline counter for rescheduling air travel to Portland," the male voice said.

"You wouldn't want them to fly if it's not safe, Chris," Susie said from her chair to his right.

"Guess not," he said, appreciating her calming effect on his fraying nerves.

It had been a trying time, the last weeks. Giving up the church he loved. Getting involved in the crazy things happening to him, to the Morgans...

"God wants us here, now, or else we would be on our way," Susie said while thumbing the pages of a *Look* magazine.

"We were in the worst possible storm," he said, almost as if to himself.

"But, that was then...this is now, Chris," his wife said. "The

Lord wants us here, not in the air right now. Can't you see that?"

"Wish I could," Christopher said. "I've never had patience. Must be an object lesson."

"Why don't you see what kind of help they can give at the American desk?" she asked, patting his hand while it rested on the arm of the chair.

"Yeah, I better do that," he said. "I'll be right back."

Christopher returned after several minutes.

"They say the next American flight to Portland is scheduled for in the morning at 8:30. If the fog lifts…"

"That's that, then. We can't do anything about it for now, so just relax, okay?"

"They will put us in a room nearby. She gave me a voucher," Christopher said. "We'll have to pick up our luggage."

They retrieved their several suitcases, and began walking toward the glass doors to find a taxi.

Christopher stumbled, almost fell, but regained his balance.

"What's wrong, Chris?!"

Susie tried to steady him, seeing that his eyes seemed to show confusion.

"I…I don't know, hon…I feel really light-headed, I guess…"

"No wonder, you've had nothing to eat but a tuna fish sandwich at noon," she said, continuing to hold his arm and hand.

"Think I'll go to the men's room, splash a little cool water on my face," he said, seeming to regain his sensibility.

"You sure? Shouldn't you wait a few minutes?" His wife brushed his forehead then his cheek with her fingertips.

"You're really clammy, Chris. We'd better sit you down for a few minutes."

"No. I'll be fine. I'll be right back," he said, looking, then seeing the black strip jutting out from above the hallway opening marked in thin, white letters, "RESTROOMS." When he reached for the appropriate door, his thoughts became surreal, his head feeling as if it would explode.

"Lord, help me!" he said, feeling his senses darken and his

body begin to collapse to the hard tile floor.

His thoughts then regathered, his vision cleared. He stood for a moment, one hand against the wall, the other holding his forehead between thumb and fingertips. If only he could get to the sink —splash cool water on his face—all would be okay.

Christopher looked at the door, then back toward the lounge area. His vision was pinpoint, as if he looked through the big end of a telescope. He shook his head, trying to make the blackness surrounding the pinpoint of sight dissipate.

His surroundings appeared totally different to him now. The lounge, as best he could see it, was a hundred times busier. It was bigger, brighter, with people scurrying in every direction.

He again shook his head, trying to clear his vision. Unable to do so, he pushed on the door to the men's room. He stumbled through the opening, then through another set of double doors, pausing to steady his movement by resting the palm of his right hand on one wall. He must find the basin and wash his senses back into his spinning brain.

The restroom was bigger, brighter than the others. Its fixtures and layout looked nothing like what he remembered in the other restrooms he had visited in Logan, or in any other airport, for that matter…

Three men, dark-complected men—probably South American…maybe Middle-Eastern—had been talking quietly when he entered. They stopped talking when he came fully into the room. They looked at him, their eyes penetrating, piercing, while he tried to straighten and walk normally. They probably thought he had been drinking…

They watched him with eyes of distrust. One said something in a language he didn't understand, and, after following him with their dark eyes while he moved to the sink, one of the three said something, and they left the washroom.

Christopher prayed, asked that he not be on the verge of a stroke, a heart attack, or something other that would end his life with Susie.

He remembered the men had had something in their hands. They had thrown something in the trash-can in one corner, before exiting the men's room. While he dried his face with the paper towels, he glanced in the bin.

Christopher felt better, the water having helped his reeling mind find its center of balance. He threw the wadded-up towel in the can, seeing three rectangular boxes just beneath the crumpled paper. He picked two of the empty packages from the can, and looked them over. Each had a picture of something. He couldn't see clearly, his vision blurred. The boxes had an instrument of some sort pictured on one side. He shook his head and blinked, but couldn't bring the objects into focus.

The three dark-complected men had been discussing the packages, he thought. His weakness and surreal thoughts had to be from lack of food, he decided. Probably a drop in blood sugar level, or something. ... He felt better, much better.

His eyesight was not yet back to normal, but the black fuzziness was clearing. He looked into the bright, stainless framed mirror that covered most of the wall. This was, indeed, unlike any restroom he had ever seen...

Christopher looked into the mirror again. He staggered backwards when his eyes met the image that reflected. He lurched forward, the heels of his hands on the porcelain of the basin.

An old man stared back at him! Almost white hair. Age creases and wrinkles around the eyes, the forehead. The jaw drooping in dewlap fashion. The image that stared at him was aged at least 30 years beyond his own.

Christopher heard a commode flush, then the door to the stall flap open, his eyes automatically going to the reflection in the mirror. A foreign-looking man, in appearance much like that of the men who had left seconds earlier, stood glaring at him. The man was a little older looking than the other three, he determined.

To his amazement, a dark, human-shaped shadow-being stepped out of the man's body, turned to face Christopher, then darted back into the man's body to assume his form. Christopher, his mouth open in astonishment, turned from watching the reflection to see the man, to defend himself if he had to do so. But, the man was not there!

His eyes searched for a number of seconds. No one in the restroom but himself. The room had changed between the time he saw the reflection and the time he turned toward the double doors.

But, no double doors existed! Just a single door. The restroom was again like all other restrooms at Logan—like all the others, in all the other airports…

Christopher turned to look again into the mirror. A face of a man in his thirties –his own face—had replaced the countenance of a man at least 65! The mirror, itself, was different, much smaller and less well lit.

Susie met him at the door when he emerged from the men's room. Her words blurted in a tone of uncharacteristic worry. "Are you okay? I thought I would have to come in and get you."

"I'm okay, now," he said.

"You were in there nearly a half-hour, Chris," she said. "Are you sure you're alright?"

"It was strange, Susie," he said glancing at his wristwatch, seeing she was right. Thirty full minutes had passed since he entered the men's room.

"I had a hallucination, or something. At least I guess that's what it was," he said, putting his arm around his wife and beginning to walk with her toward their bags.

"A hallucination?"

"Yes, I came upon three foreign-looking men. You know, Mexicans, Arabs, or something. Did you see anybody like that come out?"

"No. And I've been right here, worried about you. As a matter of fact, I've been looking for someone to go in and check on you," she said.

"These guys, they had some little boxes, some packages they had opened. I couldn't tell what were in the packages."

"What kind of hallucination is that? Is that all there was to it?"

"No. The hallucination was the men's room, itself. The place was entirely different. I've never seen one like it. Like something out of a sci-fi movie, you know, ultra-modern…"

"Anything else?"

"I saw myself in the mirror. I looked at least 65 years old, maybe older. White hair, drooping skin. It was spooky."

Susie's eyebrows raised. What could have caused such a vision…or, whatever?

Her thoughts probed further, and she asked, "These men, you say they left the washroom?"

"That's the other strange thing. I was looking in the mirror, when I saw another guy—a Mexican, or Indian…or Arab, or something, step back into the room. Then, a dark, smoky looking human-like creature—like the one that night in the storm—stepped out of the guy's body, then back into him. I turned to look at him, and he wasn't there. Not only that, but the entire men's room was changed, back to the way it is now."

Susie looked into her husband's eyes. They looked clear again. She touched his face. No fever. The clamminess—gone…

"The dark beings, again," she said, an expression of trying to recall on her face.

"Remember that old Jewish man who was killed by those terrorists?" she asked.

"Remember?! Can't get it off my mind!" Christopher said.

"You remember what he said before he died? He quoted from the Old Testament. *"Young men shall have visions, old men shall dream dreams…"*

* * *

Sharkton, June 26—early morning

Dawn painted the Atlantic in golden-yellow light. The gulls were already at it, diving and doing their aerial acrobats in preparation for another day's fishing.

Mark and Lori stood on the rocky promontory, locked arm in arm, watching the most spectacular daybreak either had experienced.

They had slept little, Mark in a room with his father and Lori in a small third-floor room that had no windows. Despite their lack of sleep, they were as wide-awake now as they had ever been. They were truly alive, like never before in their young lives.

"It was nice of Dr. Kirban to keep an eye on your dad," Lori said, snuggling against Mark, feeling his warmth fend off the chill of the breeze blowing inland with the coming of the sun.

"He wanted to examine Dad. Said he has hope for his recovery," Mark said.

"Soon?" Laura said with a smile.

"Yeah, soon," Mark said with a chuckle.

"I wonder why he only says that word," Lori said.

"I don't know. But, at least it shows he can speak. He says it very, very clearly," Mark said with another light laugh.

"The reason I mention it, is that's what Daddy said, when he was still in a state of confusion, or whatever the problem was. He only said the word, 'soon'."

"Oh?"

"They both were subjected to the helmet and who knows what other experiments. But your father was exposed since 1947, while Daddy was subjected to experiments, or whatever, for only a matter of weeks. He's completely recovered. Maybe that means your dad will just take longer."

"Maybe," Mark said, his eyes following a pair of gulls swooping beyond the high bluff, but not really seeing them.

"Let's not waste this gorgeous morning thinking about other things," she said, turning to face him, and pulling him forward with her hands behind his neck. She stood on tiptoes to kiss him.

"Yeah. This is better than talking about other stuff," he grinned, kissing her in return, while holding her close.

Lori closed her eyes again when their lips parted. She pressed her cheek against his chest and felt the warmth of his hard body, heard the soft beat of his heart.

"Thanks, Lord," she said in a whisper.

* * *

Clark Lansing stared, unblinking, in the basement laboratory, while Gessel Kirban examined him.

The once tall, straight physicist now suffered with the stooped curvature of an old man. His years of lack of physical exercise added to his poor condition. He sat on the edge of a table, without a shirt, while Kirban listened to his chest with a stethoscope.

"You still sound pretty good," the Israeli physician and scientist said, patting Clark on his shoulder, then folding the rubber tubing of the instrument and stuffing the stethoscope into the smock's side pocket.

Kirban next looked deeply into Clark's eyes with the light instrument retrieved from a nearby tabletop.

"Ah, yes. The retina still looks quite healthy," he said, then marked the fact on a chart.

"Let us get your shirt on again, Dr. Lansing. I think our examination is finished for now."

The scientist retrieved the flannel shirt from the back of a chair.

"Your son, Mark, will be pleased to hear the result of your physical exam," Kirban said, helping his patient on with his shirt, then buttoning it for him.

"I wish I could get understanding of what is blocking your cerebral progress, however," the Israeli said. "Well, soon, perhaps."

"Soon," Clark Lansing said, his eyes still fixed in a straight-ahead stare.

Kirban stepped back, kneading his chin with his thumb and index finger, a frown of concentration on his face. He tried to recall previous experience in the matter of neurological problems and word association.

"The same as with James Morgan," he said to himself. "The word, 'soon'..."

He went to a bookcase, within which he had the night before placed a number of his books. He picked a volume, and turned through its pages, the expression of concentration still etched on his face.

He read several pages in a quick scan of each page. Finally, he closed the book, and looked upward, at nothing in particular, his eyes squinting in consideration of what he had read. A knock on the door to the lab interrupted his thoughts.

"Come!" he called in the direction of the closed door.

"I have some coffee for you," Laura said, moving carefully through the doorway with a tray, upon which sat a carafe of coffee.

"Hope you like biscuits," she said. "It's about all I could find the makings for."

"Ah! From the great American South! Love them!" the scientist said, clearing a place on a small table to make way for the impromptu breakfast.

Clark Lansing seemed to respond to the smell of the biscuits.

"Want some coffee? Maybe a biscuit or two?" Laura asked Lansing, patting his arm, and looking into his eyes.

"How is he, Dr. Kirban?" she asked.

"He does not seem to be responding at the same rate as did your husband. But, we shall see. Perhaps in time."

The Israeli sipped the hot coffee after a bite of biscuit and savored both. "Perfect, my dear Laura, just perfect."

She saw on his face a look that said he was considering how to approach her with his question. After another sip on the cup, he asked, "Laura, I must ask you...do you think James would put the PND device upon his head, one more time? For the sake of learning answers to the things involving these Dimensionals, as my late colleague, Dr. Frobe, called them?"

Laura's expression hardened, her voice abrupt.

"I don't think so, Doctor. I've just gotten him back. I will not lose him again."

"I understand fully your feelings in the matter," the scientist said. "However, I feel strongly that utilizing the instrument on the particular subjects they chose, namely, your husband, Dr. Lansing, Lori, and Mark, is the only way we are going to get to the bottom of this…evil."

"Then that's what we're going to do!"

Kirban and Laura turned to see Laura's husband, who stood in the doorway.

"Whatever it takes. It's more important than any of us," James said, walking into the laboratory.

He poured the black, steaming coffee into the empty coffee mug he brought with him, then sipped with care.

"You say it's more important than any of us?" Laura said, struggling to control her anger. "Does that include our daughter?"

"I can't stand here and tell you it doesn't scare me a little. But, I know there are things we've got to find out. Those whatever they are, they've got to be exposed," James said.

"No! Jimmy, I won't have it!" Laura's adamant declaration turned to tears of pleading. "Please, Dr. Kirban, please don't put that thing on them again."

James embraced his wife. "It's going to be okay, SuperL. We can do it safely under the right controls. Dr. Kirban knows what he's doing."

He looked to Kirban for backup.

"We will be most cautious, Laura, I assure you," the Israeli scientist said.

Laura pulled away from her husband. She glared at Kirban, then at James, before leaving the laboratory without saying anything.

"She'll be okay, Doc," Morgan said. "I'll make her see it's the only way."

Laura fought her anger while she walked up the steep stares from the basement into the pantry, through the big kitchen, and into the parlor.

How could they even consider putting on those things again? It was insane! Who knew what damage was already done?

Clark Lansing…he was a vegetable. Knew only one word.

Jennifer Lansing had lost her husband. Didn't even yet know that he was alive, if the condition he was in should be considered alive.

"Dear Lord," Laura prayed. "Give me strength."

She took a deep breath while she looked out one of the huge windows that fronted the old house. She saw her daughter and Mark starting up the steps of the front porch, hand in hand.

She managed a smile, thinking, "Some things will never change, like young love."

"Morning, Mom," Lori said cheerfully when they entered the front door.

"Good morning. You kids are up and at 'em early," Laura said. "Want some biscuits? That's about all there is around here right now. We'll have to go into Sharkton."

"We'll go. Just tell us what you need," Lori said, glancing at Mark.

"Yes. Just give us your list," he said. "I've got to get my wallet and some stuff. Be right back."

With Mark gone, Lori turned to her mother.

"Okay, Mom, what's wrong?" she asked.

"What do you mean? Everything's fine."

"And that's why your eyes are swollen?" Lori said.

"It's nothing, sweetheart. We can talk about it later," Laura said. "I can see that there's nothing wrong in your life," she said with a smile.

"Oh, Mom—I love him so much," Lori said, her expression projecting fulfilled expectations.

Silence ruled for several seconds. Laura knew something important was on her daughter's mind, and she waited, saying nothing, while looking into Lori's eyes.

"Mother," Lori began, struggling for the words. "I…I've come to know that God is real. He's real in my life…"

"Sweetheart, I'm so thankful," Laura said with a bright smile. In her thoughts, she said, *Thank you, Lord.*

"He answered my prayers, even though I didn't want to know Him," Lori said. "Is there more to knowing God, than just believing in him?"

"That's the starting point, the all-important starting point, Lori. The Bible says, 'Believe on the Lord Jesus Christ, and you will be saved'."

"And, if you believe in Jesus, that's all you do to be saved from…from what?"

"From sin. The original sin, when Adam and Eve disobeyed in the Garden of Eden."

"That's why Christ came to die on the cross. Right?" Lori said.

"See? You know more than you thought," her mother said, hugging her.

"When will Rev. Banyon get here? I've got some questions," Lori said, looking into her mother's green eyes, pleased to see that she was again happy.

Chapter 18

"**P**ortland is clear, but Boston, as we see, is still heavily fogged in," Christopher said, after hanging up the phone. He stood, looking out the hotel room's window, barely able to make out the hulking form of a huge building across the street. "They won't let anything take off for at least three hours, the girl with American Airlines said."

He let himself plop heavily onto the bed.

"Fog's unusual in June," he said, crossing his legs at the ankle, and adjusting both pillows under his head.

"I wonder what it's all about," Susie said, going to the window and looking at the dense fog. "Do you think we'll find answers at the Maine house?"

"That's why we're going up there. Dr. Kirban —Randy's Israeli-scientist friend—wants to explore some things about what somebody called 'Dimensionals.'"

Susie turned from the window to her husband, and lay beside him. He removed one pillow from behind his head and handed it to her. She lay her head back after folding and fluffing the pillow.

"These things are real, aren't they?" she asked, cutting her eyes at Chris from the pillow.

"Laura's husband and Mark Lansing have seen the same things I've been seeing. I've no doubt about what the dark creatures are," he said.

"The *bene elohim*?" Susie asked, turning onto her right side, and propping her head on her hand.

"As it was in the days of Noah, so shall it be in the days of the coming of the Son of man," he answered.

"How can we find out anything more than we already know?" Susie asked.

"The Lord will see to it that we get answers He wants us to have," Christopher said. He turned to throw an arm over her, and kiss her after pulling her to himself.

"I do pray about it. I ask that we be protected, and that you be given understanding about what to do about these…crazy things happening around us."

"What a woman!" Christopher said, kissing her again. He turned more serious.

"Since I started studying prophecy, the last days, the Second Coming, Armageddon, all those things, I've seen a pattern that runs throughout God's Word like a steel cable," he said.

Susie adjusted her position beside him, moved closer, and looked into his eyes while he explained.

"God lets the enemy do nothing without allowing his own armies to intervene to the same extent the evil one intervenes."

Susie considered his words, saying, "Yes. I can believe that."

"So, no matter what, we will have the advantage, because Christ is greater…more powerful…than anything in all of creation," Christopher said.

His wife turned onto her back again, and eased her head onto the pillow. "Yes. It is true, isn't it Christopher," she said, looking at the ceiling, but seeing only the spiritual truth in her husband's words.

"The evil one, Satan, and all of the angels that fell, they have invaded again," Susie said. "It's spiritual warfare."

"But, like you said, they are real. Not just smoke, or vapor. As a matter of fact, the unseen, spiritual world is more real than this tangible world," Christopher said. "This one will pass away, prophecy says. The spiritual world is eternal."

"Then, Dr. Kirban, how can he hope to fight against the spirit world with tangible world weapons?" she asked.

"I'm not sure what he has in mind. I take it he wants to use some of the technological things he's been working with in some way against these…things."

"And, what do you think he'll do? Have any ideas?" Susie said, again turning on her side to face him.

"The Lord works in mysterious ways. I suppose He'll let us know what it's all about when the time comes, and will tell us how to use Dr. Kirban's ideas…his technological gadgets, to accomplish the Lord's will. That is, if indeed that's what He wants."

"These *bene elohim*—Dimensionals, as Dr. Kirban calls them—if they are supernatural beings, and so powerful, and so brilliant, how can mere people have a chance? Won't they take over, like in times before the Flood? Won't they know everything we're doing to oppose them?"

Christopher turned to face his wife, considering her thought.

"Like I said, I still believe that the Lord doesn't allow Satan and his forces to move without sending His own forces into action. And, God is far above every created being. He's omnipotent. He can blind them to our movement, our activity. Seems to me we've been enlisted to fight some sort of battle at this time in history."

"Seems like Satan must use human beings to accomplish his evil work," Susie said. "Makes sense, then, that the Lord chooses, now days, to use people to fight the Devil's human forces."

"The Devil's indwelt human forces," Christopher added. "Possession is real. I believe that's what I was shown in the men's room at Logan Airport. These Dimensionals possess their human hosts."

"Wonder what that was all about?" Susie said. "You really believe it was a vision?"

"Maybe we can find our answers at Mitford House," her husband said.

* * *

San Antonio, Texas, Noon June 27, 1967

Randall Prouse watched the busy construction activity going on outside the tinted tour bus window. Hemisfair—the latest of the proliferating world's fairs—was on schedule for its 1968 exposition.

Helmeted construction workers moved about in the bright, June sun, while heavy machinery muscled structural steel into place. But, his thoughts weren't on things afoot on the south side of San Antonio. His mind was on all of the things involved with Christopher Banyon and the strange trip to Israel.

He didn't hear the chatter of the 40 students he had brought to SA for a tour of the Alamo. He heard only the sound of the vicious storm that had driven Susie Banyon and him up the embankment and into the cave near Qumran. The thunderous crashes of the storm while over the Atlantic. The automatic weapons fire at the Wailing Wall, and the words of the dying Jewish religious man: "*Old men shall dream dreams...Young men shall see visions.*"

A sudden whoop of delighted college students jerked the professor from his thoughts of that appalling scene. He looked around to see the cause of the commotion. The students were laughing and talking, just having a good time. He would probably never know the reason for their outburst, nor would want to know.

The trip to the Alamo was his...how many? His one-hundredth? If he were not taking a class to the national historic site at least once a semester, he was taking one visiting relative or another.

This visit was to examine with several archaeologists who specialized in the Mexican Wars of the 1830s, archaeological finds of recent vintage. It would be exciting for the students. He preferred digs in the Middle East, in Jerusalem, in particular.

A tall, partially finished structure in the distance captured his thoughts. The Hemisfair's Tower of the Americas was almost at its full height. It would have a restaurant that revolved, according to his understanding—it would be a good place to bring friends when they visited.

Minutes later, the big tour bus pulled, to a stop in front of the world-famous mission-fortress. The place where Crockett, Bowie, and Travis, along with more than 180 other men, died fighting Santa Anna's thousands.

Leaving the air-conditioned bus made the cloudless day feel even warmer than the 90 degrees that greeted Prouse when he stepped onto the expanse of man-laid walkway in front of the Alamo. His thoughts returned again to events of the time spent in Jerusalem, and at Qumran.

Something bothered him about the time spent in the Dead Sea cave. Maybe he was making too much of it. But, he had never seen a storm like it. It came from nowhere during a season storms rarely happen. It came from the east, another nearly unheard-of thing in that locality. It drove Susie Banyon and him into the cave.

And, only Susie could go farther into the cavern once they had reached the first chamber. The whole episode was supernatural. Christopher Banyon said the fragments burst into flames, the explaining to Yadin of which was not easy. Yet his Arab-Christian friend had not seemed surprised, had only smiled, and told him not to be concerned.

What was the purpose? What went on in those rearmost chambers of the caverns? What was the deity telling them?

His analysis brought him to the realization. It was the thing that was bugging him. The Lord purposely kept him from going farther into the cave, from being a part of whatever went on in those innermost recesses of the Qumran caverns.

And, why had he not, like Christopher Banyon, seen the titanic struggle outside the airplane, in another supernaturally sent storm, this one over the Atlantic?

"Dr. Prouse."

The girl's words popped the bubble of his remembrances of the recent trip.

"Yes?"

"Dr. Martinez wants to speak to you about the artifact lecture," the co-ed said, looking up at the big archaeologist, her fingers shielding her eyes against the midday sun.

"Yeah, okay, Sherri. Tell him I'll be right there."

The cool air felt good once he entered the Alamo's front door for tourist traffic, his eyes slowly adjusting to the dark interior.

"We will go straight to the area of the newly discovered artifacts," he said. "Afterwards, be prepared with any questions for Dr. Martinez you might come up with."

He walked in front of the students, toward the rear of the Alamo complex, where the Mexican-born archaeologist, Juan Martinez, had prepared what some were calling the most exciting finds in recent years.

The prospects should excite him. In other times, he would be enthralled, no doubt. But, all he could think of now was that he had to get back into the loop in the matters of Christopher Banyon's dream-visions of the *bene elohim*…and his friend Gessel Kirban's strange helmet device…

* * *

The fog hadn't lifted within the expected 3 hours. Their flight to Portland was delayed by more than 6 hours, and the drive had taken another hour and 45 minutes.

Gessel Kirban had offered to let Lori and Mark drive his Jeep wagon to Portland to meet them. But, all had bowed to James Morgan's reasoning that the less the wagon—familiar to the Taos people—was exposed, the better.

The rental car they took from Portland could be turned in at Boothbay. Sharkton had no affiliate for leaving it there. Christopher would drive it to Boothbay tomorrow, he thought, turning the tan Plymouth off Crab Cove Road, and onto the rough, narrow road leading through the copse of trees, toward Mitford House.

"Well, there it is," he said when they emerged from the last twist of the gravel road, the headlights cutting through the darkness and illuminating the 3-story structure.

"My, it is big, isn't it?" Susie said, seeing the gothic spires and

Victorian gables.

"Told you it was spooky at night," Christopher said.

"It's beautiful," she corrected. "Because it's yours."

"It's ours," Christopher said.

"Aunt Annabel Lee was beautiful. That's for sure," Christopher said, swinging the car to the right, and pulling along by the side of the old home.

"She had no kids...she and my uncle," he said, switching off the headlights and cutting the engine.

"She left the house, everything to me. I have no idea how much, but we'll find out within a month, Mom says."

Before he could reach for the door handle, the door opened.

"Pastor!"

Laura Morgan leaned to hug him, while he sat behind the wheel. "Boy! Am I glad to see you!" she said. "Both of you," she added, reaching past the minister to pat and squeeze Susie Banyon's arm with her right hand.

"My, it's nice to be missed," Christopher said, returning her hug.

* * *

Randall Prouse brooded over the Scriptures. The piece of Biblical knowledge had grated the back of his mind while Juan Martinez lectured on the newly found artifacts of Santa Anna's assault on those who had defended the Alamo in 1836. The grating had continued, and grown more abrasive the rest of the day.

The worry had to do with Gessel Kirban's technology; Prouse knew that much. Something to do with the helmet Kirban had tried to tell him about in their brief phone conversations, when the scientist called him in Jerusalem.

He couldn't bring to the forefront of his brain exactly what part of Scripture he was looking for. But, he knew it was relevant —and that it must be remembered. The Israeli scientist had told him that the...Dimensionals...as he called them, were somehow channeling their thoughts through human brains.

The precognition neuro-diviner, Kirban had told him, was meant for use with other highly advanced technologies, to assist American and Israeli fighter pilots in air combat. But, the PND helmet was turned into some hideous instrument to control the minds of humans…At least that was the plans of the project called "Dark Dimension," the sinister brain-child of a super-secret cabal within the legitimate Taos military project. Kirban had, somehow, learned of the cabal. The Israeli couldn't tell him how he found out, because the scientist didn't know. The knowledge of the secret enclave—it was just there, in his mind-bank of knowledge.

Supernatural…had to be…

Kirban hurriedly told him, during a subsequent call, that he had found a way, he thought, to use the helmet device to channel positive thoughts that would overcome the evil thoughts.

And, that was the rub in Prouse's mind. He had finally found the Scripture. It was so simple…why had he not been able to immediately think of it?

What Gessel Kirban proposed was against God's commandments. To use mind control for channeling thoughts or anything else, seemed, Scripturally, to be as forbidden as the way the super-clandestine group planned to use the PND in the Dark Dimension project.

Prouse moved his right fingertips through the pages of his old Bible. He stopped at the portion he sought, and read. It was Deuteronomy 18: 10: *"There shall not be found among you [any one] that maketh his son or his daughter to pass through the fire, [or] that useth divination, [or] an observer of times, or an enchanter, or a witch…"*.

He quickly turned pages again, then stopped, and after several seconds of intensively exploring the passage, read from 1 Samuel, Chapter 28, verses 6 through 9: *"And when Saul enquired of the LORD, the LORD answered him not, neither by dreams nor by Urim, nor by prophets. Then said Saul unto his servants, Seek me a woman that hath a familiar spirit, that I may go to her, and enquire of her. And his servants said to him, Behold, there is a woman that hath a familiar spirit at Endor. And Saul disguised himself, and put on other raiment, and he went, and two men with him, and they came to the woman by night: and he said, I pray thee, divine unto me by the familiar spirit, and bring me him up, whom I shall name unto thee. And the woman said unto him, Behold, thou knowest what Saul hath done, how he hath cut off those that have familiar spirits, and the wizards, out of the land: wherefore then layest thou a snare for my life to cause me to die...?"*

Prouse looked up from the page, and cerebrally digested the story before he reread the passage.

Gessel had told him that he, Kirban, did not invent the PND helmet, but had made it functional for use in the fighter aircraft. Rumors were about, the Israeli scientist had told him, that the technology was a product of reverse engineering. That it had come to be out of an extensive clandestine operation called "Project Jehovah." Prouse had heard the scientist's laugh of skepticism when Kirban said that some believed it was a result of technology recovered when the disks—the UFOs—crashed near Roswell in 1947. Could it be? Could the PND device have developed from technology planted by...?

"You going to stay in here all night, again?" Ruth Prouse put her hands on her husband's shoulders, while he sat looking over the old Bible that was filled with underlined passages and his scribbled marginal notes.

"Sorry, Ruthie," he said, lifting her hand and kissing it. "There's some pretty heavy stuff going on. I've got to get a handle on it," he said, returning his attention to the opened Bible on his desk's top.

"What's the heavy stuff that keeps you from my always exciting bed chamber, my love?" Ruth said provocatively, running an index finger over his left ear.

"It's the weird goings-on with Chris, the whole strange thing," he said, ignoring her playfulness. "I believe there are some watershed prophetic things setting up here, and I can't get a grip on them—not completely."

"What's so strange? You mean the dreams, or nightmares Chris has been having?" she asked, standing behind him and massaging his neck and shoulder muscles. She felt him respond to the kneading she was providing.

"Feel good?" she asked.

"Ummmm." He moved his neck and shoulders to make the rub even better. "These creatures, I'm convinced—Chris is convinced—they are part of the whole UFO thing. The 1947 crash at Roswell, New Mexico."

"UFOs! Hope you aren't telling that to the people at the college," Ruth said with a laugh. "They won't let you deal with the precious students. Their parents will pull them out, if they think they've got a UFO kook on staff."

"Only they're not UFOs, or extraterrestrials," he said. "They're something far harder to deal with than green men from other planets."

"Oh, it's okay, then," she bantered. "If you tell the administration and the parents that you think these things are spirit beings, fallen angels, Satan and the boys, rather than little green men from outer space, it will all be okay. They'll all understand."

"Yeah. Guess they wouldn't understand either of those, would they?" he said. "I've got to tell them something, because I've got to get to Maine."

"Ever consider taking some vacation time?" she asked, with mock irritation in her voice.

He reached above his shoulders to grab both of her wrists, then pulled her forward and kissed her on the cheek. The action turned into a more serious embrace when he swiveled his desk chair and pulled his wife into his lap.

"I know, I'm a rat. I've been all over the world in these last two years, but you've been stuck here."

He looked into her eyes, and brushed her lips with his.

"Forgive me?"

She smiled. "Sure."

"Think the kiddos could stand it if we went on a vacation alone?" he asked.

"Who cares?" she said with feigned callousness. "They've been weaned. Let them forage for themselves."

Coming from the most attentive of all mothers, her words caused him to burst into laughter.

"That's my chick!" he said, hugging her and giving her a deep, theatrical kiss.

"Watch it, Tex," she said, continuing her out-of-character tone. "I don't ride with just any ol' wrangler."

"Not even to back East, Ma'am?" her husband asked in his best effort at cowboyese.

"In that case, Cowboy, when's the next stage out of town?" she asked, adding her most seductive smile.

* * *

Washington D.C., the evening of June 27, 1967

Mallory O'Rourke drummed his desk with his right fingertips. He looked upward at the white-tiled ceiling of his tiny National Security Agency office. He let his anger escape in a long, seething breath between his teeth. His patience was wearing thin, while he waited for the deputy director of Covert Operations for DOD to get on the line with him.

No, he remembered with a grimace, the man was now director, not deputy director...

O'Rourke was one of a handful of sub-strata Kennedy Administration holdovers. Never a highly publicized member of the now well-known "Irish Mafia" with which Jack Kennedy surrounded himself while President, he nonetheless was included in the inner circle of Sorenson, O'Brien, O'Donnel, Powers and the rest.

He didn't deserve this second-class citizen treatment, and he cursed Robert Cooper beneath his breath for making him hang on the phone for more than five minutes. Daniel Eganberg would have never shown such disrespect...

"Mr. O'Rourke?" the female voice on the other end of the line said.

"Yes?"

"I'm trying to run the director down. I'm sure he will be with you in a moment or two," the young woman said, hoping in her most vivacious voice to assuage the Irishman's profile-notated temper.

"We had this phone appointment, Miss..."

He waited for her response.

"Lucy Holland," she said.

"Miss Holland, tell the director that if he wants to know what the President has directed for NSA, regarding his operation, he will have to make an appointment when I can find time to talk. Got that message?"

"Yes, sir. Got it. I will certainly..."

But, the irate O'Rourke had already slammed the receiver on the cradle of his multi-buttoned phone console.

The clandestine systems director for NSA slammed the side of his fist on the desk's top. The Kennedy people were being relegated to diminishing positions of influence. No doubt because of the big, clumsy, crude Texan's preparations to win his second term.

The Presidency belonged to Robert Kennedy, not Lyndon Johnson. When Bobby became President, the Kennedy people would again be given the appropriate respect they—he— deserved.

It was the only thing keeping him holding on with fingernails and toenails to this inconsequential job. When Bobby was in the Oval Office, he, Mallory O'Rourke, would have the needed expertise in the agency's clandestine activities to—he hoped— catapult him into an office very near the new President Kennedy.

But, Johnson was a powerful man. Robert Kennedy and Lyndon Johnson hated each other. Johnson would see to it that all Kennedy appointees, at all levels, were kept under his considerable-sized thumb.

Vietnam was the only hope. The growing discontent might, just might, possibly, convince the Texas tyrant to retire, rather than seek a second full term.

Not likely, O'Rourke thought. Johnson lived for power. He, like the Kennedys, would never put aside his own love of power for the love of country.

Robert Cooper. He was a hard one to figure. A strange bird, indeed. His rise from a courier for the State Department, to Director of Covert Operations for Defense, was meteoric, phenomenal. The death of Daniel Eganberg was equally strange.

Weirder things had happened, than in-house assassination.

The President, the pretend President, wanted to know all there was to know about Covert Operations at Defense. He obviously didn't trust McNamara, a Kennedy man—and a Republican at that—to do the necessary investigative documentation of Covert Operations' doings.

Johnson—rather, somebody close to him, gave the job of finding out about Project Jehovah, and all attendant to it, to NSA. Johnson wanted to create a checks and balances system the President hoped would get to the truth, so he would know all there was to know. Lyndon Johnson always had to know it all; it was his key to ruling with an iron fist.

What they didn't realize was that the job of beginning to route out the truth of the connections flowing from Roswell in 1947, through the Jehovah Project in 1967, had been turned over to a Kennedy man.

* * *

At the same moment, Taos, New Mexico

The Director of Covert Operations would take no chances. The consequences of failure were unthinkable. He—personally—could know all that was going on, only by wearing the PND. Nothing the instrument could do to him would be worse than failure to maintain an absolute grip on the situation with regard to the fugitives.

Cooper stood on the metal platform, his mind reeling with sensations he had not experienced. Kaleidoscopic colors and shapes transformed his cognitive processes into imagined excursions that took mind and spirit from body.

He viewed the world of the Dimensionals for the first time. Before, they had entered his realm of cerebral inner-space. Now, he had entered theirs, and, through the technology, he seemed... was...transported into the time/space orbit of the dark beings who had taken him under their...wings? Was that the proper term for it?

He saw, now, not through his own eyes, which Lucy Holland, when she entered the oval chamber, noticed were turned so far upward, that only their whites could be seen between the quivering eyelids spasming beneath the precognition neuro-diviner. He saw clearly and with preternatural vision, through the transfixed eyes of Clark Lansing.

"Mr. Director," the young woman said, seeing Cooper standing atop the gleaming platform. "Are you all right?"

Cooper didn't hear or acknowledge the secretary. He saw only what Clark Lansing saw, a large room, filled with test tubes, shelves of chemicals, and myriads of laboratory paraphernalia.

"Mr. Cooper," Lucy Holland said, moving closer to the director, who continued to look toward the ovaled top of the room, his eyelids fluttering.

Lucy Holland stood at the base of the platform, riveted by the scene, wondering what she should do to get his attention. The President of the United States wanted his attention. She must, somehow, make him aware.

A dense, black mass, the shape of its host's body, emerged from Cooper. The girl's eyes widened in terror when she saw the creature, its huge eyes like burning coals, its slitted mouth widening to expose a cavernous void with fang-like teeth guarding its opening.

Chapter 19

L ori let the warm water hit her face. She reached upward to adjust the old shower nozzle. She guessed she was lucky that such an old house had a shower. And, it did seem out of place, more-or-less modern shower fixtures protruding from the wall at one end of the huge, antique bathtub.

The water felt good, and that was all that mattered.

She reached again to the fixtures, turning the left handle that was the hot water. She would make it as hot as she could stand it, because hot water streaming hard against her skin always seemed to help her relax.

She could relax now, she considered while she reminisced about time she and Mark had spent together today, enjoying the trip to Sharkton. The quaint shops that were not quaint at all to the almost stereotypical New England natives of the little town at the inward most point of the inlet.

She turned both knobs more fully to achieve a harder stream of hot water, then had to pull the shower curtain together at each end of the tub to prevent spray wetting the walls outside the tub.

This third floor bathroom was perfect. She could take her time. There were plenty of other bathrooms; no one would need this one…

Mark led his father by the arm, and directed him to be seated on the edge of the bed of the second-floor bedroom. The room was huge, with 14-foot ceilings and a large door at least 8 feet tall, with a transom above that.

Mark figured rooms of homes of this vintage were probably so constructed in order to take advantage of the sea breezes during the warmest months. But, the house was no doubt full of unwanted draftiness during the brutal cold time of year, the home sitting atop the bluff where Atlantic gales could find their way through every crack...

The place was fascinating, but the upkeep would be expensive. He and Lori would find, or build, a house of a more practical sort...

"Dad. I'm going to take my shower, now," Mark said, bending to look his father directly in the eyes. "Do you need help getting ready for bed?"

Clark Lansing glanced at his son, and then resumed his straight-ahead stare.

"Here," Mark said, unbuttoning the top two buttons of his father's shirt.

"Can you take it from here?" he questioned, trying to capture and hold Clark's attention.

His father began the process of slowly unbuttoning the remaining buttons, but continued to stare straight ahead.

"I'm turning back your bed," his son said, pulling the cover neatly back from one corner of the big bed. "See, here." He patted the area he had just cleared. "You lie down, when you're ready. I won't be long."

He looked again into his dad's eyes. His pupils were slightly dilated, but Gessel Kirban had assured it was the result of the extended use of the PND. The pupils were already decreasing in size, the Israeli had said.

What would he tell his mother? Despite his happiness at being with Lori again, the one thing that bothered him was that he had to tell his mother...

How would she react? His mother loved his father. He knew that, because of the hours she spent going through pictures, and his father's things. Mark, when a boy, often found her going through them, even when she wasn't showing her son the many tangible memories.

He would find a way to make it okay, he thought. His mother was happy with her husband, and his father was…he had another lifetime to live.

"I'll be back, Dad," Mark said, patting his father's shoulder, then bending to kiss his forehead. "Won't be long."

Thunder rumbled in the distance, and Clark turned his head to see the sheer curtain that wafted in the breeze that blew suddenly into the room through the open window.

Thunder crashed again, this time louder, the storm moving from the sea less than a quarter of a mile below.

Clark Lansing stared straight ahead again, his eyes upon the door through which Mark had walked a minute earlier. His pupils dilated wider, and his hands began shaking, as if afflicted by palsy. His eyes turned upward until the irises were all but covered by the upper lids.

His whole body convulsed in one sudden spasm before it settled to absolute stillness. Thunder rumbled above the old home again. Wind blew harder through the window, causing drapery to slap against a vase that sat on a table. The vase shattered against the portion of the hardwood floor not covered by the large oval rug.

A black mass left the man's body while the host sat on the edge of the bed. The featureless thing stood, its human-shaped limbs sparking with ominous arcs of electricity-like flashes.

The creature moved across the room and stepped through the shut bedroom door. Lori shut her eyes, turning her head upward to let the riverlets of hot water pour down her face, then her body.

A shower was not the best place to be in an electrical storm, she thought. But, it felt so good…What were the odds? A random strike that would affect her here…in this wonderful, hot shower?

When she opened her eyes, she saw the lights in the bathroom dim, then blink. They went out briefly, and then returned to full illumination.

Guess it would be best to get out, she thought, turning to face the shower knobs. The lights flickered again, before she could turn the knobs, and she reflexively turned to see if they would go out again.

The storm seemed directly over the old house, a clap of thunder shaking the dwelling to its foundation. The lights dimmed again, went out, then flashed on and off for several seconds.

Lori saw, between the shorting out of light, a black figure pass through the wall at the end of the tub. She tried to scream, but the scream got caught in her throat.

The thing stepped the rest of the way through the wall and the end of the bathtub. It stood glaring at her. Its eyes seemed to be burned, red-hot coals from the sulfurous embers of the creature's own dimension.

Lori stood, her terrorized mind calling upon the only source able to help her.

"God! Jesus! Help me!" she managed to blurt.

The monstrosity would possess her...as it had done in times past. It would have her soul!

The beast lurched forward, its limbs and tentacle-like fingers sparking while it reached for her. Lori backed as far in one corner of the ancient tub as she could, cringing, her eyes wide, her mouth unable to expel her fear.

The massive human-shaped beast slammed against her, with intention to indwell its one-time host. When the thing touched her body, the entire room flashed and crackled in a deafening electrical discharge.

Lori felt nothing. The black, convoluting form seemed to come apart, to disintegrate then quickly reform. Its mouth was agape, its shark-like teeth gnashing, its blood-red eyes pulsing with the intensity of embers fanned by a sudden rush of wind.

It reached to put its long, undulating fingers upon her arms. Again a powerful burst of electric-like discharge lit the entire room in a blinding flash.

Lori shut her eyes and prayed while she cringed, awaiting the next assault. When she again opened her eyes, she found herself alone in the shower; she heard only the running of water cascading from the shower nozzle, and muffled thunder from the storm that had passed and now receded in the distant.

She screamed... At last, she could scream!

* * *

Robert Cooper's eyelids fluttered, his eyes again able to take in his present surroundings within the oval chamber. He looked to the rounded walls. All were in place, each wearing their PND device. Something was amiss, and he tried to clear his thinking, removing the PND helmet from his own head.

Something was wrong. Something had intervened...

Cooper saw his secretary, who stood near the double doors. She was frightened, and could only stand, cowering, unable to speak or move.

He stepped from the platform and placed the PND on the platform's surface, than quickly walked to the girl.

"What are you doing here, Miss Holland?" he demanded, grabbing her forearms. She didn't respond.

"Lucy! What are you doing here?!" he shouted, shaking her.

She blinked, as if clearing her senses. She looked at him, her eyes filled with terror.

"Sir...the...the President...rather, Mr. O'Rourke has a message from the President for you..." she said in a whimper.

* * *

Lori's father was the first to arrive at the third floor bathroom door. He tried the door. It was locked.

"Lori! Are you in there?!" he shouted, shaking the doorknob.

Christopher Banyon joined James Morgan, who again shouted.

"Lori!"

He started to put his shoulder to the door, when the door unlocked and opened.

Lori stood shivering in her robe, water still beaded on her face.

Her father hugged her. "Are you okay, Sunshine?"

She said nothing, but nodded "yes."

"What happened?" Christopher asked, seeing that the girl seemed in shock.

"Lori!" Mark said, while rushing into the hallway, still dripping water, wearing only his jeans.

* * *

Morning of June 28

"I don't know, Daddy, maybe it was just the storm. Maybe lightning struck the pipes, and that's what I thought was … whatever I thought."

Lori was still frightened. Still wasn't ready to talk about the terror of the night before. But, she knew her father, the pastor, Dr. Kirban and her mother had to be told.

They had waited, let her have a night's sleep, before going over everything again, more slowly, so as to make sense of it all.

"It's okay," Mark said, while sitting with his arm around her on the sofa. "We're here. It's over. Nothing can scare you now."

"Just take your time, Baby," Lori's mother said. "We won't let anything happen to you. You won't be left alone again."

"The lights were flickering—because of the storm, I guess. Then, this dark, man-like thing. I don't know. It was probably my imagination from the lightning strike—because of the stories of the dark creatures in Mark's and Dad's nightmares, or whatever. The whole room sounded like the electric chair or something was operating. The whole room was buzzing with the sounds of electricity."

Lori's memory cleared.

"No. The thing, I saw it, before the lightning strike. Not after the lightning."

"The house was never struck by lightning," Christopher

Banyon said, giving a concerned glance to James Morgan, then to Laura and Kirban.

"We had no lightning strikes, just some browning out," Gessel Kirban affirmed.

"Then, what was it?" Lori asked.

"You say this dark being walked right through a solid wall?" the Israeli scientist asked.

"Yes, and through a solid bath tub. If I haven't gone crazy, that's what happened," Lori said.

Mark felt a shiver convulse her body, while he held her close.

"I am afraid they have found us," Kirban said. "Or something other…"

"Something other? What are you talking about, Doc?" James asked.

"Perhaps they have been with us all along, or, have come to us through Mark's father," the Israeli said.

"Dad?" Mark said

"Possibly. We shall see," Gessel Kirban said, with a scientist's resolve.

* * *

Robert Cooper had been kept waiting long enough. More than 10 minutes. The fact that he had stayed on the line meant he was worried about what was in the offing from D.C.

"Bob? You there?" the familiar voice asked through the phone receiver at Cooper's ear.

"Mal! How are you?" the heavily perspiring Cooper said, forcing a smile.

"Sorry to keep you on the line," Mallory O'Rourke lied, himself sporting a feigned smile.

"Been with the President just now," O'Rourke said, with smug satisfaction in his tone. "Wants us to do the regular check-up—nothing to fret about."

Many thoughts ran through Cooper's mind, and he dabbed at

the sweat on his face while he spoke.

"Great! We welcome the agency," he lied.

The National Security Agency was home to a bitter bunch of people whom he didn't want rummaging through his kingdom. Project Jehovah was begun at NSA. Defense had stolen it from them. Now he, Cooper, alone, had full knowledge of the true nature of the things stemming from Roswell—and before. They wanted to come in to Covert Operations and plow up all of it. They couldn't be allowed…

"Bob, now, we've had our differences in the past, and I know the position you're in, with your having just assumed the job of director. We intend to make this as quick and as painless as possible."

"No problem, Mal. We've nothing to hide at Covert Operations," the Director said with a laugh. ·

"We promise not to steal any secrets, Bob. We just want to give the President what he needs to understand everything that's happened with regard to these sightings, and so forth."

O'Rourke's feigned gentleness and singsong whine didn't fool him. NSA snoops were going to give his operation an anal exam such as it had never experienced.

"Really, the President just wants to have a clear understanding at this particular point in time, Bob, because of the change in administration head. Your taking Daniel's place, and so forth."

"Hey…understandable. As I said, we will cooperate. Whatever it takes to get Mr. Johnson the information he needs."

"Good! Good! We begin Monday. Nine o'clock, bright and early!"

When the connection was broken between Taos and Washington, D.C., Cooper sat, glaring into his surroundings, seeing nothing, his brain in hyper-drive. Two words kept stabbing into the deepest reaches of his mind: "Dark Dimension."

He was the only one who truly knew the scope and breadth of the heart of Covert Operations. The creatures from Roswell, they somehow had seen to it that no one but himself could look into the totality of "Dark Dimension."

They would have again –in their own special ways—to keep these presidentially appointed NSA bloodsuckers from getting to the project.

NSA already knew about Majestic-12, and later Jehovah, the seminal projects that came from the Roswell era. Another President –Dwight Eisenhower—had appointed NSA to handle things, then. Einstein and Oppenheimer were the geniuses who held the accumulating secrets during that era. The Department of Defense had taken over through cabinet-level maneuverings, when Einstein and Oppenheimer had passed from the scene. Project Jehovah, the name given the matters involved in the Roswell incident, seemed a gift from the Almighty. The many technologies that flowed from reverse engineering things found within the wreckage were far too crucial to be trusted to NSA.

And, now, Cooper, practically alone so far as human involvement was concerned, knew the true secrets. He, alone, knew the intricate details of "Dark Dimension," the name he gave the project the...things...chose him to implement.

But, he was no longer the only one to know the forbidden things. The things NSA wanted desperately to find out about and take back under their control. They had their methods. They were on the verge of pinpointing the location of James and Lori Morgan, Kirban, and the others.

He must bring the escapees from the complex back. Put them under lock and key, under the total control of his powerful associates. Or the fugitives would have to be eliminated. Either way, the time to move was now!

* * *

Just after noon, June 29 – Mitford House

Randall and Ruth Prouse arrived at late-morning, and although bone-tired, the archaeologist insisted on having his say. He had spent the morning on the plane rides going over his study of the matter before them.

"You can't go to the government with it, Chris. Either they won't believe what you tell them, or worse."

Prouse hesitated, trying within his thoughts to make sense of the best course of action.

"Worse?" Gessel Kirban asked from across the kitchen table. "What, worse?"

"It just hit me," Prouse said, a look of epiphany crossing his face. "That's what I was being told in my reading the account of Saul's encounter with the witch of Endor, the prophet Samuel."

"What?" Christopher Banyon said impatiently.

Prouse seemed to go into a thought-trance for a few seconds, while his partners in conversation looked at each other, than again to the archaeologist with frustration in their expressions.

"Out with it, Randy," Christopher said, even though frustrated, amused at his friend's lack of forthcoming. It was not like Randall Prouse to be at a loss for words.

"Oh! I was thinking. Saul represented the government of Israel at that time. The channeler—the witch—was terrified that the king would find out she had been doing the forbidden things... channeling, prophesying, that sort of thing. Yet, there she sat, talking to the very king she was terrified of, not recognizing him because of his disguise. Saul wanted answers. He was willing to make a deal with the Devil to get them. Saul...the government... in league with the dark forces..."

Prouse looked at Chris, then at Kirban. "Don't you see? You can't tell the government. Even if you had absolute proof. They are already in league with the powers, the principalities, with wickedness in high, supernatural places. It's there in Ephesians 6: 11-12."

"All very interesting," the Israeli said, after a moment of thought. "But, what are we then to do with the knowledge that these things are again invading?"

"Maybe it's not possible to do anything at all," Christopher said. "Maybe we can somehow delay the inevitable. I don't know.

All I know is that we've been brought to this point for some reason. We've prayed about it, taken action as best we know how. The rest is up to the Lord."

"Perhaps it is His Divine will that we use material means, the things we've been given, to get to the heart of things," Gessel Kirban said. "I have ideas...call them theories about these dark beings. I believe it is possible to turn the tables."

"What things do we have that we've been given?" Christopher said.

"The precognition neuro-diviner. I propose conversing with the thing indwelling Dr. Lansing," the scientist said.

"But, channeling...divining of every sort is expressly forbidden in God's Word," Prouse said. "We might be guilty of the same things as those interacting with these *bene elohim*..."

"But, didn't God use the evil powers of the woman at Endor, the witch, to accomplish channeling, to tell Saul he would be replaced by David as king of Israel?" Christopher said.

Prouse considered the minister's words. "Point well made," he said.

Christopher turned to the Israeli scientist. "But how can we converse...with an evil spirit? Wouldn't the thing just leave, or clam up?"

"This is where I believe forces for good will ride to the rescue," Kirban said with a smile. "Let us see if we can catch ourselves a spook."

Chapter 20

Mitford House, June 29

"I must issue a warning," Gessel Kirban said, adjusting the PND helmet on Clark Lansing's head. "If what I believe to be the case is true, we are opening up the gates of...I don't know what, exactly."

"Is it going to hurt Dad?" Mark said. "Because if it will, then we'll just have to forget this experiment, Dr. Kirban."

"No, there will be no pain. You've worn the device for long hours. Do you recall pain?"

"No, but, I don't remember much of anything of the time I wore the helmet."

"The danger I'm speaking of is from the thing that indwells your father. I believe that once the PND is switched on, the thing possessing Dr. Lansing will find itself entrapped—unable to escape the technology's hold. At least that is my theory, my sincere belief, based upon my findings," the scientist said, making final adjustments to the helmet. "I have no idea how the entity might react."

"What do you hope to accomplish by this?" Randall Prouse asked, coming close to satisfy his curiosity about the gleaming golden device.

"I am of the belief that, possibly, we can talk directly with the creature within Dr. Lansing, the thing that indwells his core being," Kirban said.

The scientist looked up from his task of adjusting the device. "Please turn the switch for the lights to its lowest setting," he instructed to Laura Morgan, who stood nearest the rheostat switch on the wall. She complied, and the laboratory dimmed until everything within the room became barely visible. Kirban took a tiny examination light from his smock's breast pocket, and shined into Clark Lansing's eyes.

The Israeli threw a switch on a table near where he sat, activating the helmet.

"See, here," he bid Prouse, James Morgan and the others to come closer. "The pupils open, almost at once, to full dilation."

"You're sure it's not hurting him," Lori said, her arm around Mark, sharing his worry.

"No...he is in no pain. Now, let us see what lies beyond those dilated pupils."

The scientist scooted his chair to in front of Clark, staring into the man's eyes.

"I call upon you who inhabit this host to speak," the scientist said. "What is your name?"

Clark Lansing said nothing, continuing to stare straight ahead, his eyes black, and unblinking.

Kirban looked away, considering his next tact. He glanced at each concerned face.

"I believe we can make contact, only if another wears the PND."

"Who?" Prouse said. "I'll try it."

"I feel very much that this is more a spiritual matter than a physical one," Kirban said. "This might sound strange coming from one who has devoted most of his life to the belief that man, alone, controls his own universe. But, I have been persuaded differently, thanks to the faith I have seen..."

He looked to each person in the room. "We must have someone with great faith to wear the helmet, to ask the questions," Kirban said.

"I'll do it," Christopher Banyon said. "Do you really think that thing will work, if one of us wears it to try to communicate to the spirit, if it does indwell him?"

"Yes," Kirban answered with confidence.

"I want to help."

All eyes went to Susie Banyon, who stepped forward.

"No! Absolutely not," Christopher said. "You're not putting that thing on. It's too dangerous."

Susie looked up at her husband, her brown eyes telling him that her volunteering was beyond either of their right to object. "I'll be okay, Chris."

"Very well," Kirban said, inferring that the minister's silence meant he agreed with his wife. The scientist got up from the chair, and helped Susie take his place. "You will feel only a bit light headed," he said. "Just relax. We will instruct as to what to ask, how to engage the entity, if it indeed indwells, as I believe."

Kirban switched on the second device when the helmet was in place.

"Ask the entity its name," the scientist instructed.

"Your name…give me your name," Susie said.

Clark Lansing's facial muscles twitched, his mouth began to move. Still, there was no sound.

Kirban started to instruct Susie again, when she spoke without prompting.

"In the name of Jesus Christ, I command you to tell me your name. Tell me your name," she said in a voice that seemed stronger, more authoritative than her own.

Christopher Banyon moved forward as if he would touch her, help her. Randall Prouse restrained him.

"She's okay, Chris," Prouse said.

Clark Lansing's eyes looked to be all black pupil. A scowl replaced his former placid expression.

The words hissed from the grinning mouth. "Our name is Legion…"

A voice from another time, another place. A growl emanating

from within the human host. They were witnessing conversation between this world and some other. Each felt the sensation. Chilling ripples of realization traversed the spine. They watched and listened in transfixed fascination within the laboratory's semi-darkness.

"Ask about…"

"Where do you come from?" Susie asked, interrupting the Israeli scientist's prompting. Kirban backed off, amazed that the questions coming from the woman seemed to originate from a source that had the authority to preempt his own.

"From a far away galaxy," the thing within Clark Lansing replied with a hiss.

"Liar!" the woman accused. "In the name of Christ…from where do you come?"

"From other dimensions. From many times and places." The voice seemed weakened, whimpering.

"Why are you here, at this time, at this place?"

A snarling, agonizing growl crawled from Clark Lansing's throat, then the voice spoke.

"To seduce," it said.

"Seduce? In what way?" Susie questioned.

The thing within Clark Lansing snickered, then snarled, "To present the taking away, when the time is come."

"Explain this taking away. How will you seduce?"

"We will not divulge."

"In the name of Jesus Christ!" Susie shouted.

Clark Lansing's body lurched backward, his head bowing forward before straightening. His pupils were huge; froth bubbled from the sides of his mouth and over his lower lip.

"In the name of the Lord Jesus Christ! Tell me about what you mean by the taking away. How will you seduce?"

The voice from within Lansing echoed. More subdued, however, it explained in a child-like whine.

"We will delude through the RAPTURE. We will show the taking away is the work of the RAPTURE," it said, the voice trailing off.

"Explain this…RAPTURE…It is not the Rapture prophesied by the Apostle Paul, is it?" Susie's voice was unlike Christopher had ever heard it. Her command of a Biblical topic he was certain she knew as little about as himself, sprang from, seemed framed by, absolute authority.

The voice groaned within Lansing, as if its source were suffering great pain.

"I command you, in the Holy name of Christ!" Susie shouted into Clark Lansing's face.

There sounded what seemed to be multiple cries rumbling within the man's throat. The many voices coalesced into one, fluid voice.

"RAPTURE is the means to delude. RAPTURE is transmolecular dissolution and reassembly. Through RAPTURE we cause flesh to vanish. To reassemble. You know," the voice said with a sly intonation, "like the Transporter on Star Trek."

The things within again chuckled quietly. "This host has experienced the RAPTURE. Soon will come the great taking away. We will explain…the RAPTURE…A great accident of physical science…"

The voices again faded until only faint sinister snickering could be heard.

"You mean 2 Thessalonians 2:9 through 12? –The strong delusion of that passage?" She questioned in the manner of a court-room prosecutor.

Christopher, like the others, stood astonished, seeing and hearing his wife interrogate the evil within Clark Lansing.

"They will believe! The Holy One's Word foretells…the fools will believe," the voice said.

Gessel Kirban started to give Susie a question to ask, but she spoke before he could say it.

"What, exactly, is this RAPTURE of which you speak?"

"It is the Rapid Atomic Particle Transmolecular Unification Reassembly Energizer," the voice that sounded like many commingled voices said. "We have used it in a few instances to accomplish certain goals."

"What goals?" Susie asked.

"To bring a top particle physicist into the magnificent one's plans."

"Who is the magnificent one?"

"There is none other. We speak of the great Lucifer, of course," the blended voices said as one in a caustic tone.

"Tell me about the plans of which you speak."

"To produce progeny for our purposes. To introduce the human realm to technologies it would take the human ones eons to otherwise produce," the voices answered in unison.

"How, and why do you wish to introduce such technologies?"

"Beginning with the…extraterrestrial matter, we interacted with the ones of flesh to see that they developed the machinery to exponentially advance physical science. Your people of science call it reverse engineering…"

"And, you needed this host?" Susie asked.

"Yes. This host has extraordinary facility for work in particle physics…A thing that was needed to develop the RAPTURE."

"But, there is another reason. What is that reason?" the prosecution continued.

The thing within Clark Lansing seemed to twist in anger and agony, but had no choice but to answer, Randall Prouse observed with amazement.

"We require his genetic make-up. The offspring of his genetics will serve us, to produce the nephilim, as in the ancient times."

"Before the Flood," Susie said, knowingly.

"Yes."

"And, how will this be done?" Susie demanded.

Again, the entity within Clark Lansing seemed to writhe in angry discomfort before it spoke.

"By entering into the daughters of men."

"As it was in the days of Noah," Christopher Banyon said barely above a whisper.

"Two are chosen to again begin producing the nephilim," the entity said. "The young Lansing was chosen from an early age, because of genetic predisposition. A female then was chosen, after it was determined that the father of the boy indeed possessed the essential genetic confirmation. The girl was chosen because there was need to keep her father subjugated to...human governmental authority, shall we say?"

"The girl is Lori Morgan," Susie said.

"Yes. We spared her father through use of the RAPTURE in order to secretly test his genetic composition. Only a perfectly matched union can produce the matrix for bringing forth the nephilim."

"But, you must indwell both the male and female at the time of conception, to produce the result you intend."

"Yes. We must assure a genetic match at every point of human physiology."

"And, tell me why you desire to produce this...nephilim," Susie said.

"No! We will not divulge!"

"Why do you try to refuse the question? The answer is known by the Holy One," she said.

"Do not make us say...We will not say it!"

"You will. I command it in Christ's Holy Name," Susie said, the order given in a calm voice.

The legion of evil beings screamed within the man, whose countenance took on a grotesque visage, his mouth wide and twisted in anguish. Mark started forward, but Gessel Kirban put out his arm to stop him.

"No, young man. Your father is well. He will not be harmed. We must continue the dialogue," the Israeli scientist said.

Lori again embraced Mark, trying to comfort him.

"I command...Christ commands you!" Susie repeated.

"We seek to contaminate the seed of man."

"Why do you seek to do this?"

"To keep the prophecy from fulfillment," the beast within

Clark Lansing said.

"The Scripture of the prophecy is Genesis 3:15, isn't it?"

"Yes."

"You intend to so contaminate the race of man that the vast majority will have souls that cannot be redeemed," Susie said.

"Yes! Yes! The first time *bene elohim* produced nephilim, before the Great Flood, the Redeemer had not yet come. Now that He has come, we will so contaminate the race that they are no longer fully the creation called man. The nephilim cannot be redeemed," the multitudinous voice confessed gleefully.

"And this...plan to repeat what *bene elohim* did in that antediluvian time, was implemented with the deception that extraterrestrials are interjecting themselves into the affairs of earth dwellers," Susie said.

"Yes."

"But, the *bene elohim* cannot indwell those who are Christ's," Susie said.

"No! No! No!" the entities within screeched, their anger rising to a higher pitch with each exclamation.

"This is why you could not possess Lori when you attempted to do so last evening."

"Yes! Yes! The Holy One dwells within her," the creatures growled with hatred.

"Those who know Jesus Christ as Savior are out of your reach."

"But, there are multitudes more within our grasp. We will have them. We have them already," the legion said as one.

"When? How do you expect to succeed?"

"When the great taking away intervenes, it will be Lucifer's time to reign!"

"The Rapture—the catching up—of Christ's believers, and the resurrection of those who have died from the time of the Cross? From the time of Pentecost—the birth of Christ's Church?"

"Yes. When they are gone, we shall prevail!"

"Ask why they haven't already sent a force here, since they

obviously infiltrated us, and kept track of us through Clark," James Morgan said.

Susie put the question to the entities within the physicist's body.

"The forces of the Holy One prevent us from doing so," the voice answered, then added with a fading, sinister giggle, "But, our colleagues now know. They will be upon this charming house in the very, very near future…"

* * *

Lori packed the few things she knew she couldn't do without, throwing them into the large sports bag. She turned, startled when her father came into the bedroom.

"We've got to move, Sunshine. No time to think about what you're going to wear tomorrow," James said, rushing to the bed and snapping suitcases shut, then lifting them and walking toward the door.

"I'll be right there, Dad," Lori said, seeing Mark stick his head through the doorway.

"I've talked to Greer. He'll be waiting for us at the dock in Boothbay," Mark said.

"Your mother and the rest are ready," James Morgan said, before leaving the room.

Gessel Kirban's Jeep wagon was loaded down. Mark drove as fast as the rutted road leading from Mitford House allowed, then turned onto Sharkton Highway. Christopher and Susie Banyon followed in the rental car, with Randall and Ruth Prouse in the back seat.

"You think we should go to Florida with them, then?" Ruth asked Christopher, who depressed the Plymouth's accelerator to the floor to catch up with the Jeep.

"We've got to see this through," he said, glancing at Ruth in the rearview mirror. "I believe it's the Lord's will that we do something. I'm not sure what."

"I agree," Randall Prouse said. "Mark says he can convince his senior officer friend to take this to a higher authority. He says the colonel will believe him."

"Well, we know one Higher Authority we can trust, don't we?" Susie said from the seat beside her husband.

"Did you hear the questions she asked those things?" Christopher asked, looking again at his passengers in the mirror. "Wasn't she something?!"

"Sure was." Prouse said. "That PND device ... did it help, do you think, Susie?"

"I honestly don't remember anything I said, not beyond the first few words I spoke once the device was turned on," she said.

"The questions were perfect to get the answers we needed," Ruth put in. "That means they came from the perfect Source."

Gessel Kirban's dirt-covered wagon creaked under the load of people, and the luggage strapped to its top. James Morgan had been thinking about it since they decided to get out of Mitford House.

"So, Dr. Kirban, you believe the thing possessing Clark are kept from escaping, and from contacting the people at Taos?"

"I am, of course, not certain. But, It seems that so long as he wears the PND, they are unable to remove from his physical being. His pupils continue to be dilated to an extent, and I believe the Dimensionals remain trapped within," the Israeli said, examining Lansing, who sat beside him in the middle row of seats.

"And, does that mean they won't be able to find us?" Laura Morgan said.

"These guys are professionals at hunting people down, SuperL. And, they have these things helping them. Who knows? Maybe it's time to ask that God of yours for help. We certainly need protection, wherever we can find it," Morgan said, more serious than joking.

"He's been helping all along, Dad," Lori said from the shotgun position.

Her father looked at her, a smile crossing his lips. "Hope

you're right, sweetheart. But, I'm not going to rule out asking for help of a more earthly sort. How about it, Mark? You think this Col. Kenyon will believe us?"

"We're pretty close. As close as a pilot and a former CO can allow themselves to get within the chain of command. He'll get our problems in front of the right people," Mark said, looking in the rearview mirror at one of their "problems" —his father's face beneath the gold-colored PND helmet.

Clark Lansing had scarcely moved since the inquisition almost an hour earlier. Mark was worried.

"Dr. Kirban," Mark said, glancing in the mirror at the Israeli scientist's face. "What do you think his chances are? Do you think these demons, or whatever they are, have done permanent damage to Dad's mind?"

"I find nothing organically amiss, neurologically speaking," Kirban said. "I see no reason to not expect a significant recovery... in due time."

* * *

Greer Swenson took the last of the load of luggage handed him by Mark, stashed it in the storage compartment, then slammed the storage area's door shut.

"Lucky thing I had to come up earlier than I thought," the pilot said. "Normally I wouldn't be back this way for another three, maybe four days."

"You know, Swen, I've come to believe that there's more to it all than dumb luck," Mark said, and jumped from the big plane's cargo doorway onto the dock.

"Yeah? How's that?"

"Somebody up there likes us, I think," Mark said, reaching to the dock's wooden-planked surface to pick up the long flashlight.

"Oh? You get religion, or something?" the pilot said with amusement.

"Something like that, I guess. I'll tell you all about it sometime," he said, beginning to walk toward the row of dilapidated buildings at the end and to one side of the dock.

He entered a doorway a minute later. He saw the white hair sticking out beneath the captain's hat, while the shop owner stood on tiptoes straightening the blue marlin displayed on the back wall.

"Mr. Maddow. I'm back."

The old man didn't turn around, but moved to the next displayed fish, and straightened it.

"What you want?" he said, without turning.

"I've brought your flashlight back," Mark said, walking to the counter and standing the instrument on its business end.

Still, the seaman said nothing, but continued straightening and dusting the trophies.

"Well, thanks again for the tour guide help, and for use of the light," Mark said.

He turned several seconds later and walked toward the door, seeing the shop owner didn't want to talk.

"Hey, boy!"

He turned to see Shad Maddow standing with his hands on the countertop, looking a lot like Popeye, Mark thought.

"Your old daddy's going to make it just fine. He's got a good boy," the old man said gruffly, then turned back to his fish, when he had refused to acknowledge Mark's thanks and wave of goodbye.

* * *

Pensacola, Florida – July 1, 1967

Christopher and Susie paid the motel manager by check. The man called the bank in San Antonio, and the check was declared acceptable.

"One town house unit for a week…seven days," the manager said, putting in the information that would give the couple a receipt marked "paid in advance."

"You got here just in time. It's our last town house," the

manager said, handing Christopher the receipt.

"You folks going to have that big unit all to yourselves?" he asked.

"No…A family gathering," Christopher answered, at the same time praying a short prayer, asking forgiveness for the lie.

They had all discussed the matter, and concluded the wrong people might be checking transactions made by Gessel Kirban, who first offered to pay for the town house. Not likely that Cooper and his operatives would be watching the preacher's bank account.

Laura stood on the front veranda with her husband's arm around her. The scenery was spectacular.

"Remember our trip here…when was that?" James asked, knowing she could remember such things. It was an ability that always amazed him.

"1946," his wife said.

The blue-green Gulf waters contrasted with the sugar-white sand to create a paradise-like setting. The brochures advertising vacations in a "A Paradise named Pensacola" were not just hype, Laura thought, enjoying her husband's embrace, as well as the gorgeous vista.

The flight had been a relatively bumpy weather-free one. But the many landings and take-offs and hours waiting for Greer Swenson to conduct his necessary business at each port had fatigued them all. Except for Mark and Lori, who explored the beach, with dungarees rolled to the calf.

"I wish this would never have to end," Lori said, holding Mark's right hand while they strolled the surf. "It seems nothing could be wrong in a world that looks and feels like this one."

They waded the edge of the gently breaking waves, enjoying the feel of the cool water while it rolled across their naked feet.

"Do you have to go?" Lori said, with one side of her face pressed against his chest while they held each other.

"You know I've got to. We can't go on with them trying to find us so they can shut us up about what's going on at Taos—and who knows where else," Mark said.

"How can your former commanding officer help?"

"I'm not sure he can. But I do know he'll listen, and will believe me. Especially when he sees the device...the helmet."

They began walking through the surf again, Lori kicking the foaming water into the air with every other step for a few steps.

"I'm glad Daddy is going with you to Holloman," she said. "Just getting back in the cockpit of an F-4 will do wonders for him."

"Yeah. I'm glad I asked Col. Kenyon to pull the strings to get him on the flight plan," Mark said.

"Of course, I had to lie, but I think Col. Kenyon will look the other way about that, once he knows the things involved, the dangers to the country."

"It's a lot deeper, a lot worse than that, Mark," Lori said. "These things are not just from other physical worlds, they're supernatural."

"Yeah, well, I'm still not sure about all that Bible prophecy stuff. Don't know what the colonel will think about that part of it. But, I do know these things are real. We've got to do something."

Chapter 21

E verything went smoothly. Mark's former commanding officer, Col. Kenneth Kenyon, had arranged for the flight of the F-4C. Mark and a Lt. Col. John Finch were authorized to ferry the bird from Egland to Holloman Air Force Base in New Mexico.

Mark and his co-pilot walked around the tail cones of the plane, half-way through the pre-flight.

"You've got some pretty good pull, kid," James Morgan said, sticking his face partially into the tail cone for the number two engine. "Getting a bird, on such short notice, for personal business…that's the stuff of generals."

"Yes, sir, well, we're not out of here yet. Let's just hope somebody doesn't decide to check out Lt. Col. John Finch."

Mark looked into the tail cone, when James had moved to the tail cone for the number 1 engine.

"And you got one that's loaded with ordnance, at that," James said. "What's that about?"

"Col. Kenyon wanted a loaded F-4C. He's getting one. That's all I know. Light on bombs, but plenty of other good stuff," Mark said, looking, then into the next tail cone.

"It was good of your friend, that pilot…"

"Swenson, Greer Swenson," Mark reminded.

"…yeah. It was nice of Swenson to load up everybody in his boat and get them away from the town house."

"It's a good move, I think. At least for a while. Until we make sure the bank transaction Christopher made wasn't somehow picked up by somebody," Mark said.

"He's got a place on a small island?"

"Kind of remote. I've spent some time there. About ten miles—maybe more—off Pensacola," Mark said, ducking to examine the belly of the F-4.

James squatted beside him and leaned his head to look for engine oil and hydraulic fluid leaks and loose or missing panel screws.

"Good. Maybe they'll be out of harm's way, in case our mission doesn't go too well," Morgan said, running his fingertips over one rear panel on the plane's bottom, then examining his fingers. Just condensation, he determined.

They stood and briefly looked at the ailerons and flaps, then ducked beneath the left wing to begin examination of the landing gear.

"The device…how are we going to get out of here without them getting a look at it?" James Morgan asked.

"I packed it in the seat pack. I'll have to open the seat pack in the cockpit before I get in. Guess I'll be flying with the PND in my lap until we get airborne, then switch helmets. Be flying the rest of the way with the Marine-issue helmet loose somewhere in the cockpit."

"What good will it do to wear the PND? I thought we're taking it just to show and tell the colonel," James said, checking the wheel-well, and pulling the red-flagged gear pin from its hole.

"I don't know why Dr. Kirban wanted me to wear it. Said something about I would know, and he would know, if it could serve any productive purpose, once we're in the air," Mark said.

* * *

"Does he have to wear this awful thing?"

Laura Morgan stood beside Clark Lansing, who stared straight ahead. She gripped his left arm, watching others pack the pick-up with the clothing and things they would need for several days on Greer Swenson's tiny island hide-away.

"Yes. The instrument apparently keeps the…entities…from escaping their host. At least, I believe and hope that is the case," Gessel Kirban said, lifting several things and hoisting them into the bed of the truck.

Lori pitched the last of her things into the truck bed and walked to her mother.

"Mark will be with us again before we know it," Dr. Lansing, she said, patting his arm. He made no indication he heard her.

"They should be leaving for Holloman about now, shouldn't they?" Lori asked.

"Their take-off time was 9:30," Laura said.

Lori looked at her watch. "It's almost 9 o'clock now," she said, walking beside Clark Lansing, opposite her mother, who guided him toward the second pick-up that had just pulled into the parking spot in front of the town house.

"The boat's ready," Randall Prouse said from the driver's seat. "Christopher, Susie and Ruth are on board. Swenson's ready to go when we get there.

* * *

Mark, sitting in the front seat, gave a thumbs-up to the men who held up the red-flagged ordnance safety pins they had just removed from the bomb racks and rockets launching devices.

James Morgan gave the thumbs-up also, then adjusted the oxygen hose and resnapped it to the side of the helmet.

"Just like the old days in 'Nam, huh, Major?" James said, watching the men salute while the F4 moved past them when Mark pushed the throttles forward and released the brakes.

James returned the salute from the back seat, and again gave the thumbs-up to the men who had made the safety checks near the end of the ramp before the F4C turned onto the taxiway.

"Only in 'Nam, we would usually be wet from now until we landed," Mark said.

"Man, it was something, that rain," said James with a grunt, remembering that often the pilot would be soaked by the time he climbed in the cockpit.

James quickly ran his eyes over the cockpit set-up. Memories of his training flooded his mind. The back seat was devoted to the radar intercept mission of the plane. There were therefore many controls for utilizing the installed radar. There wasn't much control of the radar in the front. As far as the weapons were concerned, the A/C had control of selection of the radar weapons, maneuvering and actual firing, once locked on. The bombs and such were selected in the front seat, as were the gun and sidewinder-type missiles.

Once the pilot in the rear seat had locked the equipment on target, it was mostly in the hands of the Aircraft Commander, the title most often given the man in the front seat. The flight to Holloman would be a treat, but James longed for a trip to the weapons range. Better yet, to a run over the jungles of South East Asia…

But, the time for Lt. Col. James Morgan to engage in combat had come and gone. They were to deliver one loaded Phantom to Col. Kenneth Kenyon, and, to deliver one strange device, which, maybe, the colonel would investigate, or see that someone who really counted would look into the sinister goings on at Defense, or NSA, or wherever…

"Phantom Eagle, ready for take-off," Mark's voice crackled in James' helmet earphones.

"Taxi into position and hold," the voice from the tower replied.

Mark gave the F4 throttle and it moved into position on the runway and stopped, its nose pointed down the broad concrete expanse that narrowed in perspective. He trimmed the aircraft for take-off, manipulating several levers, and buttons on the stick.

"Phantom Eagle, winds eight zero at ten knots, cleared for

take-off," the voice came from the tower.

Mark and James pushed the top of the rudder pedals, locking the brakes. Mark powered one of the General Electric J79-GE-17 turbojets to 85 percent, watching the gauges while he felt the immense power of the engine straining to move the bird. All was as it should be. He pulled the throttle to idle, then pushed the other throttle to 85 percent of power, going through the same checks as before.

"Looks good, Colonel," Mark said. "Here we go…"

He released the brakes, smoothly applying full power, then pushed the throttles into full afterburner. The F4 lifted from the runway seconds later, its engines thrusting it toward the altitude at which Mark would make the wide turn for Holloman Air Force Base. While they climbed, he turned the stick over to James Morgan, and replaced the Marine-issue helmet with the gleaming golden PND, as Gessel Kirban had instructed.

* * *

The cabin cruiser cut through the Gulf water at 20 knots, sending a spray of foam with each dive into the troughs created by the 3-foot swells. Greer Swenson scanned the distant water, feeling the cooling breeze mixed with the salt-spray that occasionally peppered his face. He steered the course for the small island he called Maryland—named after his late wife, Mary, who had died from breast cancer a year earlier. They were less than one-third of the way into the trip, and he estimated their time of arrival to be about 40 minutes away.

Below, all aboard suffered through the cabin cruiser's rough ride. Gessel Kirban reached into a green duffel bag and pulled out a covered object. He removed the blanket, exposing the PND helmet.

"My dear Lori," the scientist said in a tone that indicated he was about to make a request of her. "There is an important thing I ask that you do. You are a scientist, like myself, are you not?"

Lori didn't answer, at a loss to imagine what the Israeli could want of her. "I hope someday I'll have some of the knowledge you have," she said after a moment of hesitation, not knowing what else to say.

"Together, we might gain some of that knowledge at this very moment, if you'll agree to wear the PND for the next 20 or 30 minutes," Kirban said.

Laura Morgan stiffened from her seat beside Clark Lansing. "No, Dr. Kirban, I don't think so," she said.

"I assure that there is nothing that will harm her," Kirban said, pleading to Lori with his eyes, silently asking that she intervene on his behalf.

"Why? What do you hope to learn?"

Randall Prouse's question surprised Kirban. He turned from Lori to look at the archaeologist, who had moments before stepped outside the cabin, but now stood, his large form covering the entire doorway.

"It is my belief, my theory, because of the things we have learned from the dialogues with those creatures, that Mark's and Lori's genetic make up—that is, that each of them has certain genetic predispositions—which will make it possible for them to make contact...Mark up there," Kirban pointed an index finger toward the cabin's ceiling, "...and Lori down here."

Christopher Banyon's expression told Kirban there were more questions on the way.

"What kind of contact?" Christopher asked.

"The...you call them *bene elohim*. Dr. Frobe called them Dimensionals. These beings chose these two youngsters, according to the creatures inhabiting Dr. Lansing. Let us find out why Cooper and these creatures wanted to use the precognition neuro-diviner device in the combinations they chose. Lori, Mark, and their fathers all were chosen. Mark and Lori, especially, were chosen for the future. Let us do a small experiment. I've asked Mark to wear the device while flying to their destination."

"Yes. I'll do it," Lori said, reaching to take the helmet from the scientist.

He pulled it from her grip. "I will place it, if you don't mind, Lori. Everything must be exactly right."

"Are you sure?" Lori's mother asked. "You sure there's no danger?"

"I absolutely promise, mother," he said with compassion in his voice. Kirban adjusted the helmet on her head, and then pushed the appropriate buttons inset within the instrument's chrome-like shell.

"Power should last an hour or longer. These experimental batteries have proven themselves to be quite resilient when used with the PND technology," the Israeli said. He sat on the long bench seat built into the cabin wall across from Lori.

"Do you feel any sensations...hear anything?" he asked, looking into her eyes. Her pupils had already dilated so that they covered much of the blue irises.

"Yes. It's as if I'm in Mark's helmet. I see...I see sunlight that hurts Mark's eyes. Now, he's pulled a visor...a dark visor over his eyes."

"Yes...Yes! This is the essence of the remote viewing experiments!" The scientist was jubilant. "It is the helmet prepared for him from the first. It is configured like the pilot's helmet, with the sun visor that slides downward when needed," Kirban said with excitement.

"Our minds...they...they are like joined. He knows I...my thoughts are mingling with his," Lori said with astonishment.

The small cabin exploded in a violent flash of light and noise. All eyes of the startled occupants went to Clark Lansing, who stood, his mouth opened wide, his eyes bulging in their sockets, the blackness of their pupils seeming to cover even the corneas. His face was a twisted mask of hate beneath the PND he wore. Garbled voices raged from the possessed man's frothing mouth and gnashing teeth.

Lansing lurched toward Lori, whose concentration was broken. Randall Prouse lunged to preempt the attack. They struggled, and

Prouse slammed against the cabin's shut door, his body tossed as if a rag doll by the supernatural strength Lansing now possessed.

The demoniac faced Prouse, hatred growling within his throat. He picked a hard plastic suitcase from near Susie Banyon and flung it toward Prouse. The archaeologist dove for the floor and the case exploded open when it hit the closed door.

Gessel Kirban grabbed Lansing from behind, but was thrown aside. Christopher wrapped his arm around Lansing's throat after vaulting onto the maniac's back. Prouse attacked him from a crouched position, slamming him in the midsection with his shoulder.

Finally, Prouse, Christopher and Kirban were able to control Lansing, who relaxed and allowed himself to be seated in one corner, with all three men still holding tightly to him.

The entities that controlled Lansing began to laugh. He threw his head back, his eyes turned back in his head. The laughter was deafening in the small cabin, the demons within their host roaring.

"Oh, no!"

Lori's words caused all to look at her. Her eyes were wide, her mouth open, as if amazed. She said nothing, but stared blankly, her mouth open, as if in shock.

"What's wrong, sweetheart?" Laura Morgan said, rushing to her daughter.

"Lori!" Ruth Prouse shouted at Lori, who blinked, and turned her eyes, first to Ruth, then to her mother.

"They're coming for us," Lori whispered.

The demoniacal laughter from within Clark Lansing's throat echoed throughout the cabin.

"Who? Who's coming for us?" Randall Prouse asked, still gripping Lansing with all of his strength.

"It's them. They are in helicopters," Laura said in a quiet voice. "They want to kill us."

"They have found us," Gessel Kirban said, glancing at Prouse.

Clark Lansing's body relaxed. He stared straight ahead, his eyes almost entirely black. "We must destroy all of you," demonic voices sneered through his mouth. "You will not be allowed to tell of these things. They are of eternal importance."

"Hold him," Prouse said, bolting out of the door and onto the boat's deck. He scanned the horizon. Nothing but gulls and gray-blue skies.

"What's wrong?!" Greer Swenson shouted to be heard above the boat's loud engine and streaming wind.

"Someone's trying to find us!" Prouse shouted back.

Swenson locked the wheel and began sweeping the sky behind them with binoculars.

"There!"

He pointed to the southeast.

Prouse could not yet see them.

"Looks like a couple of them! Maybe three!" Swenson shouted above the noise.

Prouse saw them, then, three black specks, growing larger by the second, just above the horizon.

He hurried to the cabin door and stuck his head in the doorway.

"They're after us. Closing fast. Better pray," he said, hearing Lansing's witch-like cackle before ducking out again.

"You have a weapon?!" he yelled to Swenson.

"A shotgun and a pistol!" Swenson shouted. He left the boat on automatic pilot, jumped from the helm station, and dashed into the cabin to retrieve the guns. He returned to the deck and handed Randall the pistol.

"Got nine shots, that's it," Swenson said of the pistol, pulling the bolt of the Browning Sweet 16 back and letting it snap shut, thus feeding a shell into the chamber.

"Dear God," Randall said quietly. "Please stick with us."

The helicopters loomed larger now, looking like giant, black, flying insects descending upon them. Prouse and Swenson could see the racks of rockets beneath the birds. They were loaded for the hunt.

"There's nothing we can do, my friend," Swenson said. "Maybe a white flag…"

"They're bent on doing us in. Let's use what we've got," Prouse said, pulling the receiver back on the pistol and releasing it.

A blast exploded 10 feet off the stern as the choppers closed in. The second rocket whizzed over the heads of the men, who fired in the direction of the black, unmarked birds of prey while they moved ever closer. The chopper pilots were measuring for the volley of rocket and machine gun fire that would end a successful hunt.

Inside the cabin, Susie prayed, while Ruth and Laura knelt with heads bowed. Christopher prayed silently, while he and the scientist held onto the demoniac.

Lori sat transfixed, viewing through Mark's eyes, a stunning plunge toward the blue waters below.

The black helicopters, positioned for the kill, readied to fire. Prouse and Swenson could see the black helmeted people within the choppers, their eyes covered with the sun visors. It was as if they were toying with their prey, like a cat plays with its mouse-victim before the *coup de gras*.

"You got 'em?" James Morgan asked, looking into his radarscope.

"Roger," Mark responded

Mark reached downward with his left hand, manipulated several switches on the selector switches panel known as the dog bone because of its peculiar shape of two larger rotary switches separated by a row of toggles.

He visually checked the field of fire while the F4 screamed toward the enemy, then moved his thumb to push the pickle switch on the stick. He pulled the trigger with his index finger, and the AIM-9 Sidewinder infrared homing air-to-air missiles streaked toward its target.

The rocket hit the middle chopper, resulting in a massive

explosion. The fiery carnage from the fuel and ordnance of the holocaust destroyed a second chopper. The third helicopter turned sharply, breaking off its attack on the cabin cruiser. Mark brought the Phantom around in a long, looping maneuver. The jet quickly closed the distance gap.

"Locked on," James said from the back seat.

"Party's over," Mark said, pulling the trigger on the grip stick.

The Sidewinder's trail was short from the F4 launch to the black chopper, which turned instantaneously red, orange and yellow when it exploded in a fireball that plummeted into the Gulf.

* * *

Taos – the underground complex

Robert Cooper shook uncontrollably while he watched the several lab-coated people approach. He knew they were human in form only.

The innermost chamber of the complex was darkened almost to the point that the eye couldn't discern facial features. Yet, the many tiny lights of the vast chamber's technologies blinked in every conceivable color, giving the faces eerie appearance.

When they came near him, Cooper saw the pupils of the eyes. Huge, black orbs that appeared because of the pinpoints of reflected light to glow from some inner source. Now, he saw black, smoke-like wisps emanating from each—infinitesimal flickers of electricity-like sparks that the host-bodies emitted.

The creatures spoke as one through the mouths of the two men and the woman. "Your failure has delayed the magnificent one's implementation of RAPTURE," the deep, growling voices said in unison. "But, it is merely the end of our beginning. We shall prevail."

The bodies hosting the evil moved closer to Cooper, who smiled a sheepish, fleeting grin while mopping his sweat beaded forehead and mouth with a handkerchief.

"Yes, yes. It's just the beginning," he said in a meek tone of fawning agreement.

"But it shall be a new beginning without need of your failure-laden services," the seething voices said as one.

* * *

Next day—Pensacola

The colonel on the other end of the phone line was business-like. He wanted to keep his strong affection for his young friend and former pilot separated from the serious matter before them.

"The ordnance is something I will have trouble reconciling," Col. Kenyon said from his office at the center of Holloman Air Force base. "There's no report of any helicopters down in that area that I can determine."

"Sir, that's because this is an unauthorized covert operation," Mark said, feeling he should stand rather than sit, even if he wasn't physically in Kenyon's presence. "I'm sure of it. They won't report this…"

"You expended two Sidewinders, is that correct?"

"Yes sir," Mark said, looking to James Morgan, then Morgan's daughter.

"Two Sidewinders… three helicopters. Guess you won't need to spend any extra time on the range this week, son," Kenyon said sternly.

Mark smiled. The colonel was telling him—without saying it—that the matter was as good as closed.

"Everyone okay?" Kenyon asked.

"Yes, sir."

"And this Lt. Col. John Finch—What about the things you said you wanted me to know about him?" the Marine colonel asked.

"Sir, if you will please trust me on this one, I'll be forever grateful. I'm sorry I put you through the trouble of arranging things for him…for us," Mark said, hoping this by-the-book officer would let him trade—just this once—on their deep friendship.

"This young woman you're so gaga over," Kenyon said, changing the subject, much to Mark's relief. "When will the plunge take place, and will Sarah and I be invited?" Kenyon asked, still in a business-like voice.

"You know it, Colonel...You know it."

Mark turned to Lori and her father, when he hung up a minute later.

"We're in the clear, Colonel," he said, walking to Lori and putting his arms around her.

"Come here!" Laura stood in the doorway of the town house, beckoning them with a motion of her hand. She turned and hurried back to the large room.

Everyone stood, or sat, watching the program. The network anchor told the story, while the film rolled.

"The implosion was a scheduled event, a government spokesman said. The Taos, underground facility, a part of the U.S. Defense Department, was no longer in service. No one at Defense or in the government would give the nature of the operation."

Helicopter-mounted news cameras had a couple of hours earlier swept the reddish-brown and sand-colored landscape. A deep depression in the desert earth, taken from a camera shot high above, made the land look as if a giant foot had stepped where the implosion had taken place.

"It's gone. They've destroyed it," Gessel Kirban said, sitting forward in a chair to one side of the television screen.

"There is no way, after that collapse, to prove it ever was anything more than another secret government facility, no longer needed," Randall Prouse said.

"Yes. What's to tell? Who would believe?" Christopher Banyon let the question fade to nothing further to say.

"The PND? What about the helmets?" Lori asked.

"They are dead," Kirban said. "The technologies within the Taos chamber gave them their power. We could show only a broken, useless instrument."

"Who did it? Who destroyed the complex?" Laura asked holding onto her husband's arm.

"The Dimensionals did it."

All eyes turned to Clark Lansing, who sat in a chair against one wall. "The Dimensionals imploded the thing," he repeated.

"Dad!" Mark rushed to his father's side. He knelt in front of him, gripping his father's forearms.

"I'll be okay now, son," he said, squeezing Mark's hand. "Maybe we'll all be okay, now."

Epilogue

LAX, Los Angeles, California, 9:10 a.m. September 8, 2001

Lori brushed tears from her eyes while she and Mark watched their second child take care of business at the Delta counter. Morgan walk toward them, her lovely form moving with long, graceful strides just like her mother's, Mark thought, while he held Lori tightly.

"Okay, Jeddy is all settled in," she said with an upbeat smile in her voice. "The guy said he once had a Rottweiler. He promised he would see to it that Jeddy will be well taken care of until I pick him up."

She frowned with concern, seeing her mother's distress. "Now, Mom, it's not like I'm leaving the planet," she said, throwing her arms around Lori and kissing her cheek. She next embraced her father, who wanted to cry, but wouldn't.

"Remember all I've told you, baby," he said, hugging her tightly and kissing her.

"Yes, Dad, I will always keep the doors locked, and will call Uncle Mike, if there's ever a problem. And, I promise I'll check in with him when I get to New York."

Lori looked her daughter over in one last check of her attire. She brushed back a strand of Morgan's sunlight-colored hair, so that it was again in its proper place.

"We are so proud of you, sweetheart. You know that?" Lori pulled Morgan to her again, her tears spilling over her cheeks.

"I love you both so much," Morgan said, her own tears falling in thin streams from the corners of her eyes.

"I couldn't let you go, if I didn't know that it's such a great opportunity," Lori said, mopping the tears from her own eyes, then from her daughter's.

"It will be great, getting to work for a major publication. And in New York City, at that," Morgan said brightly, putting a positive spin on the departure.

"Remember, Morgan, don't leave God out of your life. Find a church."

"I will, Mom…I promise. But, I need to settle in first. Monday is going to roll around pretty quickly. I've got to be ready to hit the ground running, as Daddy always says," she said, again grabbing her father and kissing him.

Mark and Lori watched while their daughter waved a final goodbye and disappeared through the door of the tunnel-ramp that led to the Delta 757. They watched while the tug backed the big jet from its berth, and as it began to taxi on its way to take its place among the other planes awaiting takeoff clearance.

Something caused Lori to look across the concourse, to a crowd also watching departures.

There! A big man in a dark suit, a large set of binoculars to his eyes, training on their daughter's plane.

She froze, paralyzed with remembrance of the day she and Ginger Knox walked toward the University of Texas tower. The man with the field glasses! The nightmares of the large hulking figure that watched her… always the vacuuming wind that tried to draw her to him.

The man at the observation window turned and trained the binoculars on her. She forced her gaze from her self-imposed paralysis, and grabbed Mark's arm.

"Mark! That man!"

"What man?" Mark saw his wife's terrified expression.

"That man with the binoculars…" She pointed toward the crowd that continued to look out over the busy tarmac.

"I don't see anybody with binoculars, Hon," he said, continuing to look into the crowd.

Lori frantically searched, her eyes wide and darting toward the group, then around the observation area.

The man was gone!

* * *

Boston, Massachusetts – September 11, 2001 – 7:05 a.m.

Her husband's retirement as pastor of a small church near Sharkton and the sizable inheritance left him by Aunt Annabel Lee Mitford freed them to do things others could not. She must never forget to thank the Lord for His goodness, for the three children and five terrific grandchildren He had provided. Susie Banyon silently did so now.

Christopher and Susie had enjoyed the trip to Texas. San Antonio was spreading in every direction, and things had changed since he left St. Paul Church all those years ago.

"We should get to Portland by 10 at the latest," he said, touching his wife's arm.

"Should be in Sharkton by 11. It will be good to get home to Mitford House," Susie said. "But, I'll still miss San Antonio, and our friends—especially Randy and Ruth," she added.

"The kids will be glad to see Grandma," the retired minister said, stroking Susie's arm, then taking her hand and holding it, while they sat in the lobby of Logan Airport, awaiting their boarding call.

"Grandpa, too," she said.

"Wish Laura and James could've come to visit this fall, like we planned," Christopher said.

"James probably won't make it past the winter," Susie said. "The Alzheimer's has really begun to affect his mind."

"Yes. With Clark Lansing dying last year of the same thing, you have to wonder," Christopher said. "I guess it's a miracle, after undergoing that RAPTURE technology—the transmolecular experiments—and then the device they wore for so long… the PND, especially Clark, that they've lived so long."

"It's strange, the way the government provides for them, no questions. Why did they never investigate things surrounding James' supposed crash, then his reappearance?" Susie wondered aloud.

"That colonel…Kenyon, I think was his name, must have had powerful friends. Just swept everything under the rug, as they say, then, next thing you know, James and Laura, as well as Clark, had no worries for the rest of their lives. Something to do with the Defense Department, and its Covert Operations. I do know that much. A small price for them to pay to see to it that the whole thing is just dropped."

Christopher contemplated the entire matter during a few moments of silence, then spoke again. "Of course, it's all within God's will. It seems weird, the whole thing—how everything, the strange experiences, the other-worldliness…it all just seemed to cease. Yet, the scroll fragments, they plainly foretold that the end had begun once the scrolls were discovered."

"James, Lori, Mark, Clark—they came to know the Lord, that's the main thing," Susie said.

Her husband pulled her hand to his lips and kissed it. "Your faith helped change all of us," he said, looking into the soft brown eyes, and the alabaster-skinned features, the beauty of which still made his heart race.

"It was a good reunion, wasn't it?" Susie said.

"Yes. But, I do wish I could've talked one more time with Dr. Kirban," Christopher said, a frown of concentration crossing his face.

"I would like to ask him more about those technologies. How they seemed to work within the very souls of people."

"Dr. Kirban died of the same thing, Laura said his daughter told her. Alzheimer's…"

"It all seems like a dream now, a bad dream, mostly. But, some good friendships came out of it," Christopher said.

"I wonder what it all meant. The dreams, or visions, they've stopped," Susie said.

"They were real. And, the dreams...they still have significance. I just don't know what they mean for today," he said, standing. "The Lord will have to let us know, when He's ready."

He sat down again, after stretching.

"It's hard to believe that Mark is retired from Delta Airlines, now. And, that Lori is happy just being a mother and grandmother."

"What do you mean it's hard to believe that she's happy 'JUST' being a mother and grandmother?" Susie said with feigned irritation. She said then, in a more nostalgic tone, "Aren't they a happy pair?"

"Still just like when they were looking moon-eyed at each other all those years ago," Christopher said with a smile.

"We're still a lot like back then," Susie said.

"Maybe a little slower, and with a few more aches, but, yes... we've still got it," Christopher said, squeezing his wife's hand. "One thing, though, I can't wait as long as I used to on some things. I'd better go to the men's room before our boarding time."

He stood. "I won't be long," he said, then walked across the broad concourse walkway, amazed at the amount of human traffic, with people hurrying in every direction. The sights and sounds of the terminal triggered *deja vu*, while he walked into the little hallway.

He felt a bit lightheaded, and when he reached the door to the men's room, he paused for a moment, bracing himself against the wall. He held his arm straight and stiff, the heel of his hand supporting his weight on the wall's surface.

Several seconds later his mind cleared, and he walked into the outer, then the double inner doors. The dizziness came again, and he looked through whirling memories at familiar surroundings. Familiar surroundings, yet surroundings that he knew he had not experienced. Or had he?

Christopher walked to the sink, wet his hands, and splashed

his face with cool water. He looked in the mirror while he dried his hands and face with a paper towel. Again, *deja vu* hearkened his memory to something in the past...

He heard a toilet flush, and within moments the stall's door opened, and a man who looked to be about 60, dressed casually for travel, walked from the stall, paused a moment, glanced at his watch, then at Christopher.

"Pardon me, sir," the man said in accented English. "Could you be so kind as to tell me the time, please?"

The dark-eyed man, more than likely of Middle Eastern extraction, Christopher thought, looked again at his own watch.

"It's 7:21, according to my watch," Christopher said.

"Thank you very much, sir," the man said, twisted the stem of his watch, then exited the men's room.

Christopher felt uneasy. And, it wasn't just the queasiness in his stomach. Something about the man...

Christopher walked to the big trashcan sitting in the corner near the edge of a row of wash-basins. He wadded the paper towel and started to toss it in the can atop other refuse.

It came back to him, then. A sudden rush of realization. He reached into the can and picked up one of three small boxes. It was a product package, marked with the words "Box Cutter" and a picture of the instrument.

His senses darkened. What was it about? The man...the man had walked into the men's room during his weird experience at Logan all those years ago. It was that man...it was this men's room!

Only that was then...this was now. The year 2001, not 1967!

He picked up the other packages. All small, rectangular boxes that had contained box cutters. He ran his index finger in one of the boxes. He pulled from it a credit card receipt that had been stuffed there.

"Pardon me, sir, are you Christopher Banyon?"

The black man stood holding the inner door open.

"Yes, yes I am," Christopher answered.

"Your wife, she asked me to tell you that your boarding time has been announced."

"Thanks," Christopher said, glancing again at the trash-can and the packages.

Susie tugged him toward the boarding area by the shirtsleeve. "I thought you were never coming out, Chris. What were you doing in there?"

"How long was I in there?"

"Almost 20 minutes," she said leading the way past the crowd toward the American Airlines counter.

When they got in line, his attention was drawn toward another American Airlines counter across the concourse walkway. His eyes fell upon three men—young men—familiar men...

Christopher couldn't fathom how he could possibly realize such a thing. How he could remember...they were the three he had seen 34 years earlier, the dark-complected guys who had been in the men's room!

A fourth man talked to them while they stood in the American boarding check line. The same person who had asked for the time in the men's room; the same one who had come back in the men's room in the vision in 1967? Yes...the same!

"What's wrong, Chris?" Susie asked, seeing her husband's face go pale, and his dazed expression. "Are you sick?"

"No," he said, looking hard at the four men. "At least, I don't think I am," he said, as if to himself.

The *bene elohim*...He had seen it in the vision that day in the restroom at Logan. A different men's room than the one he entered that day, the same one as existed now, not 50 feet from where he stood...in 2001.

The creature...it had walked out of and back into the man that day in 1967. The same man who talked to the three younger men in the American Airlines check-in counter line.

The three packages, they were proof positive. Proof his vision 34 years earlier, and the actual experience just minutes ago, were real. And, somehow related one to another!

Could it be?!

The credit card ticket…! The ticket he took from the product box…what had he done with it?

Christopher patted his pockets, feeling the crumpled piece of paper in his right pants pocket. He withdrew it and straightened it. He read the name on the ticket: "Mustafa Kihbolah."

# # #